P9-BYR-142

# Print Reading
## for Construction
### Residential and Commercial

Write-In Text with 119 Large Prints

by

**Walter C. Brown**
Professor Emeritus
Division of Technology
Arizona State University, Tempe

Publisher
**The Goodheart-Willcox Company, Inc.**
Tinley Park, Illinois

Copyright 1997
by
**THE GOODHEART-WILLCOX COMPANY, INC.**
Previous editions copyright 1990, 1987, 1980

All rights reserved. No part of this book may be reproduced, stored in a retrieval system, or transmitted in any form or by any means, electronic, mechanical, photocopying, recording, or otherwise, without the prior written permission of The Goodheart-Willcox Company, Inc. Manufactured in the United States of America.

Library of Congress Catalog Card Number 96-47086
International Standard Book Number 1-56637-355-7
6 7 8 9 97 02 01

| **Library of Congress Cataloging-in-Publication Data** |
| --- |
| Brown, Walter Charles, |
|     Print reading for construction: residential and commercial: write-in / by Walter C. Brown. |
|       p.    cm. |
|     Rev. ed. of: Blueprint reading for construction. c1990. |
|     Includes index. |
|     ISBN 1-56637-355-7 |
|     1. Building--Details--Drawings. 2. Blueprints. I. Brown, Walter Charles, Print reading for construction. II. Title. |
| TH431.B76 1997                        96-47086 |
| 692'.1--dc21                                  CIP |

# Introduction

*Print Reading for Construction* is a training course for those who desire a knowledge of basic print reading or increased knowledge of construction drawings. The term *print reading,* as used in this write-in text, refers to interpreting and visualizing construction drawings.

*Print Reading for Construction* is a combination text and workbook. The text tells and shows *how*, and the workbook provides space for meaningful print reading, sketching, and estimating activities. Actual construction prints used with the text can be found in the *Large Prints* folder. They provide realistic job experience. The text is equally applicable for students studying construction, estimating, or construction management.

*Print Reading for Construction* is intended for technical students, apprentices, and adult workers. It also is designed to be used for self-instruction by individuals unable to attend classes.

### New features for this edition:

A list of *Technical Terms* opens each unit. Study this list before reading the unit. Pay special attention when these terms are discussed. After completing a unit, review the Technical Terms to be sure you understand all of them. All of these terms are also defined in the glossary.

*Learning Objectives* are presented to define the most important skills you will learn in the unit. After completing a unit, review these to ensure that you have mastered the new material.

Each unit is followed by *Test Your Knowledge* questions. These brief questions are used to evaluate how well you understand the topics presented in the unit.

Many new *Activities* have been added. These provide "hands-on" print reading experience.

Most of the prints in the *Large Prints* folder are new to this edition. These prints are used with the activities and will give you valuable experience at reading both residential and commercial prints.

The *Glossary* has been doubled in size. When you come across a term you are unfamiliar with, use the glossary to find its meaning.

# Contents

# MATERIALS AND SPECIFICATIONS                 Section 3

# READING PRINTS                                Section 4

## ESTIMATING                                    Section 5

## ADVANCED PRINT READING PROJECTS    Section 6

## REFERENCE SECTION                    Section 7

# Acknowledgments

The author wishes to express his appreciation to Mr. Charles O. Biggs, A.I.A. Architect, for willingly giving his time and counsel during the organizing and writing of this text. In addition to his professional assistance, Mr. Biggs furnished many of the prints contained in the text. Appreciation is also expressed to Dr. Charles W. Graham, Associate Professor, College of Architecture, Department of Construction Science, Texas A & M University, for his review of the text and helpful comments.

A number of architectural and construction companies also supplied prints and mechanical manuals on all aspects of construction. Appreciation is expressed to the following firms for their assistance: Batson & Associates Architects, Covington, Kentucky; Brick Institute of America, McLean, Virginia; Cypress Speciality Steel Company, Phoenix, Arizona; Environmental Design Consultants: Kral, Zepf, Frietag & Associates, Cincinnati, Ohio; Evans International Homes, Minneapolis, Minnesota; Garlinghouse Plan Service, Middletown, Connecticut; Gosnell Development Corporation, Phoenix, Arizona; Robert Ehmet Hayes and Associate, Architects, Fort Mitchell, Kentucky; Helgeson and Biggs, Architects, Inc., Phoenix, Arizona; Henkel, Hovel, and Schaefer, Architects-Engineer, Covington, Kentucky; Marathon Steel Company, Phoenix, Arizona; John J. Ross, A.I.A. Architect, Pittsburgh, Pennsylvania; Schweizer Associates Architect, Inc., Environmental Design, Winter Park, Florida; Don Singer Architect, Broward County, Florida; Anderson Engineering, Pheonix, Arizona; Areté 3 Ltd., Orland Park, Illinois; Christensen, Cassidy, Billington, Candelaria, Phoenix, Arizona; Foster Associates and Architects, Scottsdale, Arizona; Roberts/Jones Associates, Inc., Phoenix, Arizona.

# Section 1

# Introduction to Print Reading

©1995 L.F. GARLINGHOUSE COMPANY, INC.

# Construction Drawings

## Technical Terms

Blueprint
Computer-aided
  design and drafting
  (CADD)
Detail drawing
Elevation
Floor plan
Framing plan
Longitudinal Section

Pictorial drawing
Print
Rendering
Schedule
Section
Tracing
Transverse section
Vellum
Working drawings

## Learning Objectives

After completing this unit, you will be able to:
- Explain why drawings are important in the construction industry
- Identify what is included in a set of drawings
- Describe how prints are made
- Handle prints with proper care

Drawings are used to communicate ideas and relate directions in a construction project. Along with specifications, drawings detail the building components, materials, and methods of construction. All persons involved in the planning, supplying, or constructing of a structure must be able to read construction drawings.

A *print* is a copy of a drawing. For many years, the only type of reproduction used was the *blueprint*, which consists of white lines on a blue background. Today, the term *blueprint* is used interchangeably with *print*. Most prints have dark lines on a light background.

Prints are sometimes referred to as *working drawings* or *plans*. Original drawings are normally stored in the architect's or engineer's office. If the drawings were used at the construction site, they could be easily damaged. Therefore, prints are used to direct the workers. The term *plan* also refers to views taken from directly above the object, such as *floor plan, site plan,* or *foundation plan.*

## Construction Prints

There are two types of construction drawings—pictorial and orthographic projection. A *pictorial drawing* is used to help the viewer visualize the structure. These drawings are enhanced with trees, shrubs, and shading to make them appear more realistic. Pictorial drawings are called *renderings*, **Figure 1-1.** Pictorial drawings are used for presentations. However, they do not show any construction details.

*Orthographic projection* is a method in which different views of the subject (a building, for instance) are shown. Each view is taken from a different reference point. These reference points are selected so that the views are perpendicular to one another. This allows all the details of the structure to be shown in the fewest possible drawings.

The views used in construction drawings are the top, front, side, and back. The top view is called a *plan drawing.* Front, side, and back views are called *elevations.* A view of the interior of the building is called a *section.*

Nearly all construction drawings are created using orthographic projection. The appearance of the building is not as obvious as when shown in a pictorial drawing, but far more information can be shown. With experience, you will be able to visualize the completed structure, as well as obtain information needed for construction, from orthographic drawings.

©1995 L.F. GARLINGHOUSE COMPANY, INC.

*Figure 1-1. A pictorial drawing shows how the finished building will appear. (Garlinghouse)*

## Set of Prints

Small construction jobs usually include all necessary information on a single plan and elevation. Larger construction projects are more complicated and a single plan would become quite crowded. A set of plans is used and divided into groups according to types of construction:

- **A**—Architectural. Plot plan, elevations, framing, and building details
- **S**—Structural. Wood, concrete, and steel superstructure
- **M**—Mechanical. Plumbing, heating, ventilation, and cooling systems
- **E**—Electrical. Power and lighting systems

Some architects and engineers further divide the set of prints with additional divisions:

- **U**—Utility Site Plan. Public or municipal electrical and plumbing supply lines
- **P**—Plumbing. Waste and water supply systems
- **H**—Heating, ventilating, and air-conditioning systems

Other architects simply number the sheets of the set, and use no letter classification.

## Types of Prints

Prints are usually arranged in the approximate order of construction. A set of prints consists of civil engineering (C-1, C-2, etc.), structural engineering (S-1, S-2, etc.), architectural (A-1, A-2, etc.), electrical (E-1, E-2, etc.), mechanical (M-1, M-2, etc.), and plumbing (P-1, P-2, etc.) prints.

The civil engineering prints include plot or site plans, utilities, easements, grading, and landscaping details. A typical site plan is shown in **Figure 1-2.** The site plan can also include contour lines, walks, and driveways. Property lines, building setbacks, and utility locations are also shown.

The structural prints include the foundation, structural steel, building support system, and roof framing system. The foundation and basement plans are usually included on the same drawing, **Figure 1-3.** This plan includes the foundation walls, footings, piers, and fireplaces. Details and section drawings of the foundation wall and footings are sometimes included on the same sheet.

Architectural prints include floor plans, elevations, sections, detail drawings, and door and window schedules. In residential construction, the architectural prints make up the majority of the set.

The *floor plan* is an important drawing because it provides the most information, **Figure 1-4.** The floor plan is actually a sectional view taken on a horizontal plane 42″ to 48″ above the floor. The plane may be offset (change levels) if the building involves a split-level floor. The floor plan shows walls, doors, stairways, fireplaces, built-in cabinets, and mechanical equipment. Drawings for multistory buildings include a floor plan for each level.

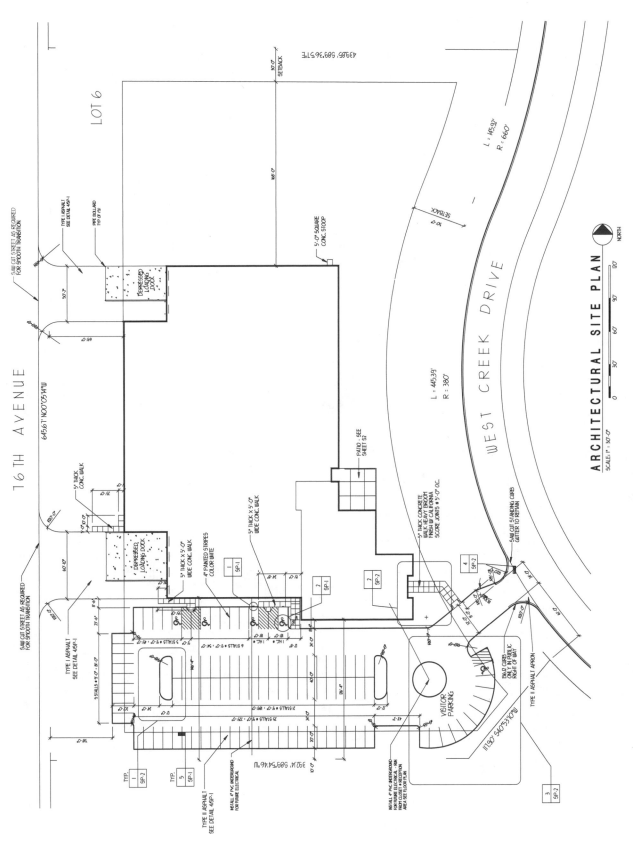

*Figure 1-2.* A site plan for an office building, warehouse, and parking lot. (Charles E. Smith, Areté 3 Ltd.)

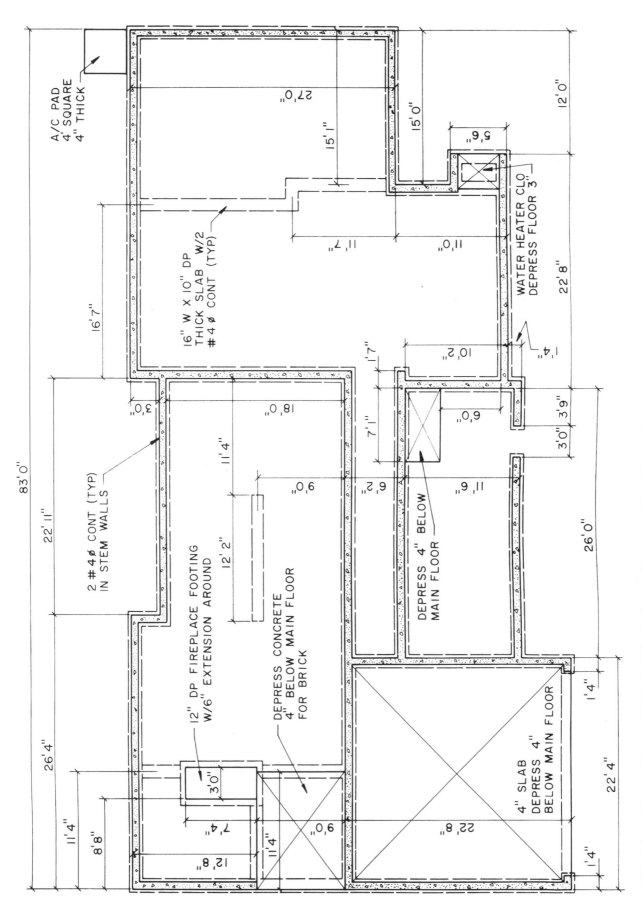

*Figure 1-3.* A foundation and basement plan includes footings, columns, and foundation walls.

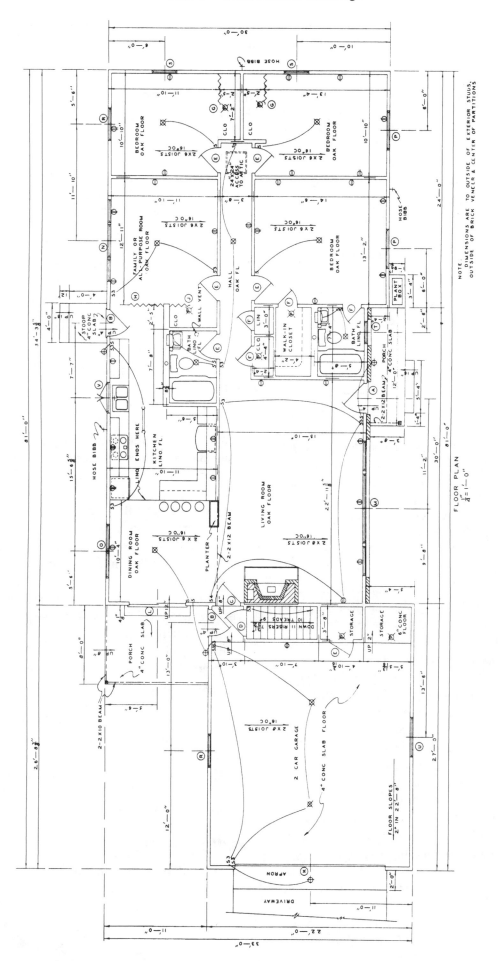

*Figure 1-4. The floor plan is one of the most informative construction drawings.*

*Elevations* are views of the exterior features of the building, **Figure 1-5.** Usually, four elevation drawings are needed to show the design of all sides of the structure. More elevation views are required for unusual designs, such as internal courtyards. Elevations of the building's interior are called *interior elevations*.

*Sections* are views showing the building as if it were cut apart, **Figure 1-6.** They show walls, stairs, and other details not clearly shown in other drawings. Sectional views are usually drawn to a scale larger than that used for the elevations and plan drawings. Sectional views taken through the narrow width of an entire building are known as *transverse sections*. Those through the long dimension are known as *longitudinal sections*.

*Detail drawings* are required for unusual construction, such as an arch, cornice, or retaining wall. Details are drawn to a large scale to clearly describe the feature. See **Figure 1-7.**

*Schedules* are lists of materials needed in the construction process. A schedule normally lists the item, an identification mark, size, number required, and any other useful information. Each item in the schedule is referenced in the plan and elevations. Different types of schedules include door schedules (**Figure 1-8**), window schedules, and lighting fixture schedules. Schedules are used for other purposes, such as the finishing schedule shown in **Figure 1-9.**

Schedules are usually included as part of a set of working drawings. Door schedules frequently are included on the plan drawings. Window schedules generally appear on the elevation drawings.

The *electrical drawings* include the electrical and lighting plan, reflected ceiling plan, and panel schedules. On larger projects, riser diagrams and load calculations may also be included. For smaller jobs, the electrical plan may appear on the floor plan itself.

The *mechanical drawings* include heating, ventilating, and air conditioning (*HVAC*) plans and plumbing plans. Sprinkler systems are also included in the mechanical drawings. Schedules for pipe and fittings, HVAC equipment, and plumbing fixtures may be included. The HVAC plan, like the electrical plan, is included on the regular floor plan for simple projects.

The *plumbing plan* shows the layout for the hot and cold water system, the sewage disposal system, and the location of plumbing fixtures. Plans for residences may have the entire plumbing plan on one drawing, and plumbing fixtures are often shown on the floor plan. For more complex structures, separate plans for each system are used.

*Framing plans* may be included in a set of plans for the framing of the roof, floors, and various

elevations or wall sections. These plans are required for more complex structures, but may be omitted for smaller, less-complicated buildings.

## Making Prints

The original drawing, also called a *tracing*, is normally made of transparent paper (*vellum*) or polyester film. Most drawings are created using *computer-aided design and drafting* (*CADD*) systems. Drawings created this way are generated on a plotter. Manual drawings are created by hand, directly on the tracing paper.

*Engineering copiers* are used extensively in industry to create prints. These copiers use an electrostatic process to reproduce drawings. Their operation is similar to common copying machines, except they are designed to handle larger sizes of paper.

Drawings can be reduced or enlarged with these copiers. A D-size (24″ × 36″) drawing can be reduced to a smaller print for easier handling. Prints are made very quickly.

Due to the nature of copying machines, these prints may not always be exact duplicates of the original drawing. Slight enlargements or reductions of portions of drawings may occur. Therefore, you should never scale a dimension from a photocopy unless you have verified that the copy has, in fact, copied to scale. This can be verified by scaling several dimensions on the print to guarantee its accuracy.

*Diazo* machines are still used today, although they are being replaced by engineering copiers. The diazo process is a photochemical process, which uses the effects of both light and chemicals to produce prints.

The diazo process consists of two steps:
1. Special light-sensitive paper is placed under the drawing. Both the drawing and the paper are inserted into the machine, where they are exposed to light. The light-sensitive chemicals on the paper that are protected from the light by the lines on the drawing remain on the paper. The remaining chemical on the paper is "burned away" by the light.
2. The paper is then exposed to ammonia vapor in the developer. The vapor causes the chemicals remaining on the paper to turn blue.

## Reading Prints

*Print reading* is the gathering of information from a print or drawing. It involves two principal elements: visualization and interpretation. These abilities are developed by reading prints. The more experience you have, the better your skill.

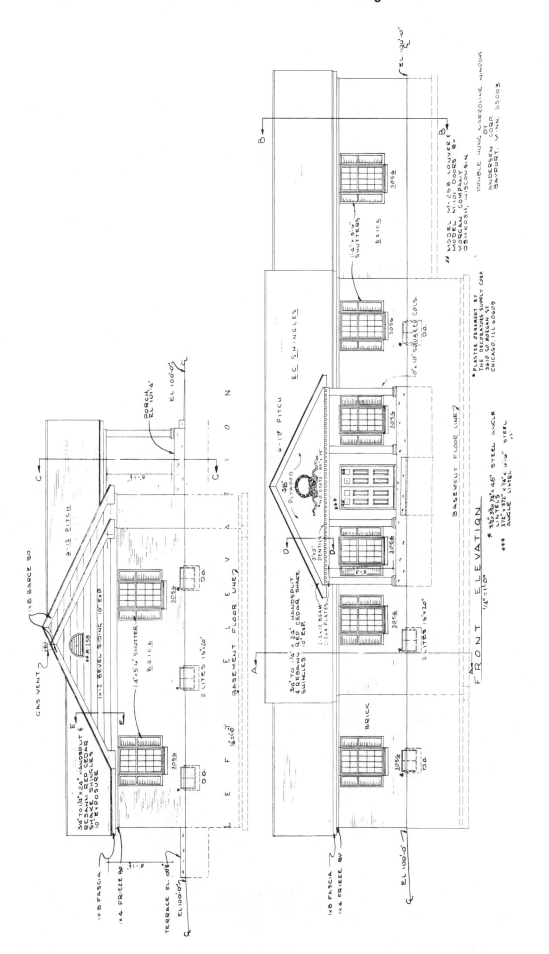

**Figure 1-5.** *These elevations show the structure from two sides.*

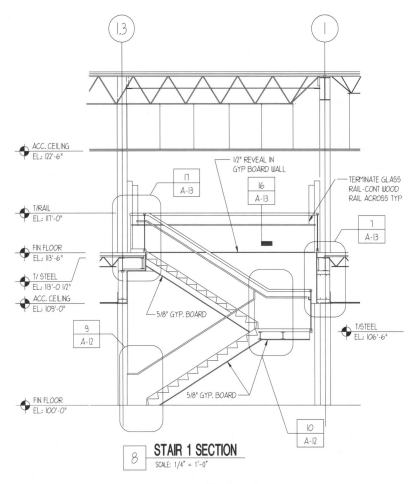

**Figure 1-6.** *This sectional view illustrates stair construction. (Charles E. Smith, Areté 3 Ltd.)*

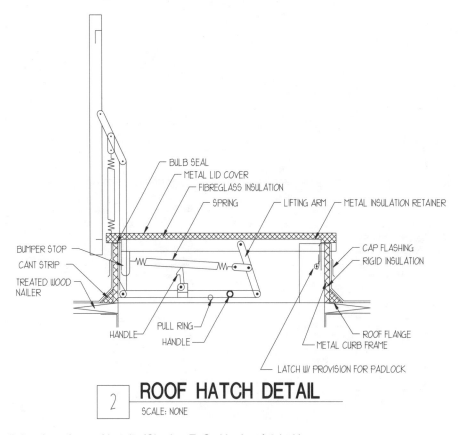

**Figure 1-7.** *A detail drawing of a roof hatch. (Charles E. Smith, Areté 3 Ltd.)*

## SHELL BUILDING DOOR SCHEDULE

| DOOR No. ⬭ | DOOR | | | | | FRAME | | | | FIRE RATING | HARDWARE | REMARKS |
|---|---|---|---|---|---|---|---|---|---|---|---|---|
| | TYPE | SIZE | THICK | MATERIAL | FINISH | TYPE | MATERIAL | FINISH | DETAIL | | | |
| 100A | A | 6'-0"x7'-0" | 1 3/4" | AL/GLASS | ENAM | - | AL | ENAM | - | | R | CURTAIN WALL - SEE SHEET A-6 |
| 121A | B | 3'-0"x7'-0" | 1 3/4" | HM | PAINT | A | HM | PAINT | 3,4/A-16 | | B,H,M,N,P,T | - |
| 122A | B | 3'-0"x7'-0" | 1 3/4" | HM | PAINT | B | HM | PAINT | 3,4/A-16 | C | B,H,M,N,P,T | 1 HOUR |
| 122B | B | 3'-0"x7'-0" | 1 3/4" | HM | PAINT | A | HM | PAINT | - | C | B,C,H,T | 1 HOUR |
| 127A | B | 3'-0"x7'-0" | 1 3/4" | HM | PAINT | A | HM | PAINT | 3,4/A-16 | | B,H,M,N,P,T | - |
| 127B | C | 10'-0"x12'-0" | 1 3/4" | STEEL | PREF. | - | STEEL | PAINT | 1,2/A-16 | | - | HI-LIFT O.H. DOOR |
| 127C | C | 9'-0"x10'-0" | 1 3/4" | STEEL | PREF. | - | STEEL | PAINT | 1,2/A-16 | | - | HI-LIFT O.H. DOOR |

H.M.= HOLLOW METAL, MTL.= METAL, PREF.= PREFINISHED, WD.= WOOD, AL.= ALUMINUM, ST/V.= STAIN & VARNISH, GL.= GLASS, STL.=STEEL, B. ENAM.= BAKED ENAMEL FINISH

### HARDWARE SCHEDULE

A   LCN SERIES 1010 CLOSER (STANDARD)
B   LCN SERIES 1011 CLOSER (H.C.)
C   GLYNN JOHNSON WALL STOP #60W
E   VON DUPRIN SERIES 99 PANIC BAR
F   2 PAIR BUTT HINGE McKINNEY #T2714
G   1 1/2 PAIR BUTT HINGE McKINNEY #T2714
H   1 1/2 PAIR BUTT HINGE HEAVY DUTY McKINNEY #T4A3786
K   HAGGAR #30S 3 1/2"x15" PUSH PLATE
L   HAGGER #30S PUSH PL w/ #3G PULL
M   REESE #815A POLYPRENE WEATHER STRIP
N   REESE #5424A THRESHOLD

O   HARDWARE PROVIDED BY MANUFACTURER
P   KEYED LOCK SET
Q   REESE #371C SWEEP
R   MANUFACTURER TO PROVIDE PUSH BAR, PULL HANDLE
    H.C. CLOSER, THRESHOLD, WEATHER STRIPPING, SWEEP,
    THUMB TURN LOCK SET
S   SCHLAGE S SERIES LATCH (MEDIUM DUTY)
T   SCHLAGE L SERIES LATCH (HEAVY DUTY)
    SUGGESTED HARDWARE OR EQUAL

**Figure 1-8.** *This schedule contains the details for all of the doors in the building. (Charles E. Smith, Areté 3 Ltd.)*

## ROOM FINISH SCHEDULE

| ROOM No. | ROOM NAME | FLR. | BASE | WALLS | | | | CL'G | CL'G HT. | REMARKS |
|---|---|---|---|---|---|---|---|---|---|---|
| | | | | N | E | S | W | | | |
| 100 | VESTIBULE | QT | VC | PT | GL | PT | GL | ACT | 9'-0" | SURF MTD PEDIMAT |
| 101 | WAITING | CPT | VC | PT | GL | PT | - | ACT | 9'-0" | - |
| 102 | RECEPTION | CPT | V | - | - | PT | PT/WD | ACT | 9'-0" | - |
| 103 | OFFICE | CPT | V | PT | PT | PT | PT | ACT | 9'-0" | - |
| 104 | VP SALES | CPT | V | PT | PT | PT | PT | ACT | 9'-0" | - |
| 105 | CLASSROOM | CPT | V | PT | PT | PT | PT | ACT | 9'-0" | - |
| 106 | CONFERENCE | CPT | V | PT | PT | PT | PT | ACT | 9'-0" | - |
| 107 | OFFICE | CPT | V | PT | PT | PT | PT | ACT | 9'-0" | - |
| 108 | OFFICE | CPT | V | PT | PT | PT | PT | ACT | 9'-0" | - |
| 109 | CONT. OFFICE | CPT | V | PT | PT | PT | PT | ACT | 9'-0" | - |
| 110 | ADMIN. VP | CPT | V | PT | PT | PT | PT | ACT | 9'-0" | - |
| 111 | OPEN OFFICE | CPT | V | PT | PT | PT | PT | ACT | 9'-0" | - |
| 112 | COMPUTER | CPT | V | PT | PT | PT | PT | ACT | 9'-0" | - |
| 113 | CONFERENCE | CPT | V | PT | PT | PT | PT | ACT | 9'-0" | - |

QT = QUARRY TILE
CT = CERAMIC TILE
CPT = CARPET
VCT = VINYL COMPOSITE TILE
GL = GLASS

V = 4" VINYL BASE
PT = PAINT
OPEN = EXPOSED CONSTRUCTION
ACT = 2x2 ACOUSTICAL CEILING TILE
VT = VINYL TILE

BL = CONCRETE BLOCK
CS = SEALED CONCRETE
DW = DRYWALL
VC = VINYL COVE BASE

**Figure 1-9.** *Schedules are forms that provide additional information to the builder. (Charles E. Smith, Areté 3 Ltd.)*

*Visualization* is the ability to create a mental image of a building from a set of prints. A study of print reading principles and learning to sketch will help you visualize construction details.

*Interpretation* is the ability to understand lines, symbols, dimensions, notes, and other information on the print. Each of these areas will be discussed in this text.

## Handling Prints

Prints and related specification sheets are as important as the tools you use. With proper care, prints can be kept usable for a long period of time.

There are several rules for handling prints:

- Never write on a print unless you have been authorized to make changes.
- Keep prints clean. Soiled prints are difficult to read and contribute to errors.
- Do not eat or drink near prints.
- Fold or roll prints carefully.
- Do not lay sharp tools or pointed objects on prints.
- Keep prints out of direct sunlight except when being used. Prints will fade and deteriorate if left in the sun.
- When not in use, store prints in a clean, dry place.

# Test Your Knowledge

*Write your answers in the spaces provided.*

_____ 1. Which is not a common type of drawing?
  A. Mechanical plan
  B. Plumbing plan
  C. Painting plan
  D. Foundation plan
  E. They are all common drawings.

_____ 2. Under which conditions can the electrical plan be included on the floor plan?
  A. When the building is not complex
  B. When print paper is scarce
  C. When the architect is also an electrician
  D. When a single company is doing all the construction
  E. There are no conditions when the electrical plan can be included on the floor plan.

_____ 3. Which drawing would show the location of a sprinkler system?
  A. Electrical plan
  B. Foundation plan
  C. Site plan
  D. Plumbing plan
  E. The sprinkler system would not be shown on any of these drawings.

_____ 4. Which occupation does *not* need to know how to read construction prints?
  A. Welder
  B. Construction estimator
  C. Owner of a lighting store
  D. Concrete supplier
  E. All these occupations require print reading.

_____ 5. A list of materials included on a drawing is called _____.
  A. notes
  B. an elevation
  C. a section
  D. a schedule
  E. None of the above.

_____ 6. A rendering would show all the details needed to build an office building. (True or False?)

_____ 7. The locations of utilities are shown on a site plan. (True or False?)

_____ 8. Most construction drawings are created using orthographic projection. (True or False?)

_____ 9. Prints will *not* be damaged if they are left out in direct sunlight for an extended period. (True or False?)

_____ 10. *Working drawing* is another term for *print*. (True or False?)

# Reading Measuring Tools

## Technical Terms

Centimeter      Metric rule
Fractional rule     Millimeter
Meter

## Learning Objectives

After completing this unit, you will be able to:
- Read both English (customary) and metric rules and tapes
- Convert between English and metric units

Many different types of measuring tools are used in the construction industry. These include framing squares, bench rules, steel rules, and tapes, **Figure 2-1.** This unit is designed to help you review the methods of reading these measuring tools.

In the English, or customary, measurement system, the distances are divided into feet, inches, and fractional parts of an inch. The rule used with this system is called the *fractional rule.* In the metric system, the divisions are in meters, centimeters, and millimeters. The rule is called the *metric rule.*

## Fractional Rule

Measurements in the construction industry are seldom more accurate than one-sixteenth of an inch. Therefore, the fractional rule is divided into 16ths. On the rule shown in **Figure 2-2**, the inch is divided into 16 parts; each small division is 1/16th of an inch. To read the fractional rule, follow these steps:

1. Study the major divisions of the inch numbered 4, 8, and 12. These represent 1/4″ (4/16), 1/2″ (8/16), and 3/4″ (12/16).
2. Note that there are four small divisions within

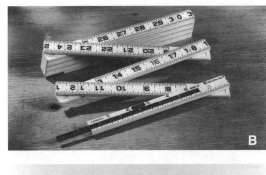

**Figure 2-1.** *Some measuring tools used in construction. A—Measuring tape. B—Folding rule. C—Steel rule. D—Plumb bob. (Craftsman)*

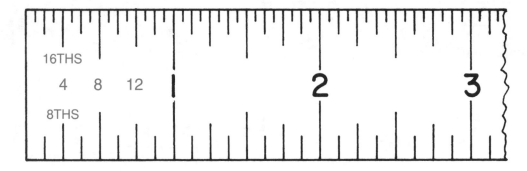

**Figure 2-2.** *Typical divisions of a fractional rule.*

each 1/4″ division. Each of these divisions represents 1/16″. Two of these divisions equal 1/8″ (2/16).

3. Further study and application of fractional parts

will enable you to locate any common fraction that is a multiple of 16ths. For example:

$$\frac{4}{16} = \frac{1}{4} \qquad \frac{8}{16} = \frac{1}{2} \qquad \frac{10}{16} = \frac{5}{8}$$

## Measurement Activity 2-1

# *Reading a Fractional Rule*

*Fill in the measurements for the eight blanks below.*
*Reduce to lowest terms and place your answers in the spaces provided.*

A ___ B ___ C ___ D ___ E ___ F ___ G ___ H ___

## Metric Rule

The basic unit of linear measure in the metric system is the **meter** (m). Other linear units are either fractions or multiples of a meter. The names of the other units consist of a prefix followed by *meter*. The most common units are the following:

| Unit | Abbreviation | Equal to |
|---|---|---|
| millimeter | mm | 1/1000 m |
| centimeter | cm | 1/100 m |
| kilometer | km | 1000 m |

In the construction field, the **millimeter** is normally used for metric drawings. Metric dimensions are better to work with because they can be added and subtracted

more easily than English units. However, the customary system is used almost exclusively in the United States because materials are manufactured to customary dimensions. A comparison of the English and metric systems will help develop an understanding of their values.

|  |  |
|---|---|
| 1 inch | = 25.4 millimeters |
| 12 inches | = 304.8 millimeters |
| 1 yard (36 inches) | = 914.4 millimeters |
| 39.37 inches | = 1000 millimeters (1 meter) |

To convert inches to millimeters, multiply by 25.4:
**Example:** Convert 14″ to millimeters.
**Solution:** 14″ × 25.4 = 355.6 mm

If the measurement is in both feet and inches, first convert the feet to inches, then convert the inches to millimeters. The millimeters can then be converted to meters by dividing by 1000:

**Example:**   Convert 11′-5″ to metric.
**Solution:**   $(11' \times 12) + 5'' = 132'' + 5'' = 137''$
$137'' \times 25.4 = 3479.8$ mm
$$\frac{3479.8 \text{mm}}{1000} = 3.48\text{m}$$

To convert millimeters to inches, divide by 25.4:

**Example:**   Convert 225 mm to inches.
**Solution:**   $225 \div 25.4 = 8.86'' = 8\ 7/8''$

When using other metric units, first convert to millimeters, then to inches, and then to feet:

**Example:**   Convert 23.45 m to customary units.
**Solution:**   23.45 m = 23,450 mm
23,450 mm ÷ 25.4 = 923.23″
912″ = 76′
923.23″ = 76′-11 1/4″

Building material sizes are given in millimeters or centimeters. For example, the nominal size of the metric brick (including joint thickness) is 225 mm × 112.5 mm × 75 mm. The standard metric modular sheet size is 120 cm × 240 cm. Metric measurements in cabinet work are usually given in centimeters.

In time, building products manufactured to standard metric sizes will become increasingly popular. Therefore, the ability to work with metric measurements will be required.

The smallest division on the metric framing square is 1/2 cm. On tapes, the smallest division is the millimeter. To read the metric rule, follow these steps:

1. Study the major divisions marked 1, 2, 3, etc. Each of these represents 1 cm.
2. Each centimeter is divided into 10 millimeters.
3. A meter is 1000 millimeters.
4. For a reading of 3.4 meters (344 mm), follow the rule to three meters (3 m) and then on to 40 cm (0.4 m), **Figure 2-3.**

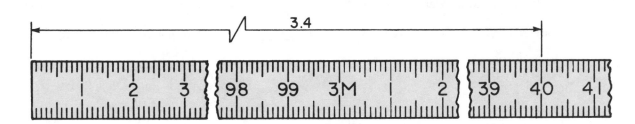

**Figure 2-3.**  *A measurement of 3.4 meters is shown.*

## Measurement Activity 2-2
# *Reading a Metric Rule*

*Fill in the measurements below in terms of millimeters. Place your answers in the spaces provided.*

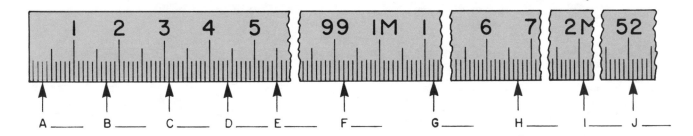

# Test Your Knowledge

*Write your answers in the spaces provided.*

_____ 1. Convert 25″ to millimeters.

     A. 25 mm

     B. 635 mm

     C. 1 mm

     D. 11.8 mm

     E. None of these answers are reasonable.

_____ 2. Convert 12′-3″ to metric measure.

     A. 307.8 mm

     B. 5.79 mm

     C. 3078 mm

     D. 3.73 m

     E. None of these answers are reasonable.

_____ 3. Convert 38 mm to customary units.

     A. 1 1/2″

     B. 965.2″

     C. 18′

     D. 3 1/8″

     E. None of these answers are reasonable.

_____ 4. Convert 17.42 m to customary units.

     A. 57′-1 7/8″

     B. 36′-10 1/2″

     C. 442 1/2″

     D. 36 7/8″

     E. None of these answers are reasonable.

_____ 5. One inch is longer than 2 cm.
(True or False?)

_____ 6. Concert 210′-6″ to metric measure.

     A. 64.2 m

     B. 5346.7 mm

     C. 2520″

     D. 5.35 m

     E. None of these answers are reasonable.

_____ 7. Convert 1.42 m to customary units.

     A. 3.6′

     B. 64″

     C. 4′-8″

     D. 1/2″

     E. None of these answers are reasonable.

_____ 8. Convert 3 1/2″ to metric measure.

     A. 88.9 cm

     B. 0.14 mm

     C. 0.14 m

     D. 8.89 mm

     E. None of these answers are reasonable.

_____ 9. One foot is longer than 30 cm.
(True or False?)

_____ 10. One yard is longer than 90 cm.
(True or False?)

# Construction Mathematics Review

## Technical Terms

Area
Circumference
Decimal fraction
Denominator
Diameter
Improper fraction

Least common
  denominator (LCD)
Numerator
Proper fraction
Radius

## Learning Objectives

After completing this unit, you will be able to:
- Add, subtract, multiply, and divide fractions
- Convert between improper fractions and mixed numbers
- Add, subtract, multiply, and divide decimal fractions

Construction workers and estimators often need to make calculations when working with prints. This unit deals with construction-oriented calculations, including fractions and decimals in both customary and metric units.

## Fractions

Fractions are written with one number over the other, such as $\frac{9}{16}$. The number on the bottom (16), is called the **denominator.** It indicates the number of equal parts into which a unit is divided. The number on top (9) is called the **numerator.** It indicates the number of equal parts taken, **Figure 3-1.** In the fraction shown (9/16), nine of the sixteen parts are taken.

A **proper fraction** is one whose numerator is less than its denominator, such as 7/16 and 3/4. An

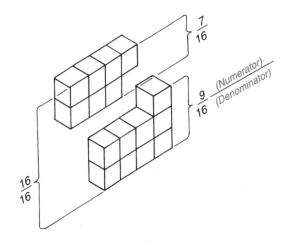

**Figure 3-1.** *The fraction 9/16 represents 9 pieces of a whole divided into 16 equal pieces.*

**improper fraction** is one whose numerator is greater than its denominator, such as 5/4 and 19/16. A **mixed number** is a number that consists of a whole number and a proper fraction, such as 2 3/4 and 5 1/8. Proper fractions represent numbers between zero and one. Improper fractions and mixed numbers represent numbers larger than one.

## Using Fractions

- Whole numbers can be changed to fractions by multiplying the numerator and denominator by the same number.

**Example:** Change 6 (whole number) into fourths.
$$\frac{6}{1} \times \frac{4}{4} = \frac{24}{4}$$

Each whole unit contains 4 fourths.
Six units contain $6 \times 4$ fourths, or 24 fourths.
The value of the number has not changed.

- Mixed numbers can be changed to fractions by changing the whole number to a fraction with the same denominator as the fractional part and adding the two fractions.

**Example:** Convert 3 5/8 to an improper fraction.

$$3\frac{5}{8} = \left(\frac{3}{1} \times \frac{8}{8}\right) + \frac{5}{8} = \frac{24}{8} + \frac{5}{8} = \frac{29}{8}$$

Three units contain $3 \times 8$ eighths, or 24 eighths. Adding the 5/8 part of the mixed number to 24/8 gives us 29/8.

- Improper fractions can be reduced to a whole or mixed number by dividing the numerator by the denominator:

$$\frac{17}{4} = 17 \div 4 = 4\frac{1}{4}$$

- Fractions can be reduced to the lowest form by dividing the numerator and denominator by the same number:

$$\frac{6}{8} = \frac{6 \div 2}{8 \div 2} = \frac{3}{4}$$

The value of a fraction does not change if the numerator and denominator are divided by the same number, since this is the same as dividing by 1.

- Fractions can be changed to higher terms by multiplying the numerator and denominator by the same number:

$$\frac{5}{8} = \frac{5 \times 2}{8 \times 2} = \frac{10}{16}$$

The value of a fraction is not changed by multiplying the numerator and denominator by the same number.

## ADDING FRACTIONS

To add fractions, the denominators must all be the same.

**Example:** $\dfrac{5}{16} + \dfrac{3}{8} + \dfrac{11}{32} = ?$

The *least common denominator* (**LCD**) into which these denominators can be divided is 32. Change all fractions to have 32 in the denominator:

$$\frac{5}{16} \times \frac{2}{2} = \frac{10}{32}$$

$$\frac{3}{8} \times \frac{4}{4} = \frac{12}{32}$$

Now that the fractions have the same denominator, add their numerators. The common denominator is used in the sum:

$$\frac{10}{32} + \frac{12}{32} + \frac{11}{32} = \frac{33}{32}$$

Convert to a mixed number:

$$\frac{33}{32} = 1\frac{1}{32}$$

**Construction Mathematics Activity 3-1**

## *Adding Fractions*

*Add the following fractions. Reduce answers to lowest form.*

1. $\dfrac{3}{4} + \dfrac{1}{8} + \dfrac{1}{2} =$

2. $\dfrac{7}{8} + \dfrac{3}{16} =$

3. $\dfrac{5}{12} + \dfrac{3}{8} + \dfrac{3}{4} =$

4. $\dfrac{3}{10} + \dfrac{9}{10} + \dfrac{1}{20} =$

5. $\dfrac{7}{16} + \dfrac{3}{32} + \dfrac{1}{4} =$

6. $1\dfrac{3}{4} + \dfrac{7}{8} + 1\dfrac{1}{16} =$

7. $\dfrac{5}{32} + \dfrac{7}{64} + \dfrac{7}{8} =$

8. $1\dfrac{3}{8} + \dfrac{3}{32} + \dfrac{7}{16} =$

9. $3\dfrac{1}{16} + \dfrac{9}{16} + \dfrac{1}{2} =$

10. $5\dfrac{1}{5} + \dfrac{3}{10} + 8\dfrac{1}{2} =$

11. $4\dfrac{5}{8} + 20\dfrac{7}{32} =$

12. $\dfrac{3}{8} + \dfrac{7}{64} + \dfrac{9}{16} =$

13. $12\dfrac{7}{8} + 25\dfrac{3}{8} =$

14. $\dfrac{21}{32} + \dfrac{9}{64} + \dfrac{1}{4} =$

15. $\dfrac{3}{8} + 1\dfrac{1}{2} + \dfrac{7}{16} + \dfrac{7}{8} =$

## SUBTRACTING FRACTIONS

To subtract fractions, the denominators must all be the same.

**Example:** $\dfrac{3}{4} - \dfrac{5}{16} = ?$

The least common denominator into which these denominators can be divided is 16.

Change 3/4 so that its denominator is 16:

$$\frac{3}{4} \times \frac{4}{4} = \frac{12}{16}$$

Subtract the numerators and retain the common denominator:

$$\frac{12}{16} - \frac{5}{16} = \frac{7}{16}$$

**Construction Mathematics Activity 3-2**
## *Subtracting Fractions*

*Subtract the following fractions. Reduce answers to lowest form.*

1. $\dfrac{3}{8} - \dfrac{1}{4} =$

2. $\dfrac{3}{4} - \dfrac{5}{16} =$

3. $1\dfrac{7}{8} - \dfrac{13}{16} =$

4. $3\dfrac{1}{2} - \dfrac{9}{16} = (borrow\ \dfrac{16}{16}\ from\ 3)$

5. $10\dfrac{3}{8} - 7\dfrac{3}{32} =$

6. $5 - 2\dfrac{3}{8} =$

7. $12\dfrac{1}{16} - 8\dfrac{1}{2} =$

8. $4\dfrac{1}{4} - 3\dfrac{1}{16} =$

9. $20\dfrac{7}{8} - 11\dfrac{3}{64} =$

10. $15\dfrac{5}{8} - 5\dfrac{1}{2} =$

## MULTIPLYING FRACTIONS

Fractions can be multiplied as follows:
1. Change all mixed numbers to improper fractions.
2. Multiply all numerators to get the numerator of the answer.
3. Multiply all denominators to get the denominator of the answer.
4. Reduce the fraction to lowest terms.

**Example:**

$$\frac{1}{2} \times 3\frac{1}{8} \times 4 = ?$$

$$\frac{1}{2} \times \frac{25}{8} \times \frac{4}{1} = \frac{100}{16}$$

$$\frac{100}{16} = 6\frac{4}{16} = 6\frac{1}{4}$$

**Construction Mathematics Activity 3-3**
## *Multiplying Fractions*

*Multiply the following fractions. Reduce answers to lowest terms.*

1. $\dfrac{3}{4} \times \dfrac{1}{2} =$

2. $2\dfrac{5}{8} \times \dfrac{1}{4} =$

3. $\dfrac{7}{8} \times 5 =$

4. $6\dfrac{3}{4} \times \dfrac{1}{3} =$

5. $12\frac{1}{2} \times \frac{1}{2} =$

8. $9\frac{5}{8} \times \frac{1}{2} =$

6. $4\frac{3}{4} \times \frac{1}{2} \times \frac{1}{8} =$

9. $10 \times \frac{4}{5} =$

7. $16 \times \frac{3}{4} =$

10. $\frac{14}{3} \times 6 =$

## DIVIDING FRACTIONS

Fractions can be divided as follows:
1. Change all mixed numbers to improper fractions.
2. Invert (turn upside down) the divisor and multiply.

**Example:**

$5\frac{1}{4} \div 1\frac{1}{2} = ?$

$\frac{21}{4} \div \frac{3}{2} =$

$\frac{21}{4} \times \frac{2}{3} = \frac{42}{12}$

$\frac{42}{12} = 3\frac{6}{12} = 3\frac{1}{2}$

Construction Mathematics Activity 3-4
## *Dividing Fractions*

*Divide the following fractions. Reduce answers to lowest terms.*

1. $2\frac{3}{4} \div 6 =$

6. $\frac{7}{8} \div \frac{7}{16} =$

2. $12 \div \frac{3}{4} =$

7. $15 \div 1\frac{1}{4} =$

3. $16\frac{1}{8} \div 2 =$

8. $21 \div 3\frac{1}{8} =$

4. $8\frac{2}{3} \div \frac{1}{3} =$

9. $5\frac{1}{4} \div \frac{3}{8} =$

5. $16\frac{1}{4} \div 20 =$

10. $3\frac{5}{8} \div 2 =$

## Decimal Fractions

The denominator in a *decimal fraction* is 10 or a multiple of 10 (100, 1000, etc.). When writing decimal fractions, we omit the denominator and place a decimal point in the numerator.

3/10 is written 0.3 (three tenths)
87/100 is written 0.87 (eighty-seven hundredths)
375/1000 is written 0.375 (three hundred seventy-five thousandths)

4375/10000 is written 0.4375 (four thousand three hundred seventy-five ten thousandths)

Whole numbers are written to the left of the decimal point and fractional parts are to the right:

5 253/1000 is written 5.253 (five and two hundred fifty-three thousandths)

## ADDING AND SUBTRACTING DECIMALS

Decimals are added and subtracted in the same manner as whole numbers. With decimals, however, the decimal points must be aligned vertically.

**Example:**
Add:
```
  7.3125
  1.25
  0.625
+ 3.375
─────────
 12.5625
```

Subtract:
```
  8.625
− 2.25
────────
  6.375
```

The decimal point in the answer is directly below the decimal points in the problem.

**Construction Mathematics Activity 3-5**
## *Adding and Subtracting Decimals*

*Solve the following problems:*

*Add:*

1. 4.5625 + 0.875 + 2.75 + 5.8137 =

2. 1.9375 + 3.25 + 0.375 =

3. 7.0625 + 0.125 + 8.0 =

4. 11.342 + 16.17 + 0.4207 =

5. 0.832 + 0.4375 + 0.27 =

*Subtract:*

6. 27.9375 − 16.937 =

7. 3.306 − 1.875 =

8. 4.0 − 0.0625 =

9. 10 − 0.75 =

10. 2.25 − 1.125 =

## MULTIPLYING DECIMALS

Decimals are multiplied in the same manner as whole numbers. The decimal points are disregarded until the multiplication is completed. To find the position of the decimal point in the answer, count the total number of decimal places to the right of the decimal point in the numbers being multiplied; then set off this number of decimal places in the answer, starting at the right.

**Example:**
```
  6.25
× 1.5   (3 decimal places in the two numbers)
────────
 9.375  (3 decimal places)
```

**Construction Mathematics Activity 3-6**
## *Multiplying Decimals*

*Solve the following problems:*

1.  4.825
    × 1.75

2.  12.05
    × 4.124

3.  167
    × 0.25

4.  .838
    × 5.9

5.  65.96
    × 0.37

6.  0.375
    × 6

7.  4.95
    × 1.35

8.  3.75
    × 100

9.  93.18
    × 0.07

10. 5639.25
    × 10

## DIVIDING DECIMALS

Dividing decimals is identical to dividing whole numbers, except that the decimal point must be properly placed in the quotient (answer).

To place the decimal point in the quotient, count the number of places to the right of the decimal point in the divisor. Add this number of places to the right of the decimal point in the dividend and place the decimal point directly above in the quotient.

**Example:** 36.5032 ÷ 4.12 = ?

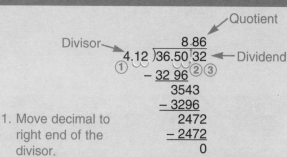

```
                          ,Quotient
Divisor→       8.86
      4.12 )36.50 32  ←Dividend
       ① ◡◡    ②③
        - 32 96
          3543
         - 3296
           2472
          - 2472
              0
```

1. Move decimal to right end of the divisor.
2. Move decimal in the dividend the same number of places it was moved in the divisor.
3. The decimal in the quotient is directly above the newly-located decimal in the dividend.

Construction Mathematics Activity 3-7
# *Dividing Decimals*

*Solve the following problems:*

1. $9.45 \div 2.7 =$

6. $25924.64 \div 31.6 =$

2. $7.9392 \div 0.96 =$

7. $331.266 \div 80.6 =$

3. $654.5 \div 35 =$

8. $821.7 \div 83 =$

4. $172.8 \div 2.4 =$

9. $4401.25 \div 503 =$

5. $1386.0 \div 1.65 =$

10. $2585.52 \div 26.6 =$

# Area Measurement

Often, it is necessary to know the amount of floor or wall space in a particular room or building. This measurement is known as *area*, and it is given in square units (square feet, square yards, square meters, for example).

## Square and Rectangular Areas

To compute the area of a rectangle or square, multiply the length of one side times the length of an adjacent side (length × width). The lengths must have the same units. The units of area are the same as units of length. For example, if you multiply two lengths in feet together, the area will be in square feet. If the lengths are given in inches, the area would be in square inches.

**Example:** Determine the area of the room shown in **Figure 3-2(A)**.

$$12 \text{ ft}^2$$
$$\underline{\times\ 10 \text{ ft}^2}$$
$$120 \text{ ft}^2$$

The area of a wall is computed in the same way, except that the area of all openings (doors and windows) are subtracted from the total.

**Example:** Determine the area of the wall surface shown in **Figure 3-2(B)**.

Total Wall Area:

$$20 \text{ ft}^2$$
$$\times \ 8 \text{ ft}^2$$
$$160 \text{ ft}^2$$

Window Area:

$$5 \text{ ft}^2$$
$$\times \ 4 \text{ ft}^2$$
$$20 \text{ ft}^2$$

(Total Wall Area) – (Window Area)
$$160 \text{ ft}^2$$
$$- 20 \text{ ft}^2$$
$$140 \text{ ft}^2 \text{ of wall surface}$$

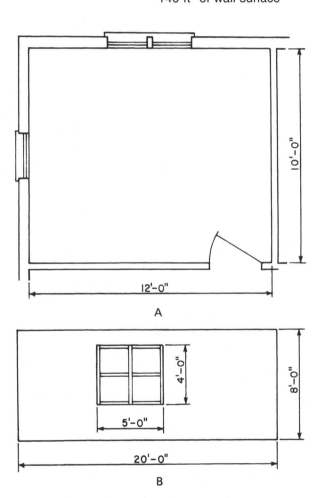

**Figure 3-2.** *A—Formula for finding area of a floor: A = L × W. B—Area of a wall: A = L × W – area of openings.*

## Triangular Area

A triangular area can be computed by multiplying the height times the base and dividing by two. **Figure 3-3** illustrates the formula.

**Example:** Compute the area of the end of the gable roof shown in **Figure 3-3**.

$$5 \text{ ft} \times 24 \text{ ft} = 120 \text{ ft}^2$$
$$120 \text{ ft}^2 \div 2 = 60 \text{ ft}^2$$

## Circular Area

The characteristics of circles are shown in **Figure 3-4**. The *circumference* is the distance around the circle. The *diameter* is the length of a line running between two points on the circle and passing through the center. The *radius* is one-half the length of the diameter.

When determining the circumference, area, or volume of a circular object, the number π (pi) is used in the formulas. Pi is the ratio of circumference to diameter, and is equal to 3.1416. The area of a circle can be found by multiplying π times the radius squared.

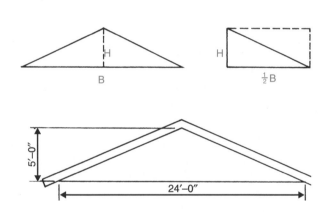

**Figure 3-3.** *Formula for finding area of a triangular area: A = (B × H) ÷ 2.*

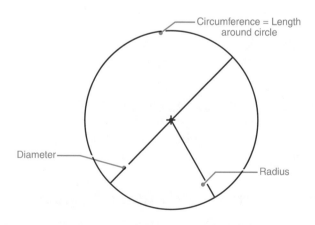

**Figure 3-4.** *In order to determine areas of circles, you must be familiar with the properties of circles, such as radius and diameter.*

**Area of a Circle = $\pi \times r^2$**

**Example:** Determine the area of the patio shown in **Figure 3-5**.

Patio diameter = $30^2$, radius = $15^2$
$3.1416 \times 15$ ft $\times 15$ ft = Area
$3.1416 \times 225$ ft² = Area

$$\begin{array}{r} 3.1416 \\ \times\ 225 \text{ ft}^2 \\ \hline 706.86 \text{ ft}^2 \text{ patio} \end{array}$$

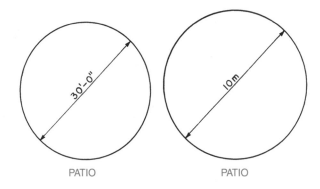

PATIO                    PATIO

**Figure 3-5.** *Formula for finding area of a circle: $A = \pi \times r^2$.*

# Volume Measurement

Volume is a cubic measure. It is found by multiplying area by depth. We will compute the volume of ready-mix concrete required for a 4″ slab for the patio in the last example. When calculating volume, you must be certain that all of the numbers being multiplied together have the same units. Since we know the area of the patio is 706.86 ft², we will change the 4″ depth to 0.333′.

$$\begin{array}{r} 706.86 \text{ ft}^2 \ \text{(area of patio)} \\ \times\ 0.333 \text{ ft.} \\ \hline 235.38 \text{ ft}^2 \ \text{in patio slab} \end{array}$$

Since concrete is sold by the cubic yard, it is necessary to change the cubic feet to cubic yards. There are 27 cubic feet in a cubic yard, so we divide cubic feet by 27:

$$\begin{array}{r} 8.71 \approx 8.7 \text{ yd}^3 \\ 27\ \overline{)235.38} \\ -216\phantom{..} \\ \hline 193\phantom{..} \\ -189\phantom{..} \\ \hline 48\phantom{.} \\ -27\phantom{.} \\ \hline 21\phantom{.} \end{array}$$

Area and volume measurements in metric are figured in the same manner using appropriate units.

**Example:**

Patio diameter = 10 meters;
    thickness = 10 centimeters.

Determine area of patio:
    $$\begin{array}{r} 3.1416 \\ \times\ 25 \text{ m}^2 \ \text{(radius squared)} \\ \hline 78.54 \text{ m}^2 \ \text{(area of patio)} \end{array}$$

Convert thickness to meters:
    10 cm = 0.1 m

Multiply area by thickness:
    $$\begin{array}{r} 78.54 \text{ m}^2 \\ \times\ 0.1 \text{ m} \\ \hline 7.854 \text{ m}^3 \ \text{(volume of patio)} \end{array}$$

Note that fewer calculations are required with metric units.

# Test Your Knowledge

*Write your answers in the spaces provided.*
*Reduce all answers to lowest terms.*

_____ 1. Add: $\dfrac{3}{8} + \dfrac{3}{8}$

    A. $\dfrac{6}{64}$

    B. 0

    C. 1

    D. $\dfrac{3}{4}$

    E. None of the above.

_____ 2. Subtract: $\dfrac{13}{16} - \dfrac{3}{8}$

    A. $\dfrac{7}{16}$

    B. $\dfrac{10}{8}$

    C. $1\dfrac{2}{3}$

    D. $\dfrac{19}{16}$

    E. None of the above.

_____ 3. Multiply: $\dfrac{2}{3} \times \dfrac{9}{16}$

    A. $\dfrac{1}{3}$

    B. $\dfrac{11}{48}$

    C. $\dfrac{11}{19}$

    D. $\dfrac{3}{8}$

    E. None of the above.

_____ 4. Divide: $\dfrac{4}{9} \div 3$

    A. $1\dfrac{1}{3}$

    B. $\dfrac{4}{27}$

    C. $\dfrac{7}{27}$

    D. $\dfrac{1}{9}$

    E. None of the above.

_____ 5. Add: $3\dfrac{3}{4} + 2\dfrac{1}{3}$

    A. $5\dfrac{4}{7}$

    B. $5\dfrac{3}{12}$

    C. $6\dfrac{1}{12}$

    D. $5\dfrac{1}{4}$

    E. None of the above.

_____ 6. Add: 23.98 + 1.123 + 4.003

    A. 29.403
    B. 7.524
    C. 75.24
    D. 29.106
    E. None of the above.

_____ 7. Subtract: 23.837 − 4.77

    A. 23.360
    B. 19.067
    C. 19.063
    D. 233.60
    E. None of the above.

_____ 8. Multiply: 1.23 × 2

    A. 2.23
    B. 24.6
    C. 246
    D. 2.46
    E. None of the above.

_____ 9. Divide: 12.64 ÷ 4.

    A. 316
    B. 50.56
    C. 16.64
    D. 3.16
    E. None of the above.

_____ 10. Divide: 88.56 ÷ 2.4

    A. 36.9
    B. 212.544
    C. 90.76
    D. 3.69
    E. None of the above.

## Construction Mathematics Activity 3–8
# *Problems in Construction Mathematics*

*Solve the following problems. Show your work.*

1. A triangular frame has sides that measure 15.7, 20.4, and 26.2 centimeters. What is the total length of the three sides?

2. A carpenter had a board 2′–10 3/4″ long. To fit the space for a shelf, he cut 7/16″ off one end. How long was the board after the piece was removed?

3. Fifteen strips, 1 1/4″ wide, are to be ripped from a sheet of plywood. If 1/8″ is lost with each cut, how much of the plywood sheet is used in making the 15 strips? (Assume 15 cuts are necessary.)

4. An interior wall of a building is made up of metal studs with 5/8″ wallboard on each side. See the drawing below. If the actual width of a stud is 3 3/8″, what is the total thickness of the wall?

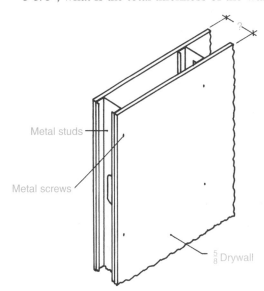

Metal studs

Metal screws

$\frac{5}{8}$ Drywall

5. A carpenter worked 10 weeks on a particular job, 5 1/2 days per week and 7 3/4 hours per day. How many hours did he work on the job?

6. What is the area of a rectangular floor that is 7.3 meters long and 4.2 meters wide?

7. There are 15 risers in a set of stairs running from the basement to the first floor. Each riser is 7 1/4″ high. What is the distance between floors?

8. The distance between two floors is 9′-0 1/2″. If 14 risers are to be used in a set of stairs, what is the height of each riser?

9. How many 1×2 shelf cleats 8″ long can be cut from a 1×2 board 16′ long? How much is left? (Disregard waste in saw cut.)

10. A contractor removed 35.7 m³ of earth from a building site. If his trucks can haul 1.7 m³ per load, how many truck loads of earth were moved?

11. Figure the amount of concrete (in cubic yards) required to pour a floor slab of the following dimensions: $18' \times 24' \times 4''$.

12. How much concrete is needed to pour a slab $6 \text{ m} \times 8 \text{ m} \times 10 \text{ cm}$?

13. How many gallons of paint are required to paint one side of a block wall of the following dimensions: $6' \times 172'$? The paint being used will cover 200 ft$^2$ per gallon.

14. Compute the liters of sealer required to seal a floor 12 m $\times$ 25 m. The sealer being used will cover 7 m$^2$ per liter.

15. How much concrete is required to pour the slab shown below?

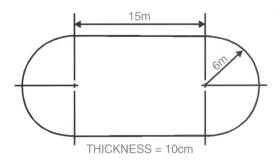

15m

6m

THICKNESS = 10cm

# Section 2

# Print Reading Basics

©1995 L.F. GARLINGHOUSE COMPANY, INC.

# Lines and Symbols

## Technical Terms

Alphabet of lines
Center line
Dimension line

Extension line
Hidden line
Symbols

## Learning Objectives

After completing this unit, you will be able to:
- Identify features from different lines
- Match drawing symbols with their meanings

Reading construction prints begins with an understanding of lines and symbols that appear on drawings. Drafters use a defined system of lines and symbols. The different types of lines and symbols are defined and discussed in this unit.

## The Alphabet of Lines

Several types of lines are commonly used on construction drawings. These are known as the *alphabet of lines.* All lines are drawn in the same color. Some vary in width. Some are solid, some are a combination of broken lines. Each conveys a different meaning. **Figure 4-1** illustrates some common lines and symbols.

PROPERTY LINE

- *Property Line:* The property line is an extra heavy line with long dashes alternating with two short dashes. The length and bearing (direction) of each line usually is identified on the site plan.

BORDER LINE

- *Border Line:* Border lines are located near the edge of the sheet of drawing paper. They are also used to separate the various portions of the drawing, such as the title block, notes, and the revision block.

OBJECT LINE

- *Object Line:* Object lines represent the main outline of the features of the object, building, or walk. The object line is a heavy, continuous line, showing all edges and surfaces.

HIDDEN LINE

- *Hidden Line:* Hidden lines are medium weight and composed of short dashes. They define edges and surfaces that are not visible in a particular view. The worker must look for another view in the set of drawings to find where these edges occur. Often, these hidden parts will be revealed in an elevation or sectional view. Hidden lines are omitted if they do not clarify the drawing.

CENTER LINE

- *Center Line:* The center line is used to indicate centers of objects such as columns, equipment, and fixtures. Normally, these objects are located by dimensioning to the center. The center line is also used to indicate a finished floor line. This line is lightweight and composed of alternating long and short dashes.

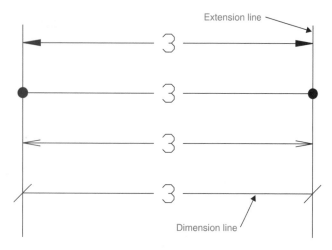

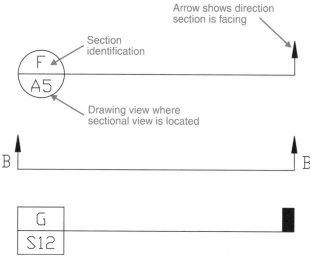

CUTTING-PLANE LINES

- *Dimension and Extension Lines:* Dimension and extension lines are thin lines that indicate the extent and direction of dimensions. Dimension lines extend for the length of the distance being measured. A marking device—such as an arrow, dot, or tick—is placed at each end of the dimension line. Extension lines are drawn perpendicular to the dimension line to specify the features between which the dimension applies. A *leader* is a line that has an arrow at one end and a text note at the other end. The arrow points to the feature or detail to which the note refers. Leaders are the same weight as dimension and extension lines.

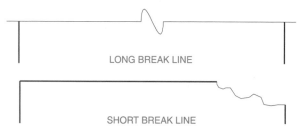

LONG BREAK LINE

SHORT BREAK LINE

- *Break Lines:* Break lines are used to show that only a portion of an object is shown. There are two instances when break lines are used: to indicate that an object continues but is not shown on the drawing, and to indicate that the full length of the object has been omitted to save space. When the break on the drawing is lengthy, long break lines with freehand "zigzags" are used. Short break lines are thick, randomly-curving lines used when the break is short, such as across a joist or beam.
- *Cutting-Plane Lines:* These lines are used with sectional views. A cutting-plane line marks the part of the drawing being "cut" to create a sectional view. Arrows on the end of the cutting-plane line indicate the direction from which the

section is being viewed. If the sectional view is on another drawing, the drawing number is included with the section identification.

- *Section Line:* Section lines, also called *cross-hatch lines,* are thin lines usually drawn at a 45° angle. They are used in a sectional view to show material that has been "cut" by the cutting-plane line.

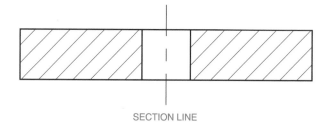

SECTION LINE

## Symbols

In addition to the various lines, a number of symbols are commonly used on construction drawings. These symbols represent building materials and fixtures. Most companies have their own set of symbols, but common items will have similar symbols.

Normally, symbols are identified in a legend, **Figure 4-2.** The legend is a list of symbols and their corresponding meanings. Sometimes, the legend for all of the symbols used in a set of prints is included on the cover sheet. When the legend is on a sheet other than the one you're reading, it is helpful to copy the legend onto a smaller sheet and keep it handy for reference.

Many common symbols are shown in *Section 7, Reference.* Look at this section now to become more familiar with symbols.

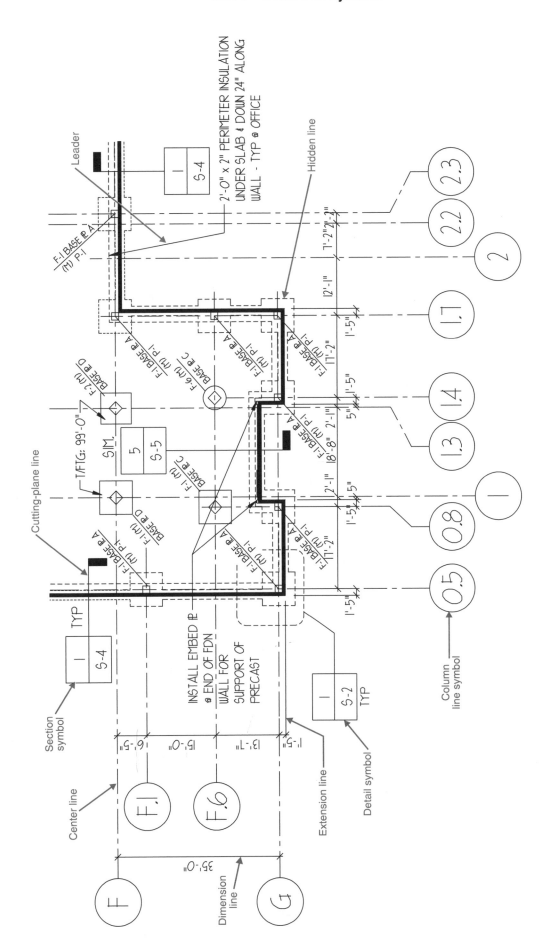

**Figure 4-1.** *Many types of lines and symbols are shown in this small portion of a foundation plan. Notice that the column lines (center lines) also serve as extension lines. (Charles E. Smith, Areté 3 Ltd.)*

| LIGHTING SYMBOLS | |
| --- | --- |
| SYMBOLS | DESCRIPTION |
| 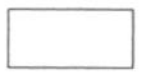 ▭ | 2'-0"x4'-0" RECESSED LIGHT FIX. W/LENSE |
|  ◨ | 2'-0"x4'-0" NIGHT LIGHT FIXTURE |
|  ⊗ | DUAL POWERED EXIT LIGHT |
|  ⌒ | EXHAUST FAN |
|  ⊔ | DUAL POWERED EMERGENCY WALL PAK LIGHT |
| ◎ | 150 W RECESSED CAN LIGHT |
| ⊕ | 100 W RECESSED CAN LIGHT |
|  ◪ | STAIR NIGHT LIGHT FIXTURE |
| ☐ | 2'-0"x2'-0" RECESSED LIGHT FIX. W/LENSE |
| ◣ | 2'-0"x2'-0" NIGHT LIGHT FIXTURE |
| 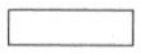 ▭ | 1'-0"x4'-0" RECESSED LIGHT FIX W/ACRYLIC LENSE |

**Figure 4-2.** *Legends are used to identify symbols.*
*(Charles E. Smith, Areté 3 Ltd.)*

## Test Your Knowledge

*Match the following terms and descriptions. Write your answers in the spaces provided.*

A. Hidden line     F. Alphabet of lines     K. Break line
B. Border line     G. Property line     L. Extension line
C. Center Line     H. Object line     M. Section line
D. Legend     I. Dimension line
E. Symbol     J. Cutting-plane line

_____ 1. Illustrates the boundaries of a plot of land.

_____ 2. Used to mark the feature for which a dimension is given.

_____ 3. Accepted convention for describing an object or a building.

_____ 4. Represents an edge that exists but is blocked from view.

_____ 5. A list of symbols included on a print.

_____ 6. Shows where material has been "cut."

_____ 7. Represents a fixture or object, replaces a note.

_____ 8. Line of symmetry.

_____ 9. Defines the drawing limits.

_____ 10. Identifies a section view.

## Line Activity 4–1

# *Alphabet of Lines*

*Draw freehand, in the spaces provided, the various lines.*
*Pay special attention to the form and weight of each line.*

1. Property Line

2. Object Line

3. Hidden Line

4. Center Line

5. Dimension and Extension Line

6. Broken Line

7. Section Line

8. Cutting-Plane Line

## Symbols Activity 4–2

# *Construction Drawing Symbols*

*In the spaces provided, draw the symbol for each item listed.*
*Refer to Section 7, Reference for the correct symbols.*

1. Duplex Receptacle Outlet

2. Push Button

3. Sliding Door

4. Telephone Outlet

5. Three-Way Switch

6. Shower Stall

7. Floor Drain (Plan View)

8. Water Heater

9. Hot Water Line

10. Fence

11. Concrete, Cast

12. Concrete, Block

13. Dimension Lumber

14. Gate Valve

15. Fire Brick

16. Second Floor Return Air Duct

17. Aluminum

18. Stove

19. Thermostat

20. Glass, Elevation

# Freehand Technical Sketching

## Technical Terms

Graph paper          Proportion
Inclined line        Unit Method

## Learning Objectives

After completing this unit, you will be able to:
- Use proper sketching techniques
- Sketch lines, circles, arcs, and ellipses
- Sketch objects and construction drawings

Sketching is used by craftspeople, suppliers, architects, and engineers to communicate ideas and construction details. This unit presents the basics of sketching. By mastering the art of sketching, you will be able to communicate your thoughts and ideas quickly and clearly.

## Sketching Technique

When sketching, sharpen your pencil to a conical point, as shown in **Figure 5-1.** When drawing a thin line, use a sharp point. When drawing a thick line, the point can be rounded.

It is important to hold the pencil properly. Grip it firmly enough to control the strokes but not so rigidly as to stiffen your movements. Your arm and hand should move freely and easily. The point of the pencil should extend approximately 1 1/2″ beyond your fingertips, **Figure 5-2.**

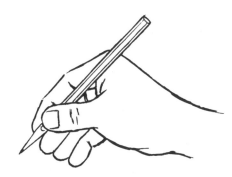

*Figure 5-2. The pencil must be held properly—your grip should be firm enough to draw smooth lines and relaxed enough so that your hand remains comfortable.*

Rotate your pencil slightly between strokes to maintain the point. Initial lines should be firm and light, but not fuzzy. Avoid making grooves in your paper by using too much pressure. In sketching straight lines, your eye should be on the point where the line will terminate. Make a series of short strokes (lines), rather than one continuous stroke. See **Figure 5-3.**

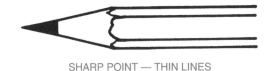

SHARP POINT — THIN LINES

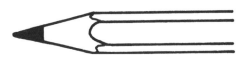

ROUNDED POINT — THICK LINES

*Figure 5-1. Pencils must be sharpened differently for different types of lines.*

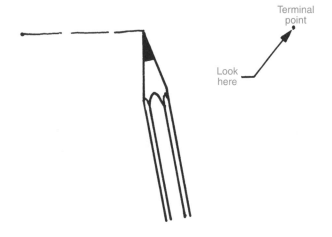

**Figure 5-3.** *Sketch lines as a series of short strokes first. Then go over the strokes to make the line solid.*

## Sketching Horizontal Lines

Horizontal lines are sketched by positioning your forearm perpendicular to the line being sketched. You then move your arm and hand parallel to the line. See **Figure 5-4.**

While following this procedure, refer to **Figure 5-5:**

### Horizontal Lines

1. Locate and mark the end points of line to be sketched.
2. Position your arm by making trial movements from left to right (left-handers, from right to left) without marking the paper.
3. Sketch short, light lines between the points. While sketching the line, look at the point where the line is to end.
4. Darken the line to form a continuous line with uniform weight. Your eye should lead the pencil along the lightly sketched line.

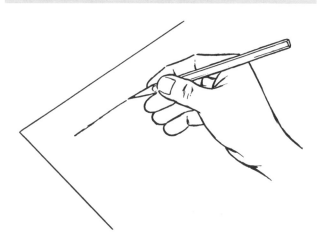

**Figure 5-4.** *Sketching a horizontal line.*

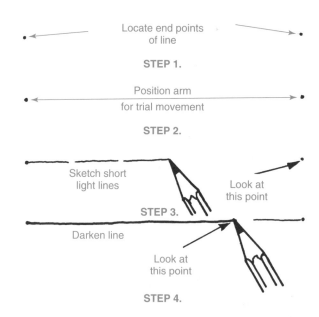

**Figure 5-5.** *Steps in sketching horizontal lines.*

## Sketching Vertical Lines

Vertical lines are sketched from top to bottom, using the same short strokes as horizontal lines. When making the strokes, position your arm comfortably, approximately 15° from vertical, **Figure 5-6.**

Refer to **Figure 5-7** as you read through the following procedure:

### Vertical Lines

1. Locate and mark the end points of the line to be sketched.
2. Position your arm by making trial movements from top to bottom.
3. Sketch short, light lines between the points. Keep your eye on the point where the line ends.
4. Darken the line to form one continuous line of uniform weight. Your eye should lead the pencil along the lightly sketched line.

You may find it easier to sketch horizontal and vertical lines if the paper is rotated slightly counterclockwise.

## Sketching Inclined Lines and Angles

All straight lines that are neither horizontal nor vertical are called *inclined lines*. You can sketch inclined lines between two points or at a designated angle. The same strokes and techniques used for sketching horizontal and vertical lines are used for inclined lines. If you prefer, rotate the paper to sketch these lines horizontally or vertically.

Angles can be estimated by first sketching a right angle (90°), and then subdividing its arc to get the desired angle. **Figure 5-8** illustrates how to get a 30° angle.

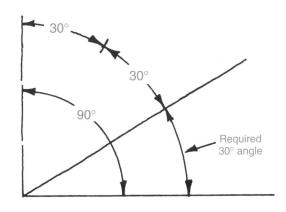

*Figure 5-6.* Position for sketching vertical lines. Paper may be rotated slightly counterclockwise for greater ease.

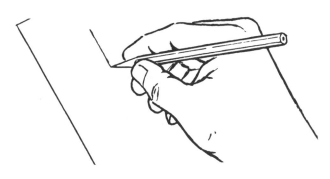

*Figure 5-7.* Sketching a vertical line.

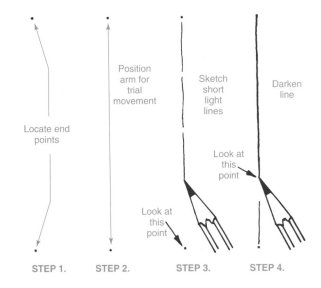

*Figure 5-8.* Estimating angle sizes.

# Sketching Arcs and Circles

There are several methods of sketching arcs and circles. One of the most-used is the Triangle-Square Method.

## Sketching Arcs between Lines

Use the following procedure to sketch an arc between two lines. See **Figure 5-9.**

### Arcs

1. Project the two lines until they intersect.
2. Lay out the arc radius from the point of intersection of the lines.
3. Form a triangle by connecting these two points and locate the center point of the triangle.
4. Sketch short, light strokes from the point where the arc is to start on the vertical line through the center point to the point on the horizontal line where the arc ends.
5. Darken the line to form one continuous arc, which should join smoothly with each straight line. Erase construction lines.

## Sketching Circles

When sketching circles, follow this procedure. See **Figure 5-10.**

### Circles

1. Locate the center of the circle and sketch the center lines. Then, approximate half the diameter on each of the center.
2. Sketch a square lightly at the diameter ends.
3. Across each corner, sketch a diagonal line to form a triangle. Then, locate the center point of each triangle.
4. Sketch short, light strokes through each quarter of the circle, making sure the arc passes through the triangle center point and joins smoothly with the square at the diameter ends.
5. Darken the line to form a smooth, well-formed circle. Erase construction lines.

# Sketching Ellipses

Sketching an ellipse is similar to sketching a circle. Refer to **Figure 5-11** as you follow the procedure.

## Ellipses

1. Locate the center of the ellipse and sketch center lines.

2. Lay out the major axis of the ellipse on the horizontal center line and the minor axis on the vertical center line.

3. Sketch a rectangle through the points on the axes.

4. Sketch tangent arcs at the points where the center lines cross the rectangle.

5. Complete the ellipse and darken the line, then erase the construction lines.

# Proportion in Sketching

*Proportion* is the relationship of the size of one part to the size of another part, or to the size of the entire object. The width, height, and depth of your sketch must be kept in proportion so the sketch conveys an accurate description of the object being sketched.

One technique useful in estimating proportions is the *Unit Method*. This method involves establishing a relationship between measurements on an object by breaking each of the measurements into units. Compare the width to the height, and select a unit that will fit each measurement, **Figure 5-12.** Unit lengths should be in the same proportion.

Proportion is a matter of estimating lengths on a part or assembly, then setting these down on your

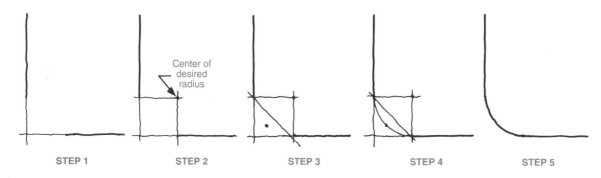

*Figure 5-9. Sketching an arc.*

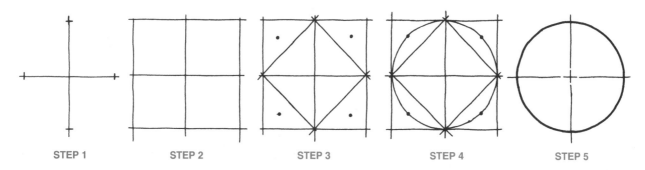

*Figure 5-10. Sketching a circle.*

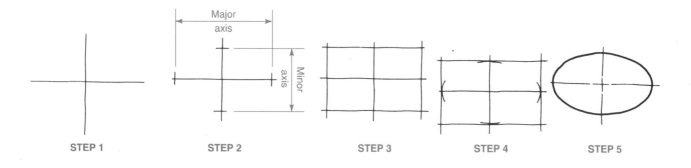

*Figure 5-11. Sketching an ellipse.*

sketch in the same ratio of units. Practice this method of establishing proportion in sketches. It will help you to represent the objects you sketch accurately.

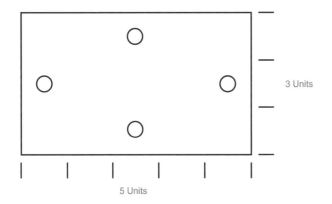

**Figure 5-12.** *Proportioning an object using the Unit Method.*

## Steps in Sketching an Object

The following steps will help you in laying out and completing your freehand sketches. **Figure 5-13** illustrates these steps for sketching an ellipse containing three circles.

### Sketching an Object

1. Sketch a rectangle or square of the correct proportion.
2. Sketch major subdivisions and details of the object.
3. Erase unnecessary lines.
4. Darken lines to correct weight.

## Sketching Aids

Many aids can be used to make your sketching more efficient and effective. *Graph paper,* which has a grid of light lines on it, helps to keep lines straight and makes proportioning easier. Straightedges are used to sketch lines. Rules help to keep proportions. If a rule or straightedge is not handy, a piece of folded paper or cardboard can be used to measure proportions or determine distances.

You should eventually develop your sketching skill to a point where aids are no longer needed.

## Test Your Knowledge

*Write your answers in the spaces provided.*

_____ 1. It is important to have good sketching skills in order to _____.
   A. impress people with your artistic ability
   B. communicate ideas
   C. read prints properly
   D. not waste drafting supplies
   E. All of these answers are correct.

_____ 2. When sketching a horizontal line, you begin by sketching short, light lines. When drawing these initial construction lines, your eyes should focus on _____.
   A. the endpoint of the line
   B. the tip of the pencil
   C. the beginning of the line
   D. your thumb
   E. None of these answers are correct.

_____ 3. In the Unit Method of proportioning, the longest dimension of an object is set equal to one unit. The other dimensions are then estimated as fractions of that unit. (True or False?)

_____ 4. The more experience you gain sketching, the more tools and aids (such as rules and graph paper) you should use. (True or False?)

_____ 5. The point of the pencil should be sharpened differently for different weights of lines. (True or False?)

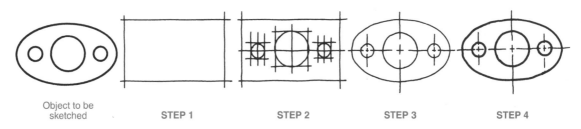

Object to be sketched          STEP 1          STEP 2          STEP 3          STEP 4

**Figure 5-13.** *Sketching an object.*

## Sketching Activity 5–1

# *Horizontal Lines*

*Sketch horizontal lines between points A–A′ through J–J′.*

A ·                      · A′     B ·                      · B′

C ·                      · C′     D ·                      · D′

E ·                                                         · E′

F ·                                                         · F′

G ·                                                       · G′

H ·                                                       · H′

I ·                                                       · I′

J ·                                                       · J′

## Sketching Activity 5–2
# *Vertical Lines*

*Sketch vertical lines between points K–K′ through T–T′.*

K M O P Q R S T

K′ M′
L N

L′ N′ O′ P′ Q′ R′ S′ T′

## Sketching Activity 5–3

# *Angles*

*Start at the indicated point and sketch the required angles.*

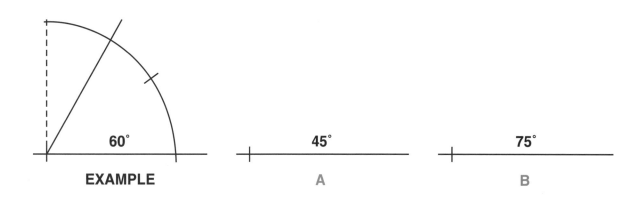

**60°**

**EXAMPLE**

**45°**

A

**75°**

B

**20°**

C

**100°**

D

**120°**

E

**22½°**

F

**85°**

G

**50°**

H

**30°**

I

**15°**

J

**90°**

K

## Sketching Activity 5–4

# *Arcs and Circles*

Sketch arcs joining the sets of lines A through F. Show construction lines for A through C. Erase
construction lines for D through F. Sketch circles G through L. Show construction lines for
circles G through I. Erase construction lines for J through L.

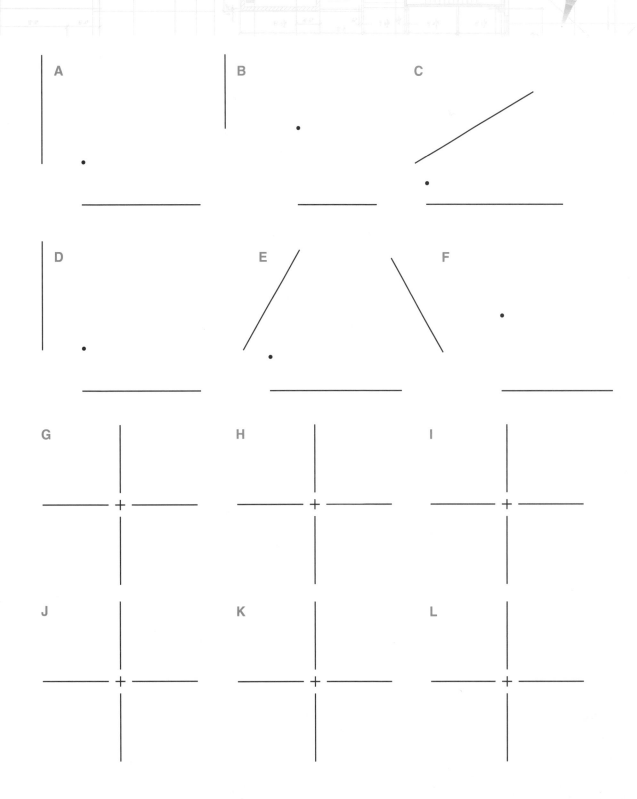

## Sketching Activity 5–5

# *Swimming Pool*

*Sketch the layout for the swimming pool in the space below the drawing.*
*Estimate the proportions. Do not measure or dimension the sketch.*

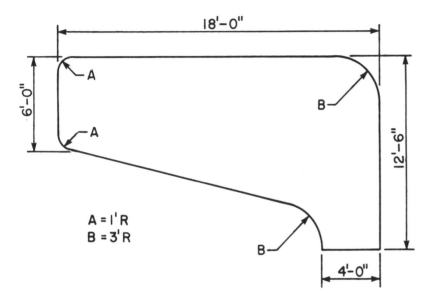

## Sketching Activity 5–6

# *Floor Plan*

*Sketch the floor plan in the space below the drawing.*
*Estimate the proportions. Do not measure or dimension the sketch.*

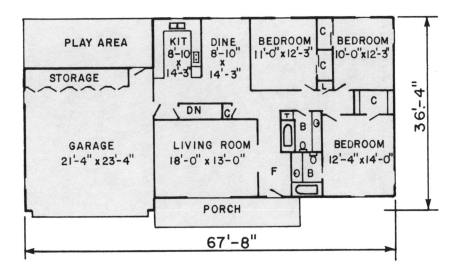

## Sketching Activity 5–7

# *Parking Lot*

*Sketch the parking lot in the space below the drawing. Estimate the proportions.*
*Do not measure or dimension the sketch.*

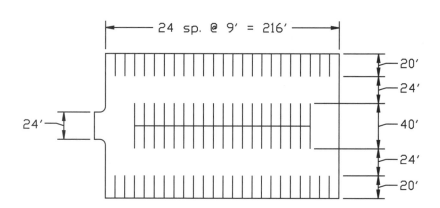

# Pictorial Drawings

## Technical Terms

Angular perspective
Cabinet oblique
Cavalier oblique
Exploded pictorial
  drawings
Isometric drawings
Horizon
One-point perspective

Parallel perspective
Perspective drawings
Pictorial drawings
Oblique drawings
Orthographic drawings
Two-point perspective
Vanishing point

## Learning Objectives

After completing this unit, you will be able to:
- Recognize pictorial drawings
- Sketch isometric and oblique drawings
- Identify the difference between cavalier oblique and cabinet oblique
- Draw objects and structures using one- and two-point perspective

*Pictorial drawings* show an object as it appears in a photograph, or as if you were viewing it, **Figure 6-1.** Several sides of the object are visible in one composite view.

Pictorial drawings are easy to understand. They give a 3-dimensional view of a room or structure, showing relationship in construction and assembly. Therefore, you will find this unit on pictorial sketching useful in helping you to visualize two- and three-view *orthographic drawings*, as well as in communicating your ideas on technical problems to others.

There are three common types of pictorial drawings:
- Isometric
- Oblique
- Perspective

Each of these can be shown as exploded pictorial drawings, which are discussed later in this chapter.

## Isometric Drawings

*Isometric drawings* are the most common pictorials. An isometric drawing is constructed with its two faces projected at angles of 30° above the horizontal, **Figure 6-2.** The isometric axes are equally spaced, with 120° between each axis.

Lines that are horizontal in an orthographic drawing are drawn at an angle of 30° in an isometric drawing. These lines are often the same length as they would be drawn in orthographic projection, or they can be shortened. Vertical lines remain vertical. Lines that are not horizontal or vertical are drawn by locating their endpoints on the isometric axes and connecting the two points.

### Constructing an Isometric Sketch

When sketching isometric drawings, remember that lines that are horizontal are drawn at a 30° angle from horizontal. Vertical lines remain vertical. The following procedure can be followed to create an isometric drawing. Refer to the sketch of the sawhorse in **Figure 6-3** as you read. After selecting the position of the object that presents to most detail, begin the sketch:

### Isometric Sketching

1. Start the sketch by laying out the axes from the lower corner.
2. Make overall measurements in their true length on the isometric axes or on lines parallel to the axes.

*Figure 6-1. A pictorial sketch of a kitchen. (St. Charles Manufacturing Co.)*

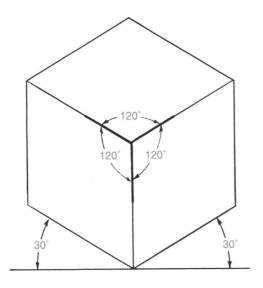

*Figure 6-2.* A cube shown in isometric view.

3. Construct a "box" to enclose the object.
4. Sketch the isometric lines of the object.
5. Sketch the nonisometric lines by first locating the endpoints of these lines, and then sketching the line between the endpoints.
6. Darken all visible lines and erase the construction lines to complete the isometric sketch.

## Isometric Circles and Arcs

Isometric circles and arcs are sketched in the same manner as the orthographic circles and arcs discussed in Unit 5, except you start with an isometric square. Follow **Figure 6-4** as you read through this procedure.

## Isometric Circles

1. Sketch an isometric square to enclose the location of circle.
2. Locate the midpoints of the sides of the isometric square and connect these midpoints.
3. Locate the midpoints of the triangles formed, then sketch isometric arcs through each to form an isometric ellipse.
4. Erase the construction lines and darken the circle.

Ellipses can be sketched in all planes of the isometric drawing in the same manner, **Figure 6-5**.

The procedure for drawing isometric arcs is similar to the procedure for drawing orthographic arcs. Refer to **Figure 6-6** as you read the following procedure:

## Isometric Arcs

1. Lay out the radius of the arc from the corner.
2. Draw a line connecting the two points, forming a triangle.
3. Locate the midpoint of triangle and sketch an arc through this point to smoothly join with the sides.
4. Erase the construction lines and darken the arc.

## Isometric Dimensioning

The dimension lines on an isometric drawing are parallel to the isometric axes. Extension lines are extended in line with these axes, **Figure 6-7**.

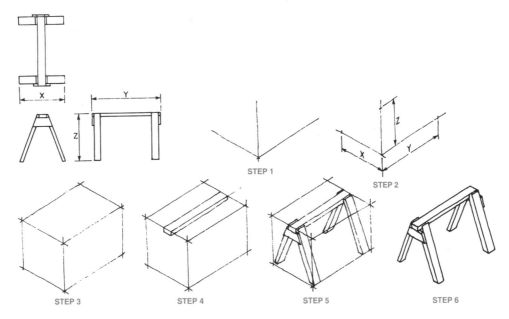

*Figure 6-3.* Constructing an isometric sketch.

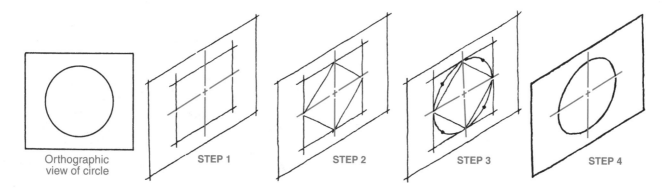

**Figure 6-4.** *Sketching an isometric ellipse.*

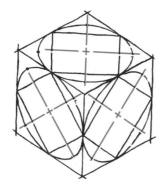

**Figure 6-5.** *Isometric ellipses in three planes.*

# Oblique Drawings

***Oblique drawings*** are another type of pictorial drawing. When an object is presented in oblique form, the front view is drawn as it would be using orthographic projection. This view shows all features with true shape and size. The top and side views are then projected back from the front view. These views can be projected at any angle—a 15°, 30°, or 45° angle is often used, **Figure 6-8.**

Oblique drawings are useful when the front contains more details and features than the side views. Circles and arcs can be drawn more easily in the front

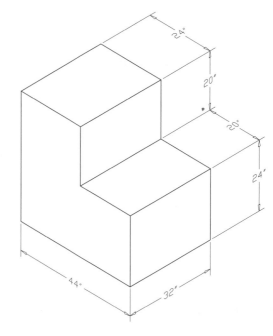

**Figure 6-7.** *Isometric dimensioning.*

view of an oblique drawing than in an isometric drawing. A mental image of an object can be more quickly created from an oblique drawing than orthographic projection.

There are two principal types of oblique drawings: cavalier and cabinet.

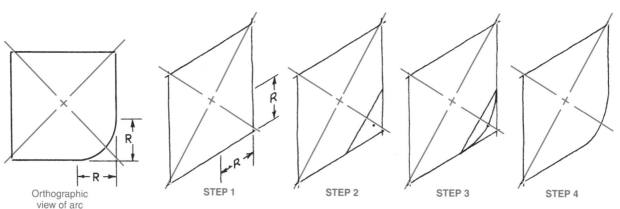

**Figure 6-6.** *Sketching an isometric arc.*

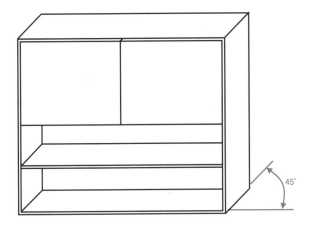

*Figure 6-8.* An oblique drawing.

## Cavalier Oblique

*Cavalier oblique* drawings are drawn with their receding view to the same scale as the front view, **Figure 6-9(A).** This creates a distorted appearance, but it does have the advantage of using one scale throughout.

## Cabinet Oblique

For *cabinet oblique* drawings, measurements made on the receding axes are reduced by half, **Figure 6-9(B).** This results in a more visually realistic representation. This type of drawing is often used for drawing cabinets, from which it gets its name.

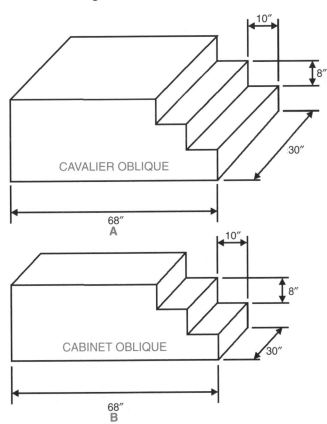

*Figure 6-9.* Types of oblique drawings.

## Oblique Circles and Arcs

Circles and arcs are sketched as true circles or arcs in the front plane of oblique drawings, **Figure 6-10.** When located in the receding planes, circles and arcs are sketched in the same manner as isometric circles and arcs (they are drawn as ellipses).

The procedure for sketching circles and arcs is the same in cabinet oblique drawings as it is for cavalier oblique except the oblique square is reduced on the receding axes.

### Oblique Circles

1. Sketch an oblique square, **Figure 6-10.**
2. Connect the midpoints of the sides of the square.
3. Locate the midpoints of resulting triangles, then sketch oblique ellipses or arcs through these midpoints to join smoothly with sides of square.
4. Erase the construction lines and darken ellipses and arcs.

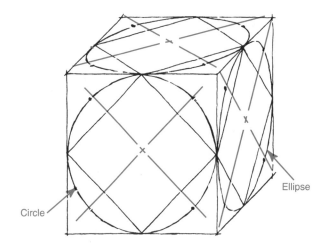

*Figure 6-10.* Sketching oblique circles and arcs.

## Perspective Drawings

The *perspective drawing* is the most realistic of all pictorial drawings. Instead of remaining parallel (as in isometric and oblique drawings), receding lines in the perspective drawing converge (meet at a vanishing point), **Figure 6-11.** This eliminates the distorted appearance that occurs at the back part of most other pictorial drawings.

To assist you in developing the technique of this type of sketching, both parallel and angular perspective sketches are discussed and illustrated.

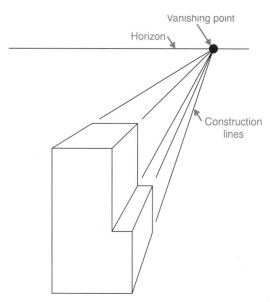

Figure 6-11.  Perspective drawing.

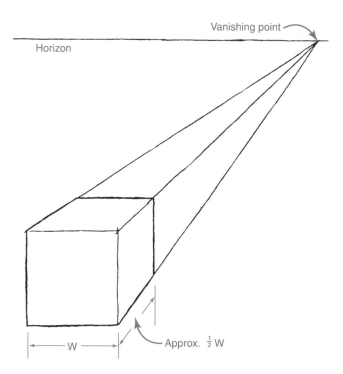

Figure 6-12.  Parallel or one-point perspective.

## Parallel Perspective (One-Point)

*Parallel,* or *one-point perspective,* is similar to oblique drawings. One face of the object is shown as a front view. True shape and size are shown in the front view, and lines parallel to the front view remain parallel. Lines that are perpendicular to the front view (which are parallel in the top and side views) converge to a single *vanishing point.* See **Figure 6-12.**

The following procedure describes one method of creating a one-point perspective drawing. See **Figure 6-13.**

### One-Point Perspective

1.  Sketch the front view of the object in its true size and shape, as it would appear in an orthographic sketch.
2.  Sketch a horizontal line (called the *horizon*) at the assumed eye level of the viewer. This line may be above, behind, or below the object, depending on which part of the object is being shown.
3.  Select a vanishing point (VP) on the horizon.
4.  Sketch lines from the front view to the vanishing point.
5.  Enclose the object in a "box" by sketching rear vertical and horizontal lines. To estimate depth of the side and top views, use your judgment to determine a distance that appears reasonable. Diagonals may be used to divide perspective planes in half. To sketch lines that aren't horizontal or vertical, locate the endpoints on the perspective axes and then connect the points.
6.  Block in features such as drawers and doors.
7.  Darken visible lines and erase construction lines.

## Angular Perspective (Two-Point)

*Angular,* or *two-point perspective,* is similar to isometric drawings. One edge of the object is placed in front. The two faces that meet at this edge recede to different vanishing points. All lines parallel to each face go to different vanishing points. **Figure 6-14** illustrates an object drawn in two-point perspective, located above the horizon line.

The following procedure can be used to create a two-point perspective drawing. Remember that vertical lines remain parallel and horizontal lines converge at one of the two vanishing points. Refer to **Figure 6-15.**

### Two-Point Perspective

1.  Sketch the horizon line at the assumed eye level of the viewer. This line may be above, behind or below the object, depending on the level from which you want to view the object.
2.  Select the position from which the object is to be viewed and sketch a vertical line for front corner of a "box".
3.  Establish right and left vanishing points on the horizon line. If the object is to be positioned so that the two sides can be viewed equally, then the vanishing points will be equidistant on each side of the object. If one side is to be favored (front view in **Figure 6-15**), the vanishing point for that side will be extended out while the

vanishing point on the other side will be shortened. However, both vanishing points must remain on the horizon line.

4. Sketch receding lines from front vertical line to the two vanishing points.
5. Enclose the object in a "box" by sketching rear vertical lines. To estimate the depth of the side and top views, use your judgment to determine a distance that looks reasonable. The reduction is not as great for the side being favored.
6. Sketch lines that aren't horizontal or vertical by locating the two endpoints on the perspective axes and then connecting the points.
7. Block in features such as drawers and doors.
8. Darken visible lines and erase construction lines.

## Perspective Circles and Arcs

Perspective circles and arcs are sketched in the same way as isometric circles and arcs. First sketch the perspective square or block, then join the midpoints of the sides to form triangles. The perspective circle or arc is sketched through the midpoints of the sides and the center of the triangles. See **Figure 6-16.**

## Exploded Pictorial Drawings

*Exploded pictorial drawings* are used to show the relative position of parts or construction details, **Figure 6-17.** They are used to clarify assembly sequence. Appliance and cabinetry service manuals also use exploded pictorial drawings.

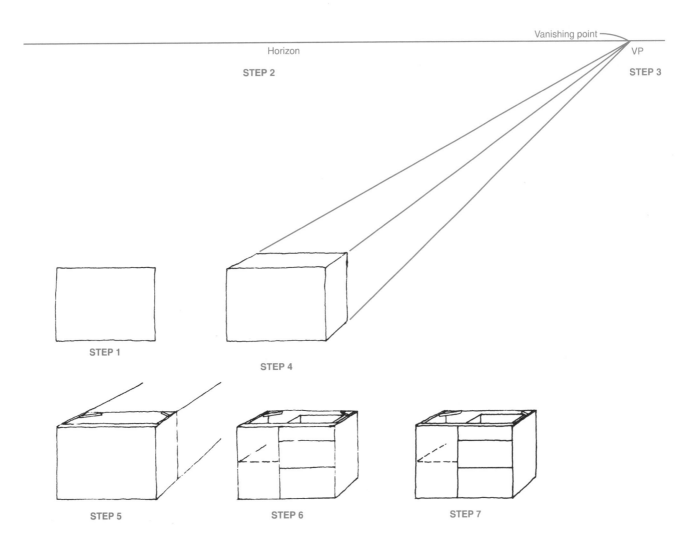

*Figure 6-13. Sketching a parallel, or one-point, perspective.*

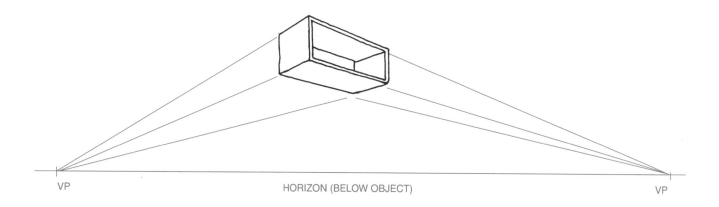

**Figure 6-14.** *Perspective view of wall cabinet with horizon below object.*

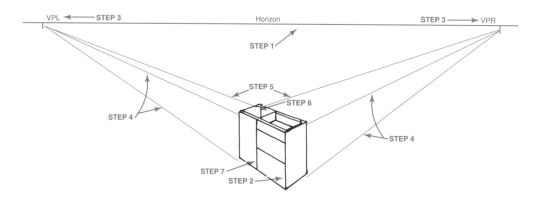

**Figure 6-15.** *Steps in sketching an angular or two-point perspective.*

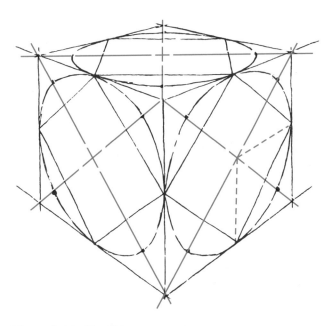

**Figure 6-16.** *Sketching perspective circles and arcs.*

# Test Your Knowledge

*Write your answers in the spaces provided.*

_____ 1. In an isometric drawing, lines that would appear horizontal in an orthographic drawing are drawn at a _____ angle from the horizontal.

A. 15°

B. 30°

C. 45°

D. 60°

E. The lines can be drawn at any angle, as long as it looks reasonable.

_____ 2. An isometric circle is not actually a circle. It is a(n) _____.

A. rhombus

B. dodecahedron

C. oval

D. ellipse

E. An isometric circle *is* a circle.

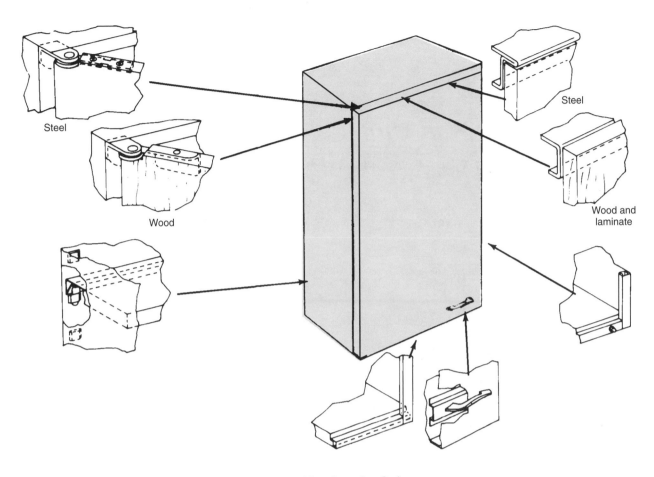

Steel

Wood

Steel

Wood and
laminate

*Figure 6-17.* *An exploded pictorial drawing. (St. Charles Manufacturing Co.)*

_____ 3. When the true shape of one face of an object must be shown, a(n) _____ drawing should be used.

    A. isometric
    B. oblique
    C. two-point perspective
    D. exploded pictorial
    E. All of these drawings would show the true shape of the face.

_____ 4. The pictorial drawing most realistic in appearance is the _____ drawing.

    A. perspective
    B. isometric
    C. exploded oblique
    D. cabinet oblique
    E. None of these are pictorial drawings.

_____ 5. Pictorial drawings are normally three-dimensional. (True or False?)

_____ 6. A perspective drawing appears more distorted than an oblique drawing. (True or False?)

_____ 7. In a perspective drawing, the vanishing point(s) must be located on the horizon line. (True or False?)

_____ 8. The three most common types of pictorial drawings are isometric, orthographic, and oblique. (True or False?)

_____ 9. A cabinet oblique drawing uses the same scale along the receding faces as for the front face. (True or False?)

_____ 10. *Angular perspective* is another name for *two-point perspective.* (True or False?)

## Sketching Activity 6–1

# *Open Shelving Wall Unit*

*Make an isometric sketch of the open shelving wall unit. Omit dimensions.*

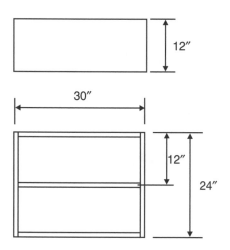

## Sketching Activity 6–2

# *Mantelpiece*

*Make an isometric sketch of the mantelpiece. Omit dimensions.*

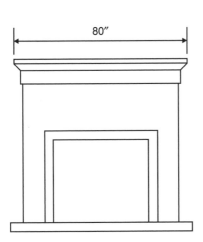

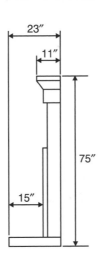

## Sketching Activity 6–3
# *Wall Unit*

*Make a cavalier oblique sketch of the wall unit (no shelf). Do not dimension.*

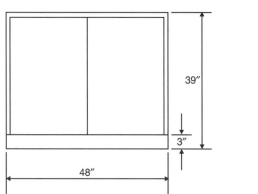
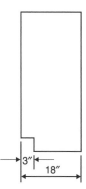

## Sketching Activity 6–4

# *Wall Cupboard*

*Make a cabinet oblique sketch of the wall cupboard (less doors).*

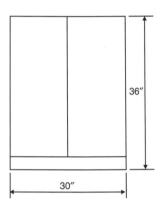

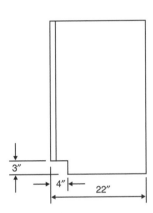

## Sketching Activity 6–5

# *Open Shelf Wall Unit*

*Make a parallel perspective sketch of the open shelf wall unit in the space below.*
*Do not dimension.*

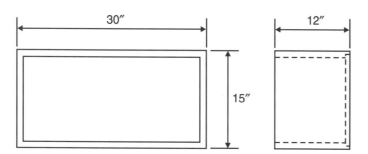

## Sketching Activity 6–6
# *Open Shelf Wall Unit*

*Make an angular perspective sketch of the open shelf wall unit in the space below. Dimension the sketch.*

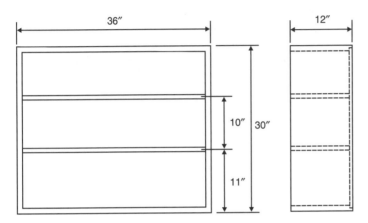

## Sketching Activity 6–7
# *Hanging Cabinet*

*Make an angular perspective sketch of the hanging cabinet in the space below.*
*Place the horizon below the cabinet. Do not dimension the sketch.*

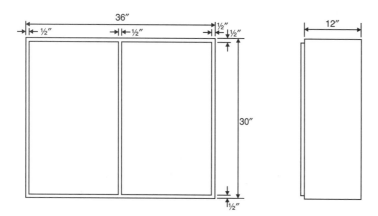

# Orthographic Drawings

## Technical Terms

Electrical plans
Elevations
Floor plans
Foundation plans
Framing plans
Mechanical plans

Perpendicular
 projectors
Plan view
Plumbing plans
Sections

## Learning Objectives

After completing this unit, you will be able to:

- Visualize orthographic objects and structures
- Create orthographic sketches
- Identify different types of orthographic drawings

Nearly all drawings used on a construction project are orthographic drawings. These drawings are created using orthographic projection, a process by which an object or structure is described using various views. Each view defines one face, or side, of the subject.

The views of an orthographic drawing are projected at right angles (90°) to each other. The best way to visualize this is by cutting and unfolding a cardboard box, as shown in **Figure 7-1.** The front view remains in position. The four adjoining views revolve 90° around the "folds", bringing them into the same plane as the front view. The rear view is shown next to the left side view, but it could be shown in several alternate positions.

Imagine placing an object inside a glass cube. If you then viewed the cube through any of its six sides, you would see only one face of the object. Each view through the sides of the cube would create one orthographic view, **Figure 7-2.**

It is easier to form a three-dimensional, mental picture of an object or structure from a pictorial drawing. However, orthographic drawings are preferred because more details can be shown. Eventually, you will learn to visualize using orthographic drawings as easily as with pictorial drawings, **Figure 7-3.**

## Creating Orthographic Drawings

Orthographic drawings are not difficult to create. Each view should be carefully drawn. Begin with the front view, then move to the top and side views. Lines parallel to the plane of the view being drawn are drawn at true size.

A notched block is shown in **Figure 7-4.** The orthographic drawing of the block is shown in **Figure 7-5.** Refer to the figure as you work through the following procedure:

### Orthographic Views

1. Begin by drawing the front view. All views should be drawn to scale. Select the object's position so that most of its features are located on the front, right side, and top.
2. At every edge and feature shown on the front view, *perpendicular projectors* are drawn in the vertical and horizontal directions. These construction lines are drawn lightly, and erased when the drawing is complete.
3. Draw the top and side views. The projection lines connect common features between views.
4. From the front edge of the top view, draw a horizontal projection line. Draw a vertical projection line from the front edge of the side view.

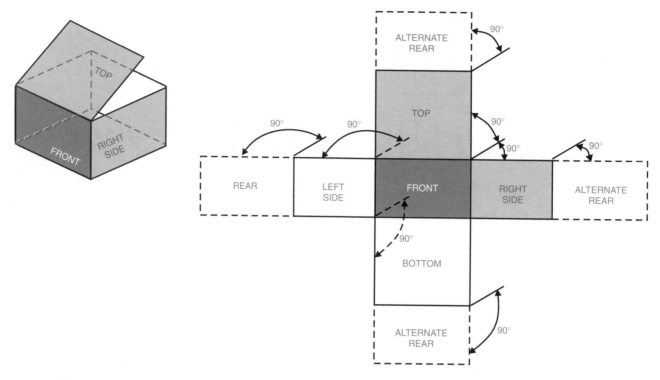

***Figure 7-1.*** *Projection of orthographic views shown by unfolded box.*

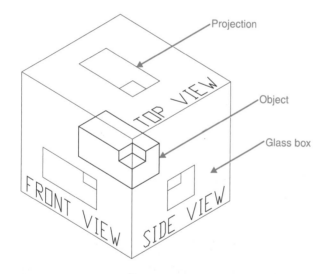

***Figure 7-2.*** *Imagining an object within a glass cube can help you visualize orthographic views.*

5. At the intersection of these lines, draw a line at a 45° angle. Projection lines for features common to the top and side views will intersect at this line.

## Construction Drawings

For construction drawings, different views of the building (floor plans and elevations) are obtained using orthographic projection. Imagine a building enclosed in a large glass box, **Figure 7-6(A).** Each view is projected toward its viewing plane, **Figure 7-6(B),** then unfolded and brought into plane with the front view, **Figure 7-6(C).**

Due to the size of most buildings and the amount of information that needs to be shown, the different views usually are separated and placed on individual sheets. Prints are made from these separate drawings and fastened together to form the set of prints for a particular job. The bottom view is not shown and the top, or *roof plan*, is shown only for complex structures.

## Plan Views

The top view of the building is called a ***plan view.*** Plan views are taken at different levels throughout the building. For example, one plan view may show only the third story, while another would show the basement. In more complicated buildings, each floor may require multiple plan views to illustrate all construction details.

There are several different classifications of plan drawings (which are often referred to simply as *plans*). Only the most complicated buildings use all types of plans. Some basic buildings can fit all of the required information on a single plan.

### Floor Plans

The ***floor plan*** shows the layout of the building, **Figure 7-7.** Walls, doors, windows, rooms, and stairs are shown. When space is available, other materials

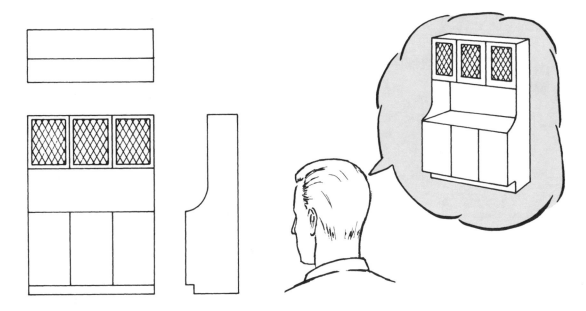

**Figure 7-3.** *Forming a mental picture of an object from an orthographic drawing.*

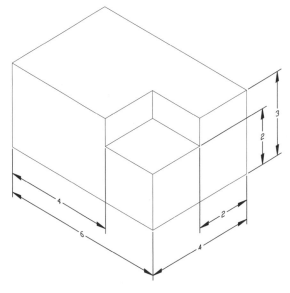

**Figure 7-4.** *This simple notched block can be easily described using orthographic projection.*

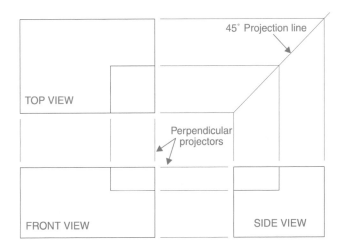

**Figure 7-5.** *Orthographic views of the notched block shown in Figure 7-4.*

(such as plumbing and electrical) can also be shown on the floor plan.

The floor plan is normally the first drawing in a set of prints. Many other section and detail drawings can be referenced from the floor plan.

Your study of a floor plan should start with a review of the general layout. Get an idea of the room sizes, halls, and storage before studying details of construction. This will help you to understand the complete set of plans.

Floor plans are drawn to scale (usually 1/48 size—1/4″ = 1′-0″). However, you should rely on the dimensions shown and not scale the drawing. A separate drawing is made for each floor, including the basement.

## Foundation Plans

The *foundation plan* is similar to the floor plan, except it shows the foundation for the building. Foundation walls, slabs, piers, and footings are shown. The basement is shown on the foundation plan, **Figure 7-8.** The locations of all wall openings, stairs, and chimneys are given.

## Framing Plans

*Framing plans* show the layout of the structural members supporting a floor or roof. A framing plan is often included for each floor. There may be a note defining the types of material to be used. If there is room, detail drawings of the connections between members may be included.

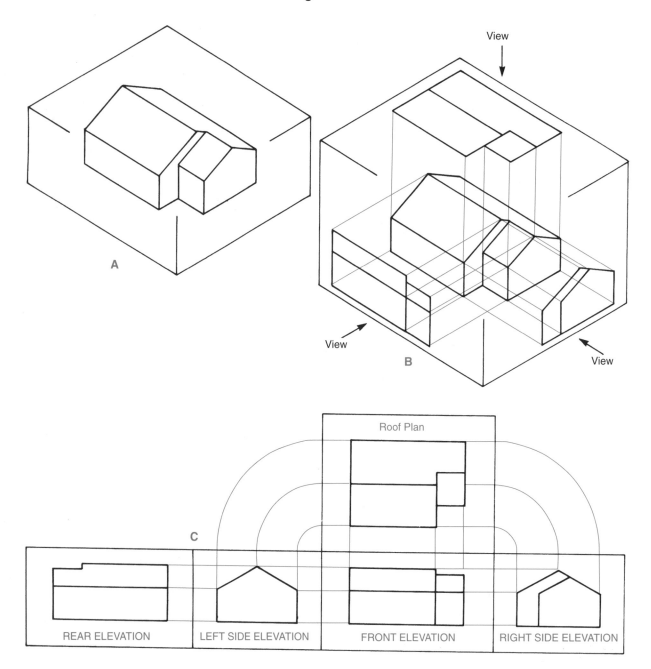

**Figure 7-6.** *Orthographic projection of a building. A—Imagine the building within a glass box. B—Each building face is projected onto a side of the box. C—The box and projections are unfolded into one plane. A view of the bottom is not needed.*

## Electrical Plans

*Electrical plans* are often created by the electrical contractor. Locations of receptacles, switches, and fixtures are included on the drawing. Another type of electrical plan, the *reflected ceiling plan,* illustrates ceiling-mounted light fixtures.

## Plumbing Plans

The *plumbing plan* shows where the water pipes enter the building, heating and circulating equipment, supply and waste systems, and plumbing fixtures. The type of piping material to be used is often included on the plumbing plan.

## Mechanical Plans

*Mechanical plans* show the heating, ventilating, and air-conditioning system (HVAC) and any mechanical equipment and systems located in the building. Piping systems are also sometimes shown on the mechanical plan.

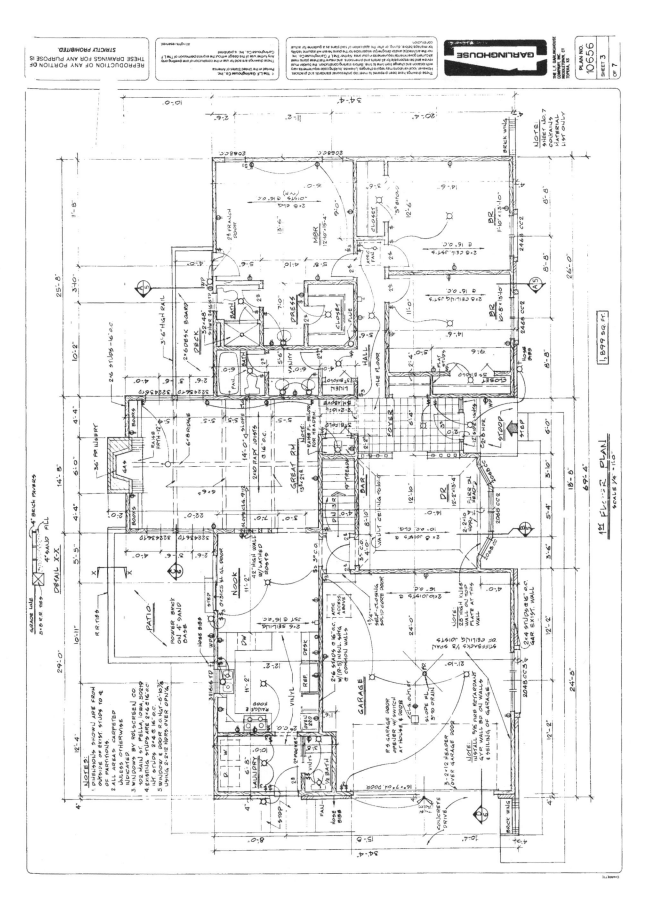

*Figure 7-7. The floor plan of a building. (Garlinghouse)*

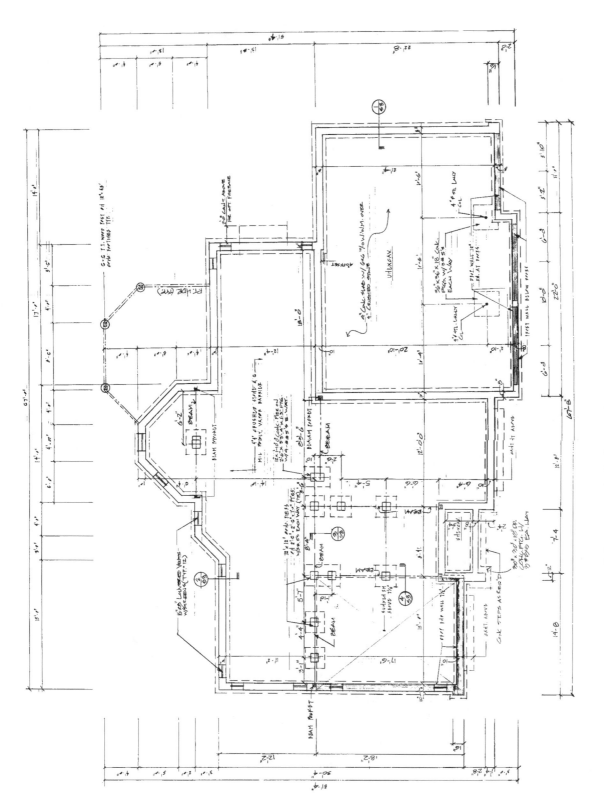

*Figure 7-8.* *A foundation plan of a building. (Garlinghouse)*

# Elevations

*Elevations* are orthographic, exterior views of a building, **Figure 7-9.** Elevations show features such as the style of the building, doors, windows, chimneys, and moldings. Any feature on an elevation that does not have sufficient clarity is shown at a larger scale in a detail drawing.

Elevations are designated as *Front, Right Side, Left Side,* and *Rear.* They also may be identified by the compass direction the elevation *faces.* When the building faces *east,* the front elevation would be the *East Elevation.*

Interior elevations may be provided to show the construction of a particular interior wall or area. Underground features of the building, such as the basement or foundation walls and footings, are shown with hidden lines on elevations.

# Sections

The purpose of a set of prints is to show the construction details of a building. Plans and elevations give most of the information needed. Sometimes, however, it is necessary to show the "inside" of a wall, cabinet, or roof structure to clarify construction procedures. When the drawing is an imaginary "cut" through a wall or other feature, it is known as a sectional view, or *section.* See **Figure 7-10.**

Sections are provided for walls, cabinets, chimneys, stairs, and other features whose construction is not shown clearly on the plan or elevation. Sectional views show how various components and materials are assembled.

# Details

Due to the scale at which construction drawings are usually made, certain features are not clearly shown on the plan, elevation, or sectional views. These features require a large-scale illustration to provide information necessary for construction. In these situations, a detail drawing is used. *Details* are drawn at a larger scale than plans, elevations, and sections, **Figure 7-11.**

Detail drawings may be placed on the same sheets as the plan or elevation views. Otherwise, the detail is found on a separate sheet and referenced.

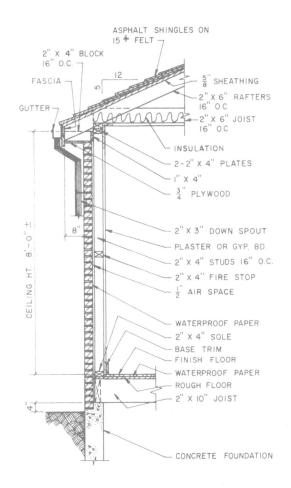

*Figure 7-10. A sectional view shows construction details not included in the plan or elevation.*

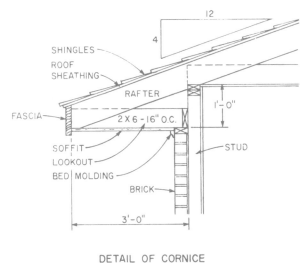

DETAIL OF CORNICE

*Figure 7-11. A detail drawing of a cornice.*

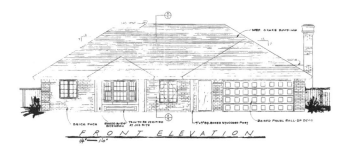

*Figure 7-9. A front elevation of a building. (Garlinghouse)*

# Test Your Knowledge

*Write your answers in the spaces provided.*

_____ 1. Why are orthographic drawings used for construction, rather than pictorial drawings?

A. Orthographic drawings are easier to create.
B. Pictorial drawings are too large to fit on the drawing sheets.
C. More details can be shown on orthographic drawings.
D. Most standards require orthographic drawings.
E. Pictorial drawings are more commonly used.

_____ 2. The maximum number of orthographic views of an object is _____.

A. two
B. three
C. four
D. five
E. None of the above.

_____ 3. Which type of drawing is a view taken from directly above the building?

A. Sectional view
B. Elevation
C. Plan view
D. Detail
E. None of the above.

_____ 4. Which type of drawing shows the building as if part of it were removed?

A. Sectional view
B. Elevation
C. Plan view
D. Detail
E. None of the above.

_____ 5. Which type of drawing is used when there isn't enough room on another drawing to illustrate something?

A. Sectional view
B. Elevation
C. Plan view
D. Detail
E. None of the above.

_____ 6. Which type of drawing illustrates the building as if you were standing on the ground looking at it?

A. Sectional view
B. Elevation
C. Plan view
D. Detail
E. None of the above.

_____ 7. The location of light switches would be found on the _____.

A. foundation plan
B. framing plan
C. electrical plan
D. plumbing plan
E. None of the above.

_____ 8. The type of floor joists would be found on the _____.

A. foundation plan
B. framing plan
C. electrical plan
D. plumbing plan
E. None of the above.

_____ 9. The size of the basement wall would be found on the _____.

A. foundation plan
B. framing plan
C. electrical plan
D. plumbing plan
E. None of the above.

_____ 10. The location of hose bibs would be found on the _____.

A. foundation plan
B. framing plan
C. electrical plan
D. plumbing plan
E. None of the above.

# Print Reading Activity 7–1
# *Matching Views*

Study the pictorial views and match each orthographic
drawing by inserting the correct letter in the space provided.

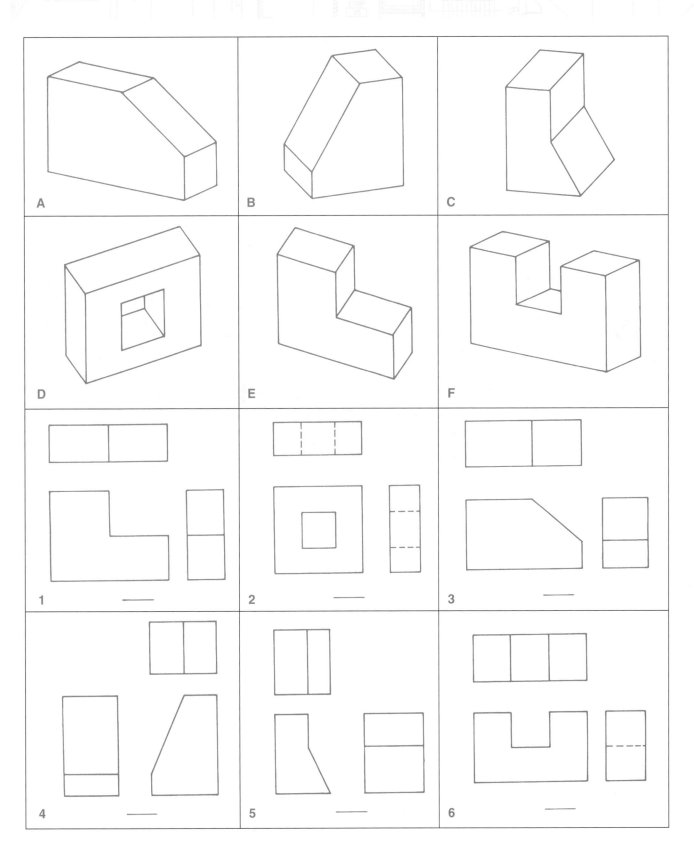

80

# Print Reading Activity 7–2
# *Residential Plan and Elevation*

*Use Figure 7-12 and Figure 7-13 to answer the following questions.*

©1995 L.F. GARLINGHOUSE COMPANY, INC.

**Figure 7-12.** *Pictorial drawing of residence to be used in Activity 7-2.*

1. Which elevation would show the windows in the master bedroom?

1. _____

2. What two sides of the building are shown in the pictorial view?

2. _____

3. What room provides access to the deck?

3. _____

4. In which elevation would the garage door be shown?

4. _____

5. How many windows are there in the great room?

5. _____

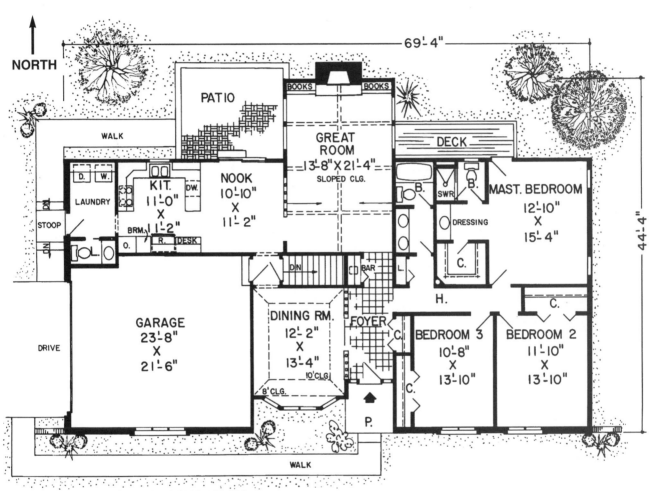

©1995 L.F. GARLINGHOUSE COMPANY, INC.

**Figure 7-13.** *Floor plan for Activity 7-2.*

6. How many bedrooms are there?  6. _____

7. How many windows would be shown in the west (left side) elevation?  7. _____

8. In which room is the desk located?  8. _____

9. How many closets are there?  9. _____

10. What are the dimensions of the dining room?  10. _____

# Print Reading Activity 7–3

# *Sketching Orthographic Views*

*Sketch the plan view and the two elevation views shown in each pictorial. The views should be correctly positioned.*

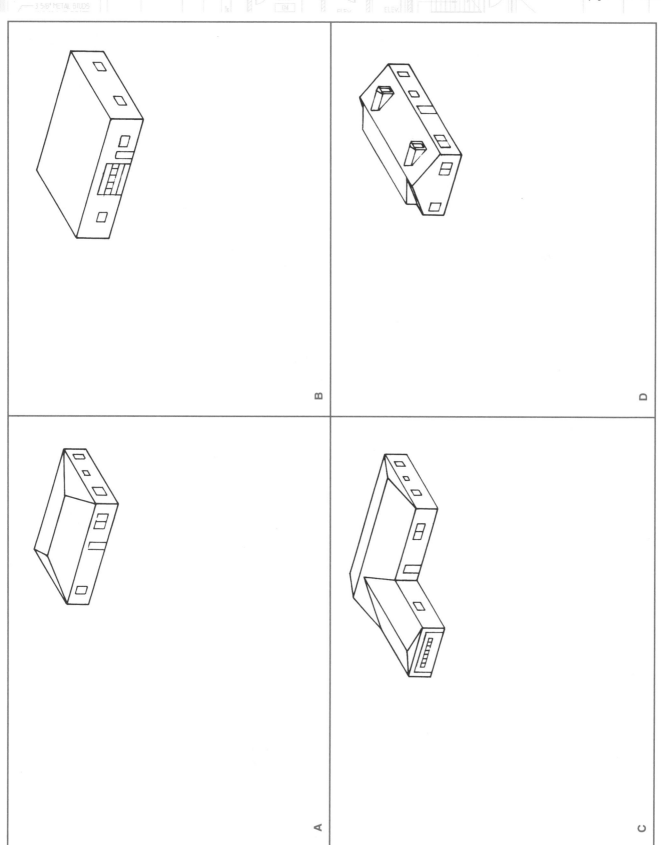

B

D

A

C

# Dimensioning

## Technical Terms

Metric scale          Scale
Rise                  Sheathing
Run

## Learning Objectives

After completing this unit, you will be able to:
- Scale dimensions from a print
- Read dimensions on a print
- Identify the items that should be dimensioned on different drawing types

Dimensions are an essential part of drawings. The person reading a print must understand various dimensioning techniques. You will find that drafting standards vary greatly from company to company, even though a considerable effort is being made to unify procedures.

Standard procedures for dimensioning are discussed in this unit. A careful study of these procedures will enable you to properly interpret construction drawings.

## Dimension Lines

Dimension and extension lines were described in Unit 4, *Lines and Symbols*. Drafters use various means of terminating dimension lines at extension lines, **Figure 8-1**. The slash method, **Figure 8-1 (C)**, is becoming the most common. Other forms are used to give individuality to the work. Normally, the dimension is shown above the dimension line.

## Drawing Scale

Construction projects are drawn to a reduced scale. The *scale* of a particular floor plan, elevation, or detail is indicated on the sheet, either in the title block or beneath the drawing itself.

On the drawing, the scale is defined in the following manner: SCALE: 1/4″ = 1′-0″. This means that a 1/4″ length on the drawing is equal to a 1′ length in reality.

The scale most commonly used for floor plans in the customary (English) measurement system is 1/4″ = 1′-0″, or 1/48 size (there are forty-eight units of 1/4″ in 12″). This is commonly referred to as the quarter scale. Normally, scales for detail drawings range from 1/2″ = 1′-0″ to full size.

## Metric System

The metric system of measurement has seen little use in the U.S., primarily because metric construction standards have not been established. Industry groups are at work developing metric standards. Once metric standards have been adopted and metric modular materials become available, metric dimensioning will be used extensively.

The *metric scale* most closely representing the quarter-inch scale (1/48 size) is the 1:50 scale (1/50 size) in which a two-centimeter length on the drawing equals a one-meter (100 cm) length on the actual object.

## Reading a Customary Scale

In addition to referring to the relative size a drawing has been drawn, the term *scale* also refers to the instrument (ruler) used to measure distances on a drawing.

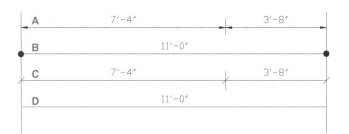

*Figure 8-1.* *Several types of marks are used at the end of dimension lines.*

As a construction worker, you will be reading dimensions given on a print and laying off measurements on the job. The needed dimensions should be provided on the print. However, there may be times when a particular dimension is desired but has been omitted or not considered necessary. Also, you may be required to sketch a detail, or lay it out to scale. In these situations, it is necessary to use a scale.

The following steps illustrate how to measure a distance on a quarter-inch scale drawing, using a scale. Refer to **Figure 8-2** as you read:

### Reading a Scale

1. Locate the scale marked 1/4.
2. Starting at zero, the scaled measurements of feet are numbered to the left, such as 2, 4, 6, 8 and so on. Inches are marked in the section to the right of zero.

3. To lay off a measurement of 6′-3″, start with the line indicating 6′ and move to the zero, and on to 3″.
4. A measurement of 11′-8″ would start at the line indicating 11′ feet and extend past zero to 8″ inches.

Architectural details frequently are drawn to larger scales, such as 1 1/2″ = 1′-0″. See **Figure 8-3.** This scale is read in the same manner as the quarter-inch scale.

### The Fractional Rule As a Scale

When an architect's scale is not available, a fractional rule can be used to take measurements. For a measurement on the 1/4″ = 1′-0″ scale, let each 1/4 inch on the rule represent one foot of actual measurement on the project. Fractional parts of the 1/4″ would represent the appropriate number of inches on the project. For example, a scaled reading of 5′-6″ would be five quarters of an inch for the 5′ and one eighth of an inch for the 6″, or 1 3/8″, **Figure 8-4.**

A properly prepared drawing will include all necessary dimensions. Caution should be exercised in scaling a print for measurements not provided. All such measurements should be cross-checked with other dimensions and verified by your supervisor.

Readings on the metric scale are made in the same manner as on the customary scale. The unit of metric linear measure is the meter. A reading of 2.5 meters on

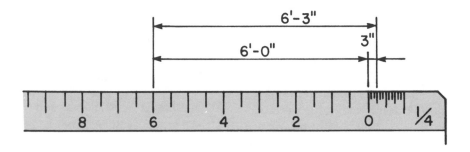

*Figure 8-2.* *Laying off a measurement on an architect's scale.*

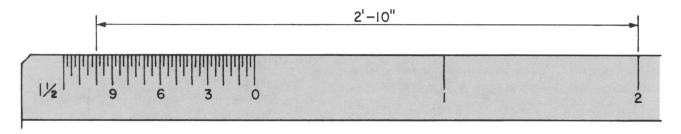

*Figure 8-3.* *A measurement on the 1 1/2″ = 1′-0″ scale.*

the 1:50 metric scale is shown in **Figure 8-5.** The unit of metric linear measure in cabinet work is the centimeter (cm). A measurement of 82 centimeters on the 1:20 metric scale is shown in **Figure 8-6.**

# Dimensioning Technique

As stated earlier in the chapter, drafting and dimensioning styles vary greatly from country-to-country, company-to-company, and drafter-to-drafter. However, certain practices remain fairly common. Although drafting is fairly standardized, personal preference and style still exist.

Individual style is often used when drawing dimensions. A dimension line can terminate in an arrowhead, dot, or tick mark. The dimension can be written above, below, or within the dimension line. Lengths can be listed in several different ways.

However, the selection of objects to be dimensioned and the techniques used to dimension them are fairly standard. Any dimension that may be needed during construction should be included on the drawing. Unnecessary dimensions should not be included.

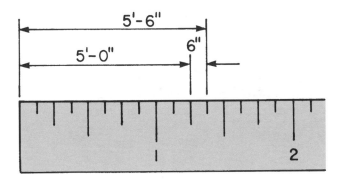

**Figure 8-4.** Using a fractional rule to scale measurements on the 1/4″ = 1′-0″ scale.

## Dimensioning Floor Plans

Floor plans show the arrangement of rooms, location of walls, and placement of windows. The plan should identify the materials and construction methods needed. The dimensions on the floor plan must be correct because other drawings will use the floor plan as their basis. Dimensions of walls, windows, and doors are included. Locations of unusual features should also be shown.

When dimensioning walls, different types of walls are dimensioned differently. Masonry walls are dimensioned to their exterior surface, **Figure 8-7.** Dimensions for exterior walls of frame and brick-veneer buildings usually start at the exterior surface of the stud wall, **Figure 8-8.** Some architects show the dimension to the outside of the masonry on brick-veneer as well. This provides the workers with the dimensions necessary for laying out the sole plates over subfloors and in locating window and door openings before the *sheathing* (structural covering over studs) is added.

Some architects dimension exterior walls of single-story frame construction from the surface of the sheathing. This surface should align with the foundation wall. If the drawing scale is too small to show the dimension clearly, a note should be added, stating where the dimensions are referring. In the absence of a note or clarity of dimensions, you should calculate the exact location of the exterior dimension by referring to other prints of floor plans, elevations, or details.

Interior walls are usually dimensioned to the center or side of partitions. Some architects dimension to partition surfaces, then dimensioning the thickness of each partition.

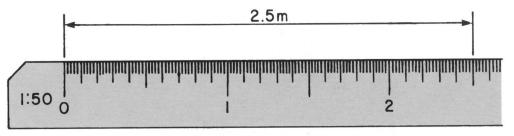

**Figure 8-5.** A reading of 2.5 meters on the metric 50 scale.

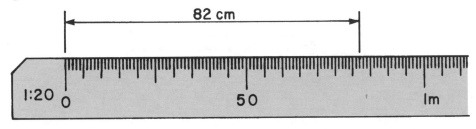

**Figure 8-6.** A reading of 82 centimeters on the metric 20 scale.

Window and door openings are located by their center lines for frame construction. For masonry construction, these openings are dimensioned to the edges of the masonry surface openings. Doors or windows in narrow areas may not be dimensioned for location if it is obvious they would be centered in the space available.

## Dimensioning Elevations

Dimensions provided on elevation drawings are those related to the vertical plane, since most horizontal dimensions are included on plan drawings. Footing thickness, depth of footing below grade, floor and ceiling heights, window and door heights, and chimney height are provided on elevation drawings, **Figure 8-9.** In addition to vertical dimensions, information is provided through notes on grade information, materials, and special details.

Roof slope usually is given on a drawing as a slope triangle. The diagram represents the ratio between the *rise* (change in elevation from top to bottom of roof) and *run* (1/2 the entire span of the building). A typical slope would be 4:12 or 4 units of rise for 12 units of run. The roof shown in **Figure 8-9** has a slope of 6:12, a rather steep roof.

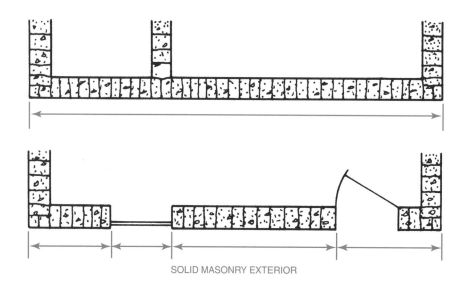

SOLID MASONRY EXTERIOR

*Figure 8-7. Dimensioning practices for masonry walls.*

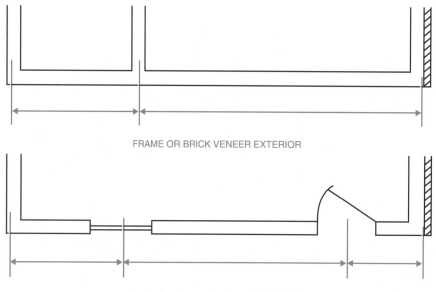

FRAME OR BRICK VENEER EXTERIOR

FRAME OR BRICK VENEER EXTERIOR

*Figure 8-8. Dimensioning windows in masonry and frame buildings.*

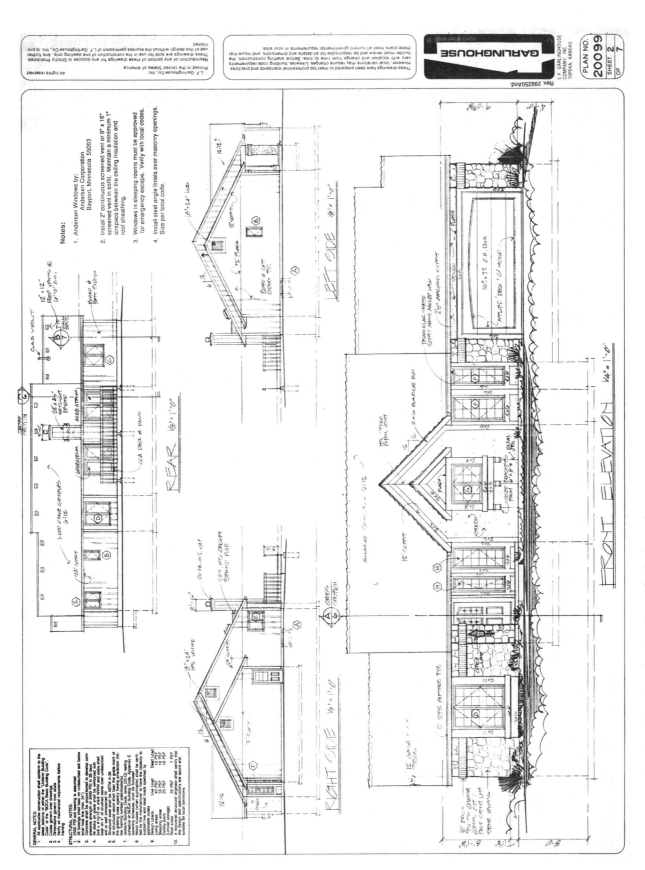

*Figure 8-9.* Typical dimensions found on elevation drawings. (Garlinghouse)

# Test Your Knowledge

*Write your answers in the spaces provided.*

_____ 1. The scale most commonly-used for floor plans is _____.

  A. 1″ = 1′-0″
  B. 1/2″ = 1′-0″
  C. 1/4″ = 1′-0″
  D. 1/8″ = 1′-0″
  E. None of these are the correct scale.

_____ 2. The metric system is rarely used in the United States because _____.

  A. it is too complicated for people to understand
  B. you must speak Spanish, French, or German to understand it
  C. it is against the law
  D. construction standards using the metric system have not been established
  E. All of these reasons are correct.

_____ 3. Which metric scale is normally used for floor plans?

  A. 1:10
  B. 1:20
  C. 1:50
  D. 1:100
  E. None of these scales are correct.

_____ 4. Which of the following dimensions *wouldn't* appear in an elevation drawing?

  A. Elevation of the second floor joists
  B. Depth of bottom of footing
  C. Thickness of a wall
  D. Height of windows
  E. None of these would appear in an elevation drawing.

_____ 5. A typical roof slope (rise to run) is _____.

  A. 1:12
  B. 4:12
  C. 12:4
  D. 12:1
  E. None of these are common roof slopes.

_____ 6. It is often necessary to scale dimensions from drawings, because normally all of the required dimensions are not shown on a drawing. (True or False?)

_____ 7. When measuring distances on a drawing, an architect's scale must be used—a normal ruler cannot be used. (True or False?)

_____ 8. Masonry walls are dimensioned to their exterior surface. (True or False?)

_____ 9. When measuring the length of a line using a scale, you position the "0" reading on the scale with one end of the line. The other line endpoint corresponds to its reading on the scale. (True or False?)

_____ 10. The scale of a drawing is the relation between the size of the drawing and the size of the actual structure. (True or False?)

**Print Reading Activity 8-1**

# *Reading Prints for Dimensions —*
# *Frame Residence*

*Refer to Prints 8-1a and 8-1b from the Large Prints supplement to answer the following questions.*

1. What is the distance between the centers of the windows on the front of the house?

1. _____

2. How wide is the fireplace?

2. _____

3. How long is the front wall of the house?

3. _____

4. What is the distance between the front of the house and the door to the laundry?

4. _____

5. How thick is the brick facade on the front of the house?

5. _____

6. How high is the foundation wall?

6. _____

7. How thick is the column footing?

7. _____

8. How far does the roof extend beyond the rear wall?

8. _____

9. How much room for the washer and dryer is there between the floor and the cabinets?

9. _____

10. What is the distance from the center of the window above the kitchen sink to the center of the door between the deck and the master bedroom?

10. _____

**Print Reading Activity 8–2**

# *Reading Prints for Dimensions —*
# *Brick Residence*

*Refer to Prints 8-2a and 8-2b from the Large Prints supplement to answer the following questions.*

1. What is the scale of the foundation and floor plan drawings?

1. _____

2. Give the overall length and width dimensions of the foundation.

2. _____

3. Locate the beam support column at the head of the stairs from the interior side of the basement fireplace and front walls.

3. _____

4. How thick are the exterior foundation walls?

4. _____

5. Give the size of the footings under the exterior foundation wall.

5. _____

6. How far below the top of the foundation wall is the recess for the brick?

6. _____

7. Give the following dimensions for the garage:

   A. Width from exterior side of walls.

7. A. _____

   B. Foundation opening for garage door.

   B. _____

   C. Greatest length inside foundation wall back to front.

   C. _____

8. Give the overall length and width of the frame wall of the house from exterior stud faces.

8. _____

9. Locate the center of the front door opening from the nearest foundation wall.

9. _____

10. What is the interior size of the living room?

10. _____

11. Locate the wall between the kitchen and dining room from the den end of the house.

11. _____

12. Give the following distances:

    A. Basement floor to underside of joists.

12. A. _____

    B. Subfloor to second floor joists.

      B. _____

    C. Second floor subfloor to ceiling joists.

      C. _____

13. What is the roof slope?

13. _____

14. With reference to the basement stairs, give the following information:

    A. Number of risers.

14. A. _____

    B. Height of risers.

      B. _____

    C. Number of treads.

      C. _____

    D. Length of treads.

      D. _____

15. What floor covering is specified for the kitchen and utility room?

15. _____

# Section 3

# Materials and Specifications

©1995 L.F. GARLINGHOUSE COMPANY, INC.

# Construction Materials

## Technical Terms

Admixture
Brick masonry
Cast-in-place concrete
Cement
Clay tile
Concrete
Concrete masonry unit
Cut stones
Float glass
Glass
Glass block
Laminate
Lumber

Nonferrous metals
Plastic
Plywood
Portland cement
Precast concrete
Prestressed concrete
Reinforcing bars
R-value
Terra cotta
Stone masonry
Structural steel
Welded wire fabric
 (WWF)

## Learning Objectives

After completing this unit, you will be able to:
- Identify the basic components of concrete
- Explain different concrete construction methods
- Describe different types of masonry brick, block, and mortar
- Classify wood as hardwood or softwood
- Recognize different structural steel shapes
- Describe various types of glass, plastic, and insulation
- Identify symbols representing materials on a drawing

Many materials are used in the construction industry. Most of these materials are carefully detailed in the project specifications. Information about materials may also be included in the drawing notes.

The purpose of this unit is to provide you with an overview of the most common materials used in construction. Also discussed are symbols used on construction drawings.

## Concrete

*Concrete* is one of the oldest building materials, having been used by the Romans as early as 100 B.C. Concrete is a mixture of cement, sand, aggregate (usually gravel), and water. When first mixed, it is *plastic* (able to flow and be shaped) and can be cast to take the shape of formwork.

Hardening of the concrete is caused by a chemical reaction between the cement and water. Most mixtures of concrete set within 12 to 24 hours, depending on the temperature, the volume of the pour, type of cement, and admixtures. When the temperature is below 70°F (20°C), the reaction slows. Very little chemical reaction takes place below 40°F (4°C). Almost none occurs at 32°F (0°C). Concrete continues to harden for months after casting, but most pours reach their load-bearing or design strength within 28 days. Forms can be removed after several days.

### Types of Cement

*Cement* binds the concrete mix together. There are many types of cement. The most common type used for general construction is called normal *portland cement.* Another variation used in construction is white portland cement. It is light-colored and used chiefly for architectural effects. White portland cement is made from carefully selected raw materials and develops the same strength as the grayish, normal portland cement.

Other types of cements, aggregates, and admixtures are available to produce special types of concrete.

Some are freeze-resistant, for setting in cold climates. Some have low-heat generation for large construction projects, such as dams. Others have high early strength to produce concrete that sets faster than normal, permitting earlier form removal and thus speeding construction. Still others are more resistant to deterioration of sulfates and alkalis in the soil.

## Concrete Mixes

A concrete mix should be designed to produce the desired result. A 1:3:4 mix contains, by volume, one part cement, three parts sand, and four parts aggregate (gravel). Enough water is added to make the mix plastic enough to flow into the forms. Too much water will reduce the strength of the concrete.

Any material added to the concrete mix other than cement, sand, aggregate, and water is known as an *admixture*. Admixtures are used to make the mix more workable, retard or speed hardening, increase freeze resistance, and increase chemical resistance.

## Reinforced Concrete

Concrete has great compressive strength but very little tensile (pulling) strength. To overcome this weakness, concrete is cast around steel bars. These bars have high tensile strength. As the concrete hardens, it grips the steel to form a bond.

*Reinforcing bars* are round with projections called deformations, formed in the rolling process to add strength to the concrete bond. Bars are placed after the forms are constructed, **Figure 9-1.** The concrete is then cast around the bars. Sheets of wire mesh are used to reinforce concrete slabs.

## Concrete Construction

Concrete members can be precast or cast-in-place. Both methods have advantages and disadvantages.

*Precast concrete* is cast at a concrete factory. After the member hardens, it is transported to the construction site, where it is installed. Because the casting is done in a controlled environment, higher quality is attained. Beams, columns, and panels can be precast. However, precast components must be small enough to allow transportation. **Figure 9-2** shows a precast wall panel being moved into place at the building site.

*Cast-in-place concrete* is cast at the construction site. Forms are built, reinforcing bars are placed, then freshly-mixed concrete is poured. The concrete hardens and never needs to be moved. Since the casting occurs outdoors, the pour can be adversely affected by cold or wet weather. Also, reinforcement placement and form

**Figure 9-1.** *After forms are constructed and reinforcing bars are placed, the concrete can be poured.*

**Figure 9-2.** *Precast wall panels are brought by truck to the building site. A crane is used to place the panels.*

dimensions are not as precise as in the controlled precast environment. Some large projects must be cast-in-place, due to transportation concerns.

# Prestressed Concrete

When a beam is loaded and bends, the upper half of the beam is pushed together (compression) and the lower half is pulled apart (tension). And, as previously stated, concrete is much stronger in compression than in tension. *Prestressed concrete* uses high-strength steel cables to push together (compress) the lower half of the beam before it is loaded. Basically, this is the same as pushing up on the bottom of the beam. The beam can then support an additional load equal to the load "pushing up" on it. Prestressing makes concrete beams much stronger, and allows them to span far greater distances than normal reinforced beams.

Concrete is prestressed by casting it around steel cables or rods that are placed under tension (pulled) to as much as 250,000 psi (pounds per in$^2$). Prestressed concrete members can be designed to use half the concrete and one-fourth the steel required for conventional reinforced concrete members of equivalent strength. Concrete bridge beams and beams in parking decks are normally prestressed.

There are two types of prestressed members: pretensioned and posttensioned:

- *Pretensioned* members are normally precast at a concrete factory and transported to the construction site. The high-strength prestressing cables are first pulled to produce tension. While the cables are held, the concrete beam is cast. Once the beam hardens, the ends of the cables are cut. The cable within the concrete tries to contract, causing compression in the concrete. See **Figure 9-3.**
- *Posttensioned* members have cables contained in tubes so that they do not bond with the concrete. The tube, with the cable inside of it, is cast in the beam. A plate is attached to the cable at one end of the beam. At the other end, a jack is used to pull the cable. When the correct tension is reached, a plate is attached to the end with the jack. The tense cable pulls on the end plates, compressing the concrete. See **Figure 9-4.** Posttensioned members can be either precast or cast-in-place.

# Masonry

Masonry products are building units such as stone, brick, concrete, tile, glass, and gypsum. Masonry construction is the assembling of these units, using mortar as a binding agent.

Almost all masonry construction must be reinforced with metals. Like concrete, masonry has good compressive strength and poor tensile strength.

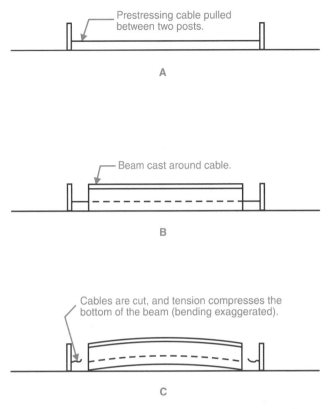

**Figure 9-3.** *Constructing a pretensioned beam. A—Cable is put under tension. B—Concrete is cast around cable and allowed to harden. C—Ends of cable are cut. Cable causes beam to compress.*

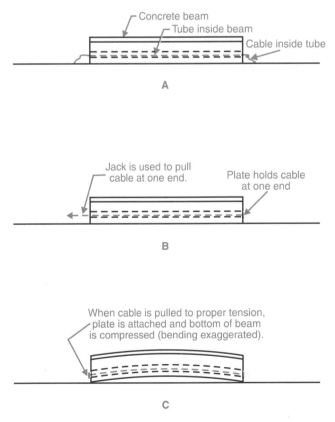

**Figure 9-4.** *Constructing a posttensioned beam. A—A tube containing the prestressing cable is cast in the beam. B—One end of the cable is pulled to create tension. C—Cable is cut and held at ends with plates.*

## Stone Masonry

The most common stones used in *stone masonry* are granite, limestone, marble, sandstone, and slate. Like concrete, stone has been used as a building material for many centuries. In the past, stones were used for structural members, roofing, and finishing. Due to the development of new materials and methods of construction, stones are now used mainly for their decorative value.

Most stones are removed from a quarry and sent to a finishing mill for final dressing. Some stones are used in their original shapes and surface finishes. Others are cut to a specific shape, size, and finish. These stones are known as *cut stones*.

## Brick Masonry

*Brick masonry* uses bricks that are manufactured, rather than removed from quarries. There are many types of bricks:

- **Adobe:** Natural sun-dried clays or earth and a binder.
- **Kiln-Burned:** Natural clays or shales (sometimes other materials are added, such as chemicals to produce color) molded to shape, dried, and fired for hardness.
- **Sand-Lime:** Composed of a mixture of sand and lime, molded and hardened under steam pressure and heat.
- **Concrete:** A mixture of portland cement and aggregates, molded into solid or cored units and hardened chemically.

There are many types and sizes of brick. Most are either building brick or face brick. Some special types are used to a lesser extent.

- **Building Brick:** Known as common brick, this is the most used brick. It is used for walls, backing, and other applications where appearance is not important.
- **Face Brick:** This is manufactured under more controlled conditions to produce bricks of specific dimensions, color, and structural qualities. These bricks are more expensive than building brick because of the care going into their manufacture. Face bricks with defects are often sold as common bricks.
- **Glazed Brick:** Used for decorative and special service applications.
- **Fire Brick:** Used where masonry units are subjected to extreme heat, such as fireplaces, incinerators, and industrial furnaces.
- **Paving Brick:** Used in driveways or areas where abrasion is a concern.

Special bricks also are available in unusual shapes for window sills, rounded corners, and other unusual applications.

## Mortar

Mortar is the binding agent used to hold masonry units together. Mortar also compensates for the differences in brick sizes. Metal ties and reinforcement are secured in mortar. Mortar consists of cement, hydrated lime, sand, and water.

The American Society for Testing and Materials has established standards for mortar. There are five different standardized types:

- **Type M** has high compressive strength and good durability. It is used for unreinforced, underground masonry.
- **Type S** is also a high-strength mortar. Although its compressive strength is not as high as Type M, it has a stronger bond and greater lateral strength. It also has the greatest tensile strength of any mortar type. Type S is used for reinforced masonry, unreinforced masonry subjected to bending, and when mortar is the only connection between face brick and backing brick.
- **Type N** is a medium-strength, general use mortar. It is best used for exposed, above-ground masonry.
- **Type O** is low-strength mortar used for interior, nonbearing masonry. This type of mortar should not be used for applications that will be exposed to freezing temperatures.
- **Type K** has very low strength and should only be used for interior applications when strength is not a concern.

Stone work usually requires a special type of mortar consisting of white portland cement, hydrated lime, and sand. This mortar prevents stains caused by ordinary cements. Mortar in the joints is normally raked back from the surface as the stone is set. Later, the joint is pointed, using the same mortar or a colored sealant.

Trade associations recommend proportions of cement, hydrated lime, and sand for mortar. Local building codes also set allowable limits. A typical mixture would be 1 part portland cement by volume, 1/4 part hydrated lime, and 3 parts sand. Water is added to make the mortar workable. Also, many brick masons use a special masonry cement containing plasticizing agents to make the mortar more workable.

## Structural Clay Tile

Structural *clay tile* is made of materials similar to brick, but it is a larger building unit. It has many uses in construction— as load-bearing walls, backup for curtain walls, and fireproofing around structural steel. Rectangular open cells pass through each unit, and tile comes in a variety of shapes and sizes.

Clay tile has largely been replaced with hollow brick and concrete masonry units. Most masonry walls today are composite walls of a finish surface material and a less expensive backup material.

*Terra cotta* is a type of structural clay tile principally used for nonbearing ornamental and decorative effects.

## Concrete Masonry Units (CMU)

Another popular and widely used building material is the *concrete masonry unit*, which is made from portland cement, sand, and gravel. By using different aggregates, such as, sand, gravel, expanded shale, and pumice, the CMUs' weight, strength, and acoustical properties can be controlled.

CMUs are made in a variety of sizes, shapes, and densities to meet specific construction needs. The standard block is 7 5/8"×7 5/8"×15 5/8". When 3/8" of mortar is used, this becomes an 8"×8"×16" module. Another common size is the 3 5/8"×7 5/8"×15 5/8" block.

Concrete block can have colored surfaces and special design features. Slump blocks, which give the appearance of rough adobe brick, **Figure 9-5,** are also available.

## Gypsum Blocks

Gypsum masonry blocks are used primarily for interior, nonbearing walls, fire-resistant partitions, and enclosures around structural steel. Made from gypsum and a binder of vegetable fiber or wood chips, they can be given a plaster finish coat. Gypsum blocks have a face size of 12"×30" and come in thicknesses of 2", 3", 4", and 6".

## Gypsum Wallboard and Plaster

Gypsum wallboard and plaster products consist of a core of air-entrained gypsum between two layers of treated paper. Wallboard comes in 4'×8' sheets. It is fastened to wood or metal studs with nails or screws, and varies in thickness from 1/4" to 1". Joints are sealed with a joint compound and paper tape to provide a smooth, even surface. The wall can be painted, papered, or given a surface texture to enhance its appearance.

Lath for gypsum plaster walls is available in 16"×48" sheets with thicknesses of 3/8" and 1/2". The lath is fastened to the studs and a three-coat gypsum plaster process—scratch coat, brown coat, and finish coat—is applied.

Building papers are available in a variety of types suitable for sheathing walls and roofs. Some papers are reinforced for strength and tear resistance. Building papers are treated with asphalt, plastic, tar, or other materials. The building paper is usually specified on the print or in the specifications.

*Figure 9-5.* *A popular type of concrete masonry unit is the slump block. (National Concrete Masonry Association)*

## Glass Block

*Glass block* is made by fusing two sections of glass together. A partial vacuum is created between the pieces, providing good insulating qualities. Edges are left rough to improve the bond with the mortar.

Glass block is used in nonbearing situations, such as interior walls, screens, curtain walls, and windows. They are manufactured in three nominal sizes: 6×6, 8×8, and 12×12 inches. Special blocks are available for forming corners and curved panels.

## Masonry Joint Reinforcement

Masonry walls are reinforced by placing various anchors, ties, and rods in the mortar joints. These reinforcing units are produced in many sizes and shapes for different applications. Reinforcing devices are called out directly on the prints or in applicable building codes.

# Wood Products

Wood continues to be one of the chief building materials used today. It is used for structural framing (rough carpentry), trim, floors, walls, and cabinetry (finish carpentry). While steps have been taken to substitute other materials in place of it, wood remains a valuable and widely-used residential construction material.

When wood is cut into pieces of specific thickness, width, and length, it is called *lumber*. Lumber products include rough framing members (at least 2″ thick), such as beams, headers, and posts; finished lumber, such as flooring, door and window trim, paneling, and moldings; and specialty items, such as decorative panels, carved doors, ornamental overlay designs, and turned balusters (stair rail posts).

## Wood Classification

Woods are broadly classified as either hardwoods or softwoods. There are many varieties used for construction:

| Hardwoods | |
|---|---|
| Ash | Gum |
| Ash, White | Hickory |
| Beech | Mahogany |
| Birch | Maple |
| Cherry | Oak |
| Elm | Walnut |

| Softwoods | |
|---|---|
| Cypress | Pine, White |
| Fir, Douglas | Poplar, Yellow |
| Fir, White | Red Cedar, Eastern |
| Hemlock | Red Cedar, Western |
| Pine, Ponderosa | Redwood |
| Pine, Southern | Spruce |

These classifications are not an exact measure of hardness or softness (because this varies) but a general classification based on type of tree. In addition to hardness or softness, woods vary in strength, weight, texture, workability, and cost. Building specifications usually indicate the type and grade of lumber to be used in different parts of the construction.

## Lumber

Lumber is classified as rough-sawn or surfaced to size. Rough-sawn has been cut to rough size but not dressed or surfaced. Surfaced lumber has been dressed or finished to size by running it through a planer. S2S refers to lumber dressed on two sides, and S4S is lumber that is surfaced or planed on four sides.

*Plywood* is a wood product made of several layers of lumber with the grain at right angles in each successive layer. An odd number of layers are bonded together (so the grain of the face and back are running in the same direction) with an adhesive. The panels are finished to thicknesses from 1/8″ to over 1″, and are usually 4′×8′ in size. Because of its modular size and uniformity, plywood speeds construction and is considered an economical building material.

Interior plywood is bonded with an adhesive that is water-resistant. It is used for cabinetry, rough flooring, and finished walls. Exterior or structural plywood is bonded with a waterproof adhesive. It is used for exterior wall sheathing, finished walls, roof sheathing, and concrete forms.

## Glue-Laminated Timber

The process of *laminating* (bonding layers of lumber together with adhesive) wood beams, arches and other members has made it possible to span larger distances and change traditional construction techniques. Wood members of nearly any size and shape can be fabricated, **Figure 9-6.** These laminated products are made of kiln-dried lumber and prepared for interior and exterior use. These beams are usually prefinished at the factory and delivered to the job with protective wrapping.

*Figure 9-6. Wood lamination has added strength and beauty to the wood construction field. (Weyerhaeuser)*

# Metal Products

Metal is used extensively in the construction industry. Large commercial buildings use structural steel. Construction jobs make use of metal windows, doors, studs, beams, joists, wall facings, roofing, plumbing, and hardware.

*Structural steel* is the term applied to hot-rolled steel sections, shapes, and plates. This includes bolts, rivets, and bracing.

Structural steel shapes are formed by passing hot steel strips (long pieces called billets, blooms, or slabs) through a succession of rollers that gradually form it into the required shape, **Figure 9-7.** Structural steel shapes are available in a number of sizes and weights. **Figure 9-8** illustrates some standard shapes and gives their identifying symbol and designation.

A typical designation for a wide-flange beam would be W12×16, which indicates a beam 12″ in depth that weights 16 pounds per linear foot. A typical designation for a lightweight beam, sometimes called an I-beam, would be S8×23. This indicates that the beam is 8″ deep and weights 23 pounds per linear foot.

Steel members are connected to form building frames, **Figure 9-9.** The frame is then hidden behind other materials, such as a masonry wall, precast panels, or sheet metal siding.

Steel *angles* (sometimes called *angle iron*) are used as bracing in steel framing and to construct open-web joists, **Figure 9-10.** Angles are designated with the letter "L", followed by the lengths and thickness of the "legs." For an angle identified as L3×3×1/2, both legs are 3″ long and 1/2″ thick.

*Figure 9-7. A structural steel beam is being formed by a series of rollers. (United States Steel)*

Steel reinforcing bars are used in open-web joists and in reinforced concrete. Small bars are identified by a number corresponding to the eighths of an inch in the diameter. That is, a No. 4 bar would have a 4/8″ (or 1/2″) diameter. Larger bars (9 through 18) don't correspond to eighths of an inch, beginning with No. 9 which is 1.128″ in diameter.

*Welded wire fabric (WWF)* is a prefabricated material used for the reinforcement of concrete slabs, floors, and pipe. It consists of a mesh of steel wires welded together. It is available in sheets and rolls.

There are two types of welded wire fabric: *smooth* (or plain), designated by a *W*; and *deformed*, designated *D*. The deformed fabric has deformations along the

| DESCRIPTIVE NAME | SHAPE | IDENTIFYING SHAPE | TYPICAL DESIGNATION<br>Height    Wt/Ft in Lb. | NOMINAL SIZE<br>Height    Width |
|---|---|---|---|---|
| WIDE FLANGE SHAPES |  I | W | W21 × 142 | 21 × 13 |
| MISCELLANEOUS SHAPES |  I | M | M8 × 6.5 | 8 × 2¼ |
| AMERICAN STANDARD BEAMS |  I | S | S8 × 23 | 8 × 4 |
| AMERICAN STANDARD CHANNELS |  [ | C | C6 × 13 | 6 × 2 |
| MISCELLANEOUS CHANNELS |  [ | MC | MC8 × 20 | 8 × 3 |
| ANGLES–EQUAL LEGS |  L | L | L6 × 6 × ½* | 6 × 6 |
| ANGLES–UNEQUAL LEGS | L | L | L8 × 6 × ½* | 8 × 6 |
| BULB ANGLES | L | BL | BL6 × 3½ × 17.4 | 3½ × 6 |
| STRUCTURAL TEES (CUT FROM WIDE FLANGE) |  T | WT | WT12 × 60 | 12 |
| STRUCTURAL TEES (CUT FROM MISCELLANEOUS SHAPES) |  T | MT | MT5 × 4.5 | 5 |
| STRUCTURAL TEES (CUT FROM AM. STD. BEAMS) |  T | ST | ST9 × 35 | 9 |
| TEES |  T | T | T5 × 11.5 | 3 × 5 |
| WALL TEE |  T | AT | AT8 × 29.2 | 4⅞ × 7¾ |
| ELEVATOR TEES |  T | ET | ET4 × 24.5 | 4⅛ × 5½ |
| ZEES |  Z | Z | Z4 × 15.9 | 6 × 3½ |

\* SIZE ONLY

**Figure 9-8.** *Some examples of structural steel shapes.*

**Figure 9-9.** *This steel frame is designed to support the entire weight of the building.*

**Figure 9-10.** *Installation of open-web steel joists.*

wire to better develop anchorage in the concrete. Previously, the fabric was specified by gage number, and some drawings still use this system.

Welded wire fabric is further designated by numbers. An example is 6×8–W8.0×W4.0. The first number (6) gives the spacing of the longitudinal wire in inches, **Figure 9-11.** The second number (8) gives the spacing of the transverse wires in inches. The first letter-number combination (W8.0) gives the type and size of the longitudinal wire. The second combination (W4.0) gives information on the transverse wire.

In the example given, the longitudinal wires are 6″ apart. The transverse wires are 8″ apart. The longitudinal wire is smooth and has a cross-sectional area of 0.08 in². The transverse wire is also smooth with an area of 0.04 in². **Figure 9-12** lists some of the common stock styles of welded wire fabric.

## Gage Metals

Wall studs, lintels, window and door frames, and floor joists are made from heavy gage metals. Thin gage metals are used for such items as roof flashing, duct work, roofing, and wall siding.

## Galvanized Ferrous Metals

Galvanized ferrous metals are produced by dipping sheet metal in hot zinc. Galvanized iron is widely used for flashing and other applications where weather tends to corrode metals.

## Nonferrous Metals

*Nonferrous metals* contain little or no iron. Aluminum alloys are used to a limited extent in structural work and framing. It is used in its natural color for windows, doors, thresholds, and siding. Aluminum can also be anodized or given a chemical finish to add color and make it more resistant to abrasion.

Aluminum alloys are made in structural shapes for use as H-beams, I-beams, and angles. Aluminum is also used for some duct work, screens, and for electrical wiring. Copper and copper alloys are used for construction items such as piping, flashing, roofing, screens, gutters, and electrical wiring. The particular metal would be indicated on the drawing as a note and most likely detailed in the specifications.

## Glass

*Glass* is a ceramic material formed at temperatures above 2300°F (1260°C). It is made from sand (silica), soda (sodium oxide), and lime (calcium oxide). Other chemicals can be added to change its characteristics.

*Float glass* is the most common type of glass. A continuous ribbon of molten glass flows out of a furnace and floats on a bath of molten tin. Irregularities melt out and the glass becomes flat. The ribbon of glass is fire-polished and annealed, without grinding or polishing. Over 90% of the world's flat glass is made by the float process.

After the float process, other processes can further modify the properties of the glass, producing several types:

- *Sheet glass* is commonly used for windows in thickness of 3/32″ (single strength—SS) and 1/8″ (double strength—DS). Thick glass is a sheet glass 3/16″ to 7/16″ in thickness.
- *Plate glass* is sheet glass that has been heat-treated during forming, producing a brilliant surface that is ground and polished when cooled.
- *Bent glass* is produced by heating annealed glass to a point where it softens so it can be pressed over a form.
- *Safety glass* has been developed to overcome

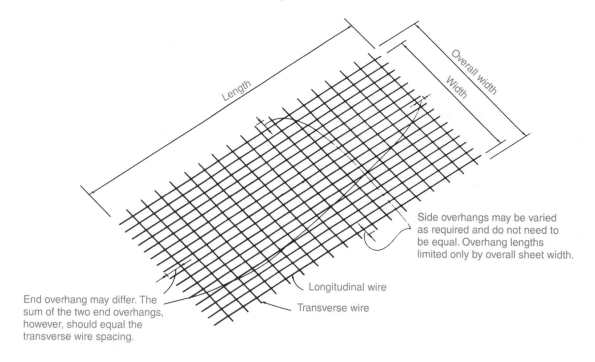

Side overhangs may be varied as required and do not need to be equal. Overhang lengths limited only by overall sheet width.

End overhang may differ. The sum of the two end overhangs, however, should equal the transverse wire spacing.

Longitudinal wire

Transverse wire

*Figure 9-11. Welded wire fabric nomenclature. (Wire Reinforcement Institute)*

## Common Stock Styles of Welded Wire Fabric

| STYLE DESIGNATION | | STEEL AREA (in²/ft) | | WEIGHT (lb/100 ft²) |
|---|---|---|---|---|
| **New Designation (by W-number)** | **Old Designation (by steel wire gage)** | **Longit.** | **Trans.** | |
| **ROLL** | | | | |
| 6x6–W1.4xW1.4 | 6x6–10x10 | .028 | .028 | 21 |
| 6x6–W2.0xW2.0 | 6x6–8x8* | .040 | .040 | 29 |
| 6x6–W2.9xW2.9 | 6x6–6x6 | .058 | .058 | 42 |
| 6x6–W4.0xW4.0 | 6x6–4x4 | .080 | .080 | 58 |
| 4x4–W1.4xW1.4 | 4x4–10x10 | .042 | .042 | 31 |
| 4x4–W2.0xW2.0 | 4x4–8x8* | .060 | .060 | 43 |
| 4x4–W2.9xW2.9 | 4x4–6x6 | .087 | .087 | 62 |
| 4x4–W4.0xW4.0 | 4x4–44 | .120 | .120 | 85 |
| **SHEETS** | | | | |
| 6x6–W2.9xW2.9 | 6x6–6x6 | .058 | .058 | 42 |
| 6xt–W4.0xW4.0 | 6x6–4x4 | .080 | .080 | 58 |
| 6x6–W5.5xW5.5 | 6x6–2x2** | .110 | .110 | 80 |
| 4x4–W4.0xW4.0 | 4x4–4x4 | .120 | .120 | 85 |

*Exact W-number size for 8 gauge is W2.1
**Exact W-number size for 2 gauge is W5.4

*Figure 9-12. Common stock styles of welded wire fabric. (Wire Reinforcement Institute)*

the hazards of sheet glass in large, exposed, or public areas. Three types of safety glass are available: tempered, laminated, and wired glass.

- Tempered glass is developed by heating annealed glass to near its melting point and then chilling it rapidly, creating high compression on the exterior surfaces and high tension internally. This makes the piece of glass three to five times as strong as annealed glass. Tempered glass can be broken, but it shatters into small, pebble-like pieces rather than sharp slivers. Tempered glass must be ordered to the exact size before tempering because it cannot be cut, drilled, or ground after it has been tempered.

- Laminated glass consists of a layers of vinyl between sheets of glass. The layers of plastic and glass are bonded together with heat and pressure. The elasticity of the plastic serves as a cushion for any object striking the laminated glass. This glass can be broken, but the plastic layers hold the small, sharp pieces in place.

- Wired glass has a wire mesh molded into its center. Wire glass can be broken, but the wire holds the small parts together. Wired glass can be obtained with an etched finish, a sandblasted finish, or a patterned finish.

- *Insulating glass* is a unit of two or more sheets of glass separated by an air space that is dehydrated and sealed. These units serve as a good insulator for heat and sound transfer. A typical insulating glass installation in a window sash is shown in **Figure 9-13.**

- *Patterned glass* is sheet glass with a pattern rolled into one or both sides to diffuse the light and provide privacy.

- *Stained glass*, sometimes called *art* or *cathedral glass*, is produced by adding metallic oxides in the molten state. This glass can be used in sheets or cut into smaller pieces and made into leaded glass for windows and decor pieces.

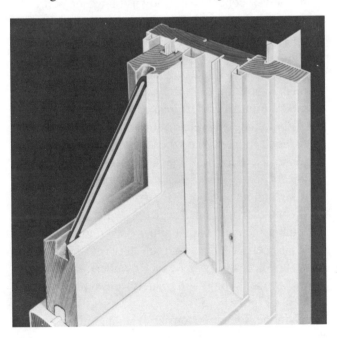

*Figure 9-13. Window with insulating glass. (Andersen Corp.)*

## Ceramic Tile

Many types of tile are used in construction. Some of these are discussed here:

- *Ceramic tiles* are used for floor and wall coverings. The tile comes in sizes from 3/8″ square to 16″×18″ units. Popular wall sizes are 4 1/4″× 4 1/4″, 4 1/4″×6″ and 6″×6″. Hexagonal and octagonal tiles are also available. The tiles can be glazed or unglazed. Glazed tiles are usually 5/16″ thick. Unglazed (faience) tiles vary from 7/16″ to 3/4″ thick.

- *Mosaic tiles* can be laid to form a design or pattern. They are normally smaller than 6″ and can be glazed or unglazed.

- *Quarry tile* is used for floor coverings and is produced from clays that provide a wear-resistant surface.

- *Fired-clay tile* is used primarily for floor coverings. It is produced from clays and is fired in a kiln to harden the surface.

Tiles are set in portland cement, latex adhesive, or epoxy mortar. The joints between the tiles are grouted.

## Plastics

*Plastics* have many uses in construction. Plastic laminates serve as counter tops, door veneer, and wall surfacing. Panels of wood or gypsum are printed, textured, and given a plastic vinyl coating. Plastic rain gutters and downspouts collect and distribute rain water. Plastic pipes are used for water-transmission, sprinkling, drainage, and sewage systems.

Plastics are also used for many trim and ornamental decor items, such as moldings on doors and simulated wood carvings. Plastic usually is noted on the drawing and detailed in the specifications.

## Insulation

The purpose of thermal insulation is to reduce heat transmission through walls, ceilings, and floors. When the outdoor temperature is warm, insulation keeps the heat from entering the structure. When the outdoor temperature is cool, insulation helps keep the warm air indoors.

Insulation is manufactured in a variety of forms and types to meet specific construction requirements. Each type will have an *R-value* (resistance to heat transfer), depending on the manner of application and amount of material. A high R-value means good insulation qualities. Insulation materials are classified as:

- Flexible (blanket or batt).
- Loose-fill.
- Reflective.
- Rigid (structural and nonstructural).

*Flexible insulation* is available in blanket and batt form, **Figure 9-14.** Blankets come in widths suitable to

**Figure 9-14.** *Flexible insulation being installed above a ceiling. A vapor barrier should always be installed on the side to be warm in cold weather. (Owens-Corning Fiberglas)*

fit 16″ and 24″ stud and joist spacing and thicknesses of 1″ to 3 1/2″. The body of the blanket is made of mineral or vegetable fiber, such as rock wool, glass wool, wood fiber, or cotton. Organic materials are treated to resist fire, decay, insects, and vermin. Blankets are covered with a paper sheet on one or both sides. The vapor barrier is installed facing the warm side of the wall. Batt insulation is made of the same material as blankets, in thicknesses of 2″ to 6″ and lengths of 24″ and 48″.

*Loose-fill insulation* is available in bags or bales. It is either poured, blown, or packed in place by hand. Loose-fill insulation is made from rock wool, glass wool, wood fibers, shredded redwood bark, cork, wood pulp products, vermiculite, saw dust, and shavings. This insulation is suited for insulating sidewalls and attics of building. It is also used to fill cells in block walls.

*Reflective insulation* is designed to reflect radiant heat. It is made from aluminum foil, sheet metal with tin coating, and paper products coated with a reflective oxide composition. To be effective, the reflective surface must face an air space of at least 3/4″. When the reflective surface contacts another material, such as a wall or ceiling, the reflective properties are lost along with its insulating value. This material is often used on the back of gypsum lath and blanket insulation.

*Rigid insulation* is made of a fiberboard material in sheet form. Common types are made from processed wood, sugarcane, and other fiber. These produce a lightweight, low-density product with good heat and acoustical insulating qualities. Rigid insulation is used as sheathing for walls and roof decks when additional insulation is needed.

# Material Symbols on Drawings

Besides showing the location and sizes of different construction components, drawings also identify the materials that are used. Materials are identified in several ways:

- A section of a drawing may contain a pattern that is unique to a specific material. See **Figure 9-15.**
- Often, materials are specified in the notes included on a drawing. This allows for easy reference.
- Materials are also included in the project speci-fications.

Concrete is represented in the section view as small dots with a scattering of small triangular shapes. On plan views, concrete is shown blank or with the concrete hatch pattern. If the concrete area is large, the pattern may be shown in portions, rather than the entire outline.

Section views that cut across structural framing members show these pieces with an "×" within each member, **Figure 9-15.** Finished lumber (trim, fascia boards, moldings) in section shows the wood end grain. For a wood frame wall on the plan view, the usual prac-tice is to leave the wall blank, **Figure 9-16(A).** Some architects shade this area lightly to better outline the building and its partitions, **Figure 9-16(B).**

When shown in small scale, plywood is represented with the same symbol as lumber. When in section and the scale permits, lines may be drawn to indicate the plies (not necessarily the exact number). In elevation views, wood siding and panels are represented as shown in **Figure 9-15.**

Symbols for glass consist of a single line on plan drawings and section drawings. The symbol may consist of several lines on large scale drawings. Glass areas in elevation views are left plain or consist of a series of random diagonal lines.

| MATERIAL | PLAN | ELEVATION | SECTION |
|---|---|---|---|
| EARTH | NONE | NONE | |
| CONCRETE | | | SAME AS PLAN VIEW |
| CONCRETE BLOCK | | | |
| GRAVEL FILL | SAME AS SECTION | NONE | |
| WOOD | FLOOR AREAS LEFT BLANK | SIDING  PANEL | FINISH FRAMING |
| BRICK | FACE / COMMON | FACE OR COMMON | SAME AS PLAN VIEW |
| STONE | CUT / RUBBLE | CUT  RUBBLE | CUT  RUBBLE |
| STRUCTURAL STEEL | | INDICATE BY NOTE | SPECIFY |
| SHEET METAL FLASHING | INDICATE BY NOTE | | SHOW CONTOUR |
| INSULATION | SAME AS SECTION | INSULATION | LOOSE FILL OR BATT / BOARD |
| PLASTER | SAME AS SECTION | PLASTER | STUD / LATH AND PLASTER |
| GLASS | | | LARGE SCALE / SMALL SCALE |
| TILE | | | |

**Figure 9-15.** *Symbols used for construction materials.*

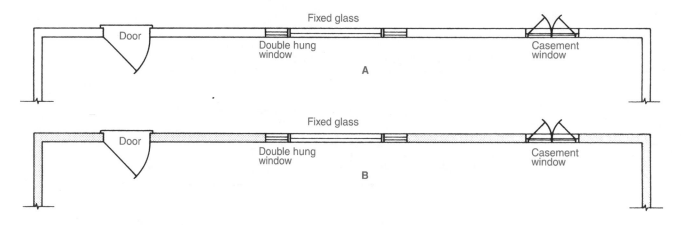

**Figure 9-16.** *A plan view of a wood frame wall.*

# Test Your Knowledge

*Write your answers in the spaces provided.*

_____ 1. Concrete is stronger in tension (pulled) than it is in compression (pushed). (True or False?)

_____ 2. When preparing a batch of concrete, which of the following would not be included?

  A. Water
  B. Cement
  C. Aggregate (sand, gravel)
  D. Chemical admixtures
  E. All of these items could be included in the mix.

_____ 3. Which mortar type is best-suited for situations requiring high lateral strength?

  A. Type M
  B. Type S
  C. Type N
  D. Type O
  E. None of the above.

_____ 4. What is the difference between interior and exterior plywood?

  A. The type of wood used
  B. The size of the sheets
  C. The type of adhesive used
  D. The thickness of the sheets
  E. Interior and exterior plywood are identical.

_____ 5. The steel beam identification W8×15 represents a wide-flange beam _____.

  A. 8″ deep and weighing 15 lbs. per linear foot
  B. 8″ deep and 15″ wide
  C. 8″ wide and 15″ deep
  D. 8″ deep and 15′ long
  E. None of the above are correct.

_____ 6. Nonferrous metals contain little or no aluminum. (True or False?)

_____ 7. Concrete completely hardens within 48 hours after it is poured. (True or False?)

_____ 8. Which of the following is *not* considered to be a type of safety glass?

  A. Wired glass
  B. Plate glass
  C. Laminated glass
  D. Tempered glass
  E. All of these are types of safety glass.

_____ 9. Prestressed concrete beams are normally larger than a standard reinforced concrete beam of equal strength. (True or False?)

_____ 10. An air space between two sealed panes of glass serves as good insulation. (True or False?)

# Specifications

## Technical Terms

American Society for
Testing and
Materials (ASTM)
Construction
Specifications
Institute (CSI)

Divisions
Documents
Specifications

## Learning Objectives

After completing this unit, you will be able to:
- Explain what is included in specifications
- Explain why specifications are needed
- Find a particular topic within specifications

*Specifications* are written statements that define the extent and quality of work to be done and the materials to be used. They supplement the drawings which, in turn, describe the physical location, size, and shape of the project. Specifications are often referred to as *specs*.

In this unit, specifications are explained. Also, a typical set of specifications is presented to acquaint you with its organization and to assist you in locating information concerning a particular phase of construction.

Specifications vary in length from a few pages to hundreds of pages. They are normally prepared by a person who is thoroughly familiar with construction procedures, building materials, and local government codes.

Specifications and drawings supplement each other so that all information needed for a construction project is included. An example would be the hardware for use on doors. The drawings would show location and direction of door swing; the specification would indicate quality or brand name, style, finish and any other information to ensure that the proper hardware is installed.

## Requirements and Scope

The architect, owner, general contractor, and subcontractors all use the specifications, as do the craftspeople engaged in the construction. The following statements are excerpts from a typical set of specifications:

**General Requirements:**

Work shall include all items (building and site) indicated on these drawings unless otherwise noted. The American Institute of Architects (AIA) General Conditions, latest edition, are hereby a part of this contract. General contractor shall remove all construction debris from the job site and leave the building broom clean.

**Structural Specifications:**

All footing shall be carried to undisturbed medium sand or rock, and to at least the depth shown on the drawings.

All concrete to attain a minimum ultimate compressive strength of 3000 PSI in 28 days. Aggregates to be clean and well-graded, maximum size of 1″. Concrete slump 3″ minimum to 5″ maximum.

Specifications, along with the drawings, ensure that the construction project will be completed in the manner it was intended.

## Specification Divisions

Specifications differ for various construction projects. However, there are certain elements that are common to any construction job. The *Construction*

*Specifications Institute (CSI)* has standardized specific *divisions* within specifications:

- Division 1—General Requirements
- Division 2—Site Construction
- Division 3—Concrete
- Division 4—Masonry
- Division 5—Metals
- Division 6—Wood and Plastics
- Division 7—Thermal and Moisture Protection
- Division 8—Doors and Windows
- Division 9—Finishes
- Division 10—Specialties
- Division 11—Equipment
- Division 12—Furnishings
- Division 13—Special Construction
- Division 14—Conveying Systems
- Division 15—Mechanical
- Division 16—Electrical

Specifications provide detailed information that cannot be shown on the drawing due to space constraints. Specifications and drawings each provide information on details of construction.

Specifications serve several purposes:

- As a guide for contractors bidding on a construction job. The specifications tell the contractor the exact materials to be used. This makes the estimate more accurate than if the contractor had to make assumptions.
- As a standard for quality of material and work to be done in a project.
- As a guide for the building inspector in checking for compliance with building codes and zoning ordinances.
- As the basis of agreement between the owner, architect, and contractors in settling any disputes that may arise regarding the construction project.

# Contents

Specifications, and the information contained in them, vary from a simple outline to elaborate sets of specifications.

The contract requirements, or *documents,* are contained within the specifications. These cover nontechnical aspects of the project, such as the terms of the contract agreement and responsibilities for inspection, insurance, permits, utilities, and supervision. It is in these areas that misunderstandings often occur. Therefore, these requirements are more detailed on complex projects.

The technical aspects of the project are listed by divisions, usually in the order the work is performed on the job. Materials are specified by standard numbers. The *American Society for Testing and Materials (ASTM)* has standards indicating test procedures used to specify materials.

In addition to specifying materials, the standards for quality of work to be done are also included. Inspection procedures and criteria are stated. Provisions may be provided for determining responsibility and corrective measures if the quality standards are not met.

# Reading Specifications

When reading specifications, first review the table of contents to become familiar with the type of information included. This will also give you an overview of what is included in the project.

Information of a general nature, such as insurance, supervision, and inspection, is found in the *General Requirements* section.

When searching for a particular topic, determine under which division it would be included. For example, if you needed to know the required concrete strength, you would look under *Division 3—Concrete.* If you needed to find the variety of shrub to be planted along a walkway, you would look under *Division 2—Site Construction.*

# Test Your Knowledge

*Use the CSI Specification Index in* Section 7, Reference, *to match the following subjects with the Division in which they would be located. Write your answers in the spaces provided.*

_____ 1. Ceramic tile

_____ 2. Prefabricated toolshed

_____ 3. Pressure-treated lumber

_____ 4. Piping material

_____ 5. Murals

_____ 6. Asphalt paving

_____ 7. Food preparation tables

_____ 8. Skylights

_____ 9. Conveyors

_____ 10. Mailbox

_____ 11. Public-address system

_____ 12. Elevators

_____ 13. Lighting rods

_____ 14. Statues

_____ 15. Acoustical paneling

_____ 16. File cabinets

_____ 17. Thermostats

_____ 18. Exercise equipment

_____ 19. Reinforcing bars

_____ 20. Flagpoles

A.  Division 1—General Requirements
B.  Division 2—Site Construction
C.  Division 3—Concrete
D.  Division 4—Masonry
E.  Division 5—Metals
F.  Division 6—Wood and Plastics
G.  Division 7—Thermal and Moisture Protection
H.  Division 8—Doors and Windows
I.  Division 9—Finishes
J.  Division 10—Specialties
K.  Division 11—Equipment
L.  Division 12—Furnishings
M.  Division 13—Special Construction
N.  Division 14—Conveying Systems
O.  Division 15—Mechanical
P.  Division 16—Electrical

## Print Reading Activity 10–1

# Reading Specifications

*Use the partial set of specifications at the end of this activity and the CSI Specifications in Section 7, Reference, to answer the following questions. Write your answers in the spaces provided.*

1. Under which division would you locate

   A. Roofing materials and processes?          1. A. _____

   B. Interior wood trim?                       B. _____

   C. Interior finishing of walls?              C. _____

2. What must all bidders do before submitting a bid?          2. _____

3. If an item is mentioned in the specification and not in the drawings, must the bidder supply it?          3. _____

4. Who has the final decision as to the interpretation of the drawings and specifications?          4. _____

5. To whom does the term *contractor* refer?          5. _____

_____

_____

6. Who is responsible for providing and paying for temporary electrical service?          6. _____

7. Who shall provide the necessary temporary heat needed to accomplish the work?          7. _____

8. If the permanent heating plant is used for temporary heat, who will pay for its operation?          8. _____

9. Who may provide and maintain temporary storage sheds for storage of all materials that may be damaged by the weather?          9. _____

10. How much of an overlap must be made between the new and existing roof?

10. _____

11. If a dimension shown as 20'-0" on the drawings is scaled as 18'-6", which dimension is used?

11. _____

12. What thickness of rigid insulation is used on flat roofs?

12. _____

13. Where can a copy of the General Conditions of the Contract be viewed?

13. _____

14. These specification are for what type of construction?

14. _____

15. If a detail drawing shows a 3'-4" wide sidewalk and the plan view shows the same sidewalk as 3'-6" wide, how wide should the sidewalk be?

15. _____

**SPECIFICATIONS FOR AN OFFICE ADDITION**
**For GOODHEART-WILLCOX COMPANY, INC.**
**At 123 Taft Drive, South Holland, Illinois**

**PLAN NO. 12275**
**Architects: Donald T. Smith & Associates**
**7227 W. 127th Street, Palos Heights, Illinois**

## INDEX

## SUPPLEMENTARY GENERAL CONDITIONS

### General:

These Supplementary General Conditions and the Specifications bound herewith shall be subject to all the requirements of the "General Conditions of the Contract for the Construction of Building," latest edition, Standard Form of the A.I.A., except that these Supplementary General Conditions shall take precedence over and modify any pages or statements of the General Conditions of the Contract and shall be used in conjunction with them as a part of the Contract Documents. The General Conditions of the Contract are hereby, except as same may be inconsistent herewith, made a part of this Specification, to the same extent as if herein written in full.

Copies of the General Conditions of the Contract are on file and may be referred to at the Office of the Architects.

### Scope of Work:

The work involved and outlined by these Specifications is for the construction work for the completion of the Office Addition for Goodheart-Willcox Co., Inc., 123 Taft Drive, South Holland, Illinois, as further illustrated, indicated, or shown on the accompanying drawings.

### Examination of Site:

Before submitting a proposal for this work, each bidder will be held to have examined the site, satisfied himself fully as to existing conditions under which he will be obligated to operate in performing his part of the work, or which will in any manner affect the work under this contract. He shall include in his proposal any and all sums required to execute his work under existing conditions. No allowance for additional compensation will be subsequently in this connection, in behalf of any contractor, or for any error or negligence on his part.

## Drawings and Specifications:

These Specifications are intended to supplement the Drawings, the two being considered complementary, therefore, it will not be the province of these Specifications to mention any portion of the construction which the drawings are competent to explain and such omission will not relieve the contractor from carrying out such portions as are only indicated on the drawings. Should the items be required by these Specifications which are not indicated on the drawings, they are to be supplied, even if of such nature that they could have been indicated thereon.

Any items which may not be indicated on the drawings or mentioned herein, but are necessary to complete the entire work, as shown and intended, shall be implied and must be furnished in place.

The decision of the architects as to the proper interpretation of the Drawings and these Specifications shall be final and shall require compliance by the contractor in executing the work.

Figured dimensions shall have precedence over scale measurements, and details over smaller scale general drawings. Should any...

## Principles and Definitions:

Where the words "approved," "satisfactory," "equal," "proper," "ordered," "as directed," etc., are used, approval, etc., by architects is understood.

It is understood that when the word "Contractor" is used in these Supplementary General Conditions, the work described in the paragraph may apply to all Contractors and Subcontractors involved with the work.

## Temporary Facilities:

Temporary Heat: Each contractor shall provide the necessary temporary heat needed for materials, water, etc., or any other heat required to accomplish his work. If the permanent heating plant is used for temporary heat, the owner will pay for its operation.

Temporary Light & Power: The general contractor shall arrange and pay for a temporary electrical service taken from the existing building for use by all trades, include 60 amp, 2 pole, 4 outlet fused panel mounted on pole or wall at the site. The electrical contractor shall provide temporary light within the structure as necessary and directed. General contractor will pay for all temporary electrical service until such time when permanent meter shall be installed.

Temporary Sheds for Storage: The general contractor may provide and maintain on the premises, where directed, watertight storage shed, or sheds, for storage of all material which may be damaged by the weather. These sheds shall have wood floors raised above the grounds.

## Division 7
## THERMAL AND MOISTURE PROTECTION

### General Conditions:

The contractor shall read the General Conditions and Supplementary General Conditions which are a part of these Specifications.

### Scope of Work:

Furnish all materials and labor necessary to complete the entire roofing as shown on the drawings or hereinafter specified.

### Roofing:

Flat roofing shall be 4 ply tar and gravel Spec. 102 of the Chicago Roofing Contractors Association, except single pour on gravel.

Carry new roofing onto existing roof a minimum of 3'-0" and roof new saddles on existing.

### Rigid Insulation:

Cover all flat roof surfaces over steel deck with 2" of rigid insulation.

Insulation board shall be Fesco or equal.

Insulation shall be installed according to Spec. 102 of the Chicago Roofing Contractors Association. Form saddles on existing roof of rigid insulation so pitch is to new roof drain.

# Section 4

# Reading Prints

©1995 L.F. GARLINGHOUSE COMPANY, INC.

# Plot Plans

## Technical Terms

| | |
|---|---|
| Assumed benchmark | Plan North |
| Bearing | Plot plan |
| Benchmark | Property lines |
| Contour lines | Second |
| Delta | Setback distance |
| Legend | Site plan |
| Minute | Topography |
| North arrow | True North |

## Learning Objectives

After completing this unit, you will be able to:
- Recognize common features of plot plans
- Identify property line descriptions
- Explain the difference between True North and Plan North

A building can be greatly enhanced by its location on the plot of land. Therefore, architects take advantage of the slope of the land, surrounding trees, view from the street, and other features to improve the appearance of a structure.

## Features of Plot Plans

A *plot plan* (sometimes called a *site plan*) is a view from above the property that shows the location of the building on the lot. See **Figure 11-1.** Many features may be shown on the plot plan:
- Lot and block number or address
- Bearing (direction) and length of property lines
- North arrow
- Dimensions of front, rear, and side yards
- Location of other accessory buildings (carport, garage, etc.)
- Location of walks, drives, fences, and patios
- Location of easement setbacks
- Location of utilities
- Elevations at the various locations
- Trees and shrubs to be retained

## North Arrow

The *north arrow* indicates the north direction. When initially looking at a plot plan, find the north arrow. This will help you to visualize the structure. This is particularly true if you are familiar with the plot of land on which the building will be constructed.

If the walls of the building are not parallel to the compass directions, a *Plan North* may be designated. The Plan North will be slightly different than the *True North,* **Figure 11-2.** A Plan North is provided so that there is a reference direction aligned with the building. This also simplifies the description of elevation views.

## Property Lines

Lines outlining the building plot are called *property lines.* The length and *bearing* (direction) of each property line is identified on the plot plan. Bearing is expressed as degrees east or west of north or south, **Figure 11-3.** Bearings are given in degrees, minutes, and seconds. (A *minute* is 1/60th of a degree, a *second* is 1/60th of a minute.)

When the property line is a curve rather than a straight line, it is identified by a radius, length of curve, and its angle of tangency. A *delta* (Δ) is the central angle formed by the radii meeting the curve at the points of tangency.

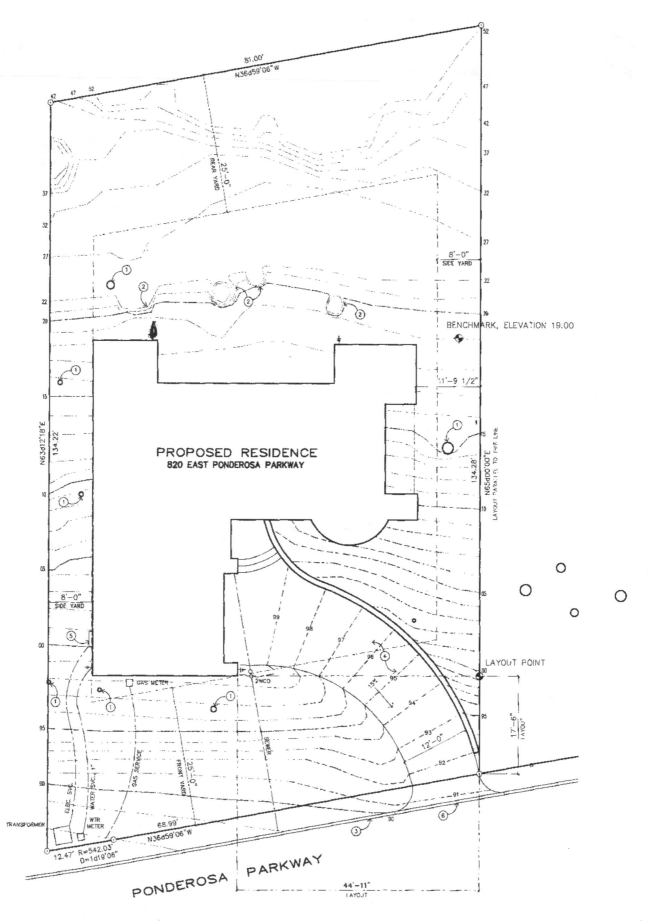

**Figure 11-1.** *A site plan locates the building on the property. (Roberts/Jones Associates, Inc.)*

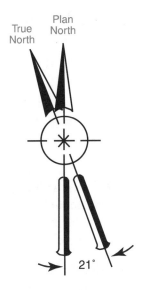

**Figure 11-2.** *The north arrow indicates the difference between True North and Plan North.*

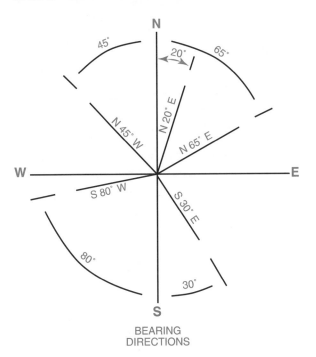

**Figure 11-3.** *Expressing directions as bearings.*

## Contour Lines

*Contour lines* are lines that identify the ground elevation. All of the points along a single contour line are at the same elevation. The elevation of the line is listed, **Figure 11-4.** Contour lines are drawn on the plot plan to indicate the changing elevation of the land.

The interval between contour lines (change in vertical distance) can represent any convenient distance such as 1', 5', or 10'. If the interval is too small, there will be too many contour lines and the drawing will become crowded. If the interval is too large, some

detail will be lost. For example, if a 10' interval is used, a 7' high mound of dirt wouldn't be shown if it was located between contour lines. This could affect the excavation estimating.

Contour lines that are far apart indicate a gradual slope of the land. Lines that are close together indicate a steep slope.

The elevations on a particular plot are referenced to a local permanent marker of known elevation, such as a survey marker plate, a fire hydrant, or a manhole cover. The marker is called a *benchmark.* To simplify the reading and laying out of elevations, some architects set the elevation of a particular point to 100.00'. All elevations are then taken with respect to this point. This elevation is sometimes called an *assumed benchmark.*

Contour lines are long, freehand dashed lines, **Figure 11-5.** When it is desired to show both the original grade and a finish grade of contour, the original is shown in short dashed lines, the finish grade in solid lines.

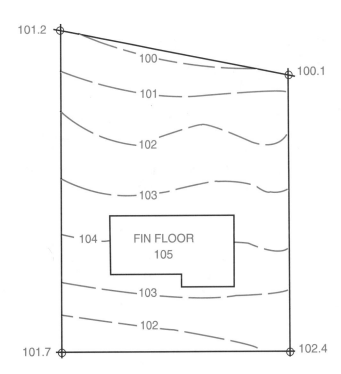

**Figure 11-4.** *Contour lines show the elevation and the general lay of the plot of land.*

## Topographic Features

The *topography* (location and elevation of features) is often shown on the plot plan. Topographic features include natural and man-made objects, such as trees, shrubs, and utility poles. **Figure 11-6** illustrates common topographical symbols used on plans. Plot plans should also include a list of the symbols used to identify features. This list is called a *legend.*

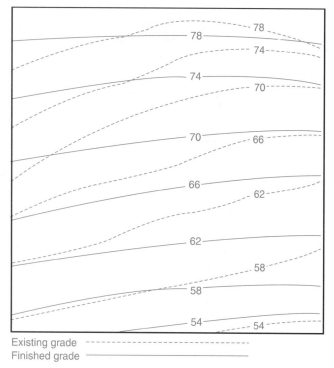

Existing grade   -------------------------------

Finished grade   ———————————————

**Figure 11-5.** *Contour lines showing the original and finished grade.*

## Building Location

An outline of the structure is shown on the plot plan. Often, the elevation of the first floor is also included. The distances from the property lines to the building are shown.

Most local building codes specify a minimum distance between the building and the property lines. This distance is called a ***setback distance.*** This can also be shown on the plot plan.

The connections between the main utility lines and the building are shown on the plot plan. Underground pipes and cables are shown as a dashed line. These lines are identified on the drawing using abbreviations defined in the legend.

# Test Your Knowledge

*Write your answers in the spaces provided.*

_____ 1. A *benchmark* is _____.
- A. used to mark the location of lawn furniture
- B. a portable device used to measure elevations
- C. a line drawn with chalk on the ground
- D. a permanent object of known elevation used to measure other elevations
- E. None of these things.

_____ 2. Plan North is defined by the creator of the drawing. (True or False?)

_____ 3. Which of the following is *not* used to define a curved property line?
- A. Radius
- B. Curve length
- C. Elevation change
- D. Central angle
- E. All of these are needed to define a curved property line.

_____ 4. If the interval between contour lines is too large, the contour lines will be crowded too closely. (True or False?)

_____ 5. Which of the following would *not* be shown on a plot plan?
- A. Location of a garage
- B. Trees
- C. Utility lines
- D. Location of the chimney on a building
- E. All of these would be shown on a plot plan.

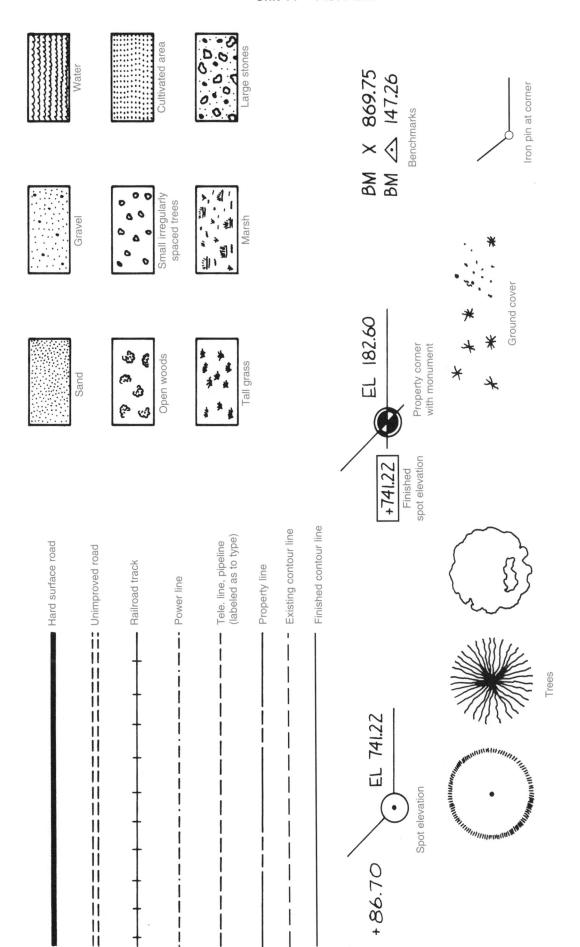

*Figure 11-6. Common symbols used on plot plans.*

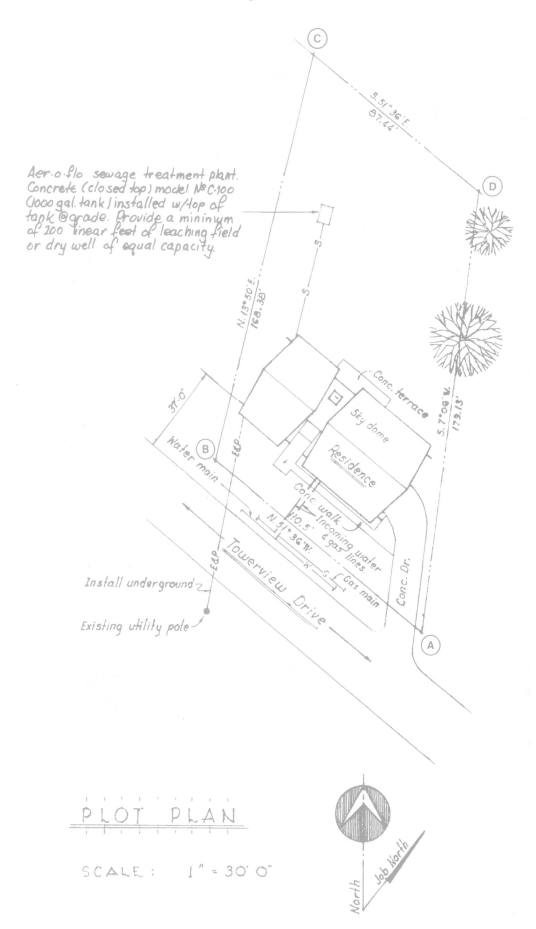

*Figure 11-7.* *A simple plot plan. (Batson & Associates Architects)*

# Print Reading Activity 11–1
## *Plot Plan for a Residence*

*Refer to Figure 11-7 to answer the following questions.*

1. What is the scale of the plot plan?

1. _____

2. Starting with the property corner marked A, give the bearing and length of each property line.

   A. A to B

   B. B to C

   C. C to D

   D. D to A

2. A. _____

   B. _____

   C. _____

   D. _____

3. The location of the residence is not aligned with True North. Which assigned direction does the front of the house face?

3. _____

4. What distance is the house set back from the street?

4. _____

5. Make a simple sketch below, showing the building centered on the lot and properly set back from the street.

**Print Reading Activity 11–2**

## *Plot Plan for an Office Building*

*Refer to Print 11-2 from the Large Prints supplement to answer the following questions. Note:* RWD *is an abbreviation for* Redwood.

1. What is the scale of the plot plan? _____

2. How many sheets are there in this set of plans? _____

3. Give the bearing and length for each property line.

   A. A to E _____

   B. E to D _____

   C. D to C _____

   D. C to B _____

   E. B to A _____

4. Based on the North Orientation Arrow, the side of the building facing the planter would be visible in which Elevation? _____

5. Explain what shaded areas F and G are and what is to be done.

   _____

   _____

   _____

6. Where would a detail of the concrete Curb J be found? _____

7. How many parking spaces are to be provided along the east side and how wide is each?

   _____

8. Which is *higher*, the driveway low point at the west or south entry? _____

9. How wide are the driveways at the curb entry? _____

10. What is the existing grade and finished floor level for the New Building?

   A. Existing _____

   B. Finished Floor _____

# Foundation Prints

## Technical Terms

Basement plan
Concrete masonry unit
Floating slab
   construction
Footing
Foundation plan

Frost line
Keyway
Monolithic slab
Slab-on-grade
Waterproofing

## Learning Objectives

After completing this unit, you will be able to:
• Identify footings on a foundation plan
• Identify various components of a foundation system
• Recognize reinforcing steel on prints

Once the building has been located on the plot and the necessary site clearing and excavation is complete, work begins on the concrete footings and foundation walls. The details of construction for the footings and foundation walls are found on the *foundation plan* (or *basement plan*).

The footings and walls must be carefully laid out because the entire structure depends on their accuracy. To make print reading easier, this unit explains how footings and foundations are located, excavated, and constructed. In addition, slab-on-grade floor construction is discussed.

## Footings

*Footings* are the "feet" upon which the entire building rests. The sizes of the footings are shown on the foundation plan or on a detail of the foundation

wall. See **Figure 12-1.** The footing size is determined by architects and engineers, based on the type of soil (determined by tests) and the weight of the building.

Footings are also required under columns. These footings frequently are wider and thicker than footings for foundation walls because the column loads are concentrated in one spot. See **Figure 12-2.** Fireplace chimneys and similar concentrations of weight also require larger footings.

Footings are located using strings attached to batter boards set back from the excavation. The footings can be trenches cut into the floor of the excavation or they can rest on the excavation floor. In the latter case, boards are used to form the sides to the proper width and height.

Footings must rest on undisturbed earth below the *frost line,* the deepest point in the ground that can freeze in a given region. The local building code will give the depth of the frost line, and how far below it the bottoms of the footings are to be placed.

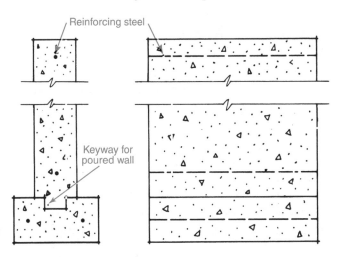

***Figure 12-1.*** *Footings are designed to carry the weight of the entire building and to transfer that weight to the earth below.*

Steel reinforcing rods are placed in the footings. This is especially important when footings must pass over earth previously disturbed due to previous excavation. When a poured concrete foundation wall is to be erected on the footing, the drawing may call for a *keyway* to be cast in the footing to anchor the wall. Refer again to **Figure 12-1.**

On a foundation plan, footings are shown as hidden lines, **Figure 12-3.** The width of the footing under the foundation walls and columns is shown. Reinforcing rods are shown as dots in sectional views. On elevation drawings, these rods are indicated by long dash lines. In addition, notes on the drawing and in the specifications must be carefully checked for details relating to construction of the footings.

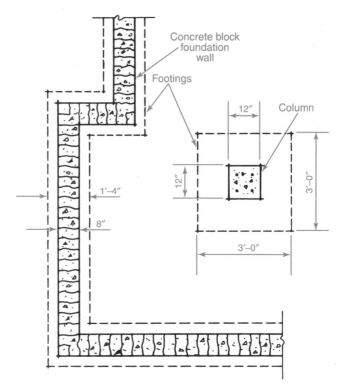

*Figure 12-3. Plan view of footings for wall and column.*

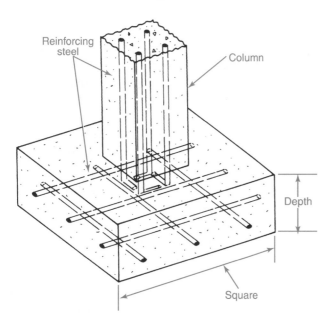

*Figure 12-2. Footings for columns have a larger cross section than wall footings. A square shape is normally used.*

## Foundation Walls

Foundation walls are the base of the building. They transfer the weight of the building to the footings and to the ground below. Foundation walls can be poured concrete or *concrete masonry units* (concrete block). Poured concrete is used where soil and weather conditions place considerable side pressure on the walls. Where applicable, concrete masonry units are an efficient way of constructing a foundation wall because no forms are required. Usually, both types of walls are reinforced with steel rods.

Foundation walls and columns are shown as solid lines on the foundation plan. The space between the lines represents the material used. Foundation walls

and footings are shown as hidden lines in elevation views, **Figure 12-4.**

A foundation wall section is shown in **Figure 12-5.** The material symbols used in the section indicate general type of material used. However, these materials will be detailed in notes on the drawing or in the specifications.

Fireplaces and chimneys are shown on the foundation plan with appropriate dimensions. Details are drawn to provide construction details, **Figure 12-6.**

## Slabs

A concrete slab poured at ground level is called a *slab-on-grade*. Concrete slabs are used as both basement floors and main floors. Basement floors are poured after the footings and foundation walls are in and, sometimes, before the rough framing starts.

*Floating slab construction* uses a *monolithic slab* (one continuous unit), **Figure 12-7.** Another method of pouring a slab floor is to first pour the foundation walls to floor height. Then, the area within the walls is filled with soil and gravel. Finally, the floor is poured within the walls, separated by an expansion joint. See **Figure 12-8.**

Load-bearing walls over slab floors require a thickened slab. These areas are indicated by hidden lines and a note, **Figure 12-9.**

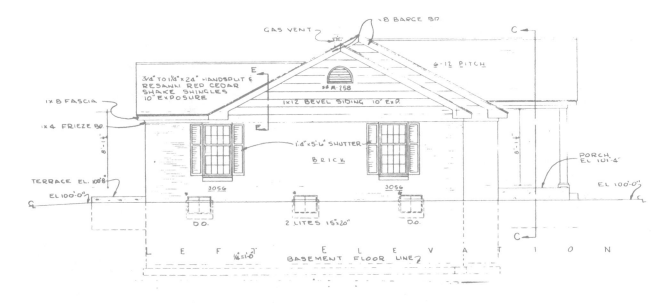

**Figure 12-4.** *Elevation view of a residence showing foundation wall and footing as hidden lines.*

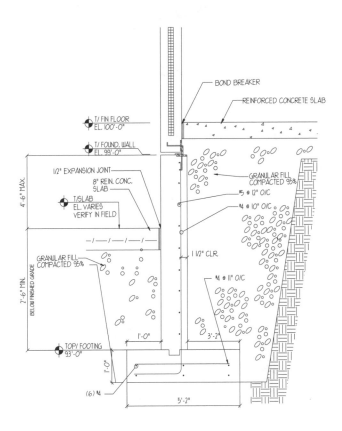

**Figure 12-5.** *A foundation wall section provides a detailed view of the footing and wall construction.*

## Reinforced Slabs

When a concrete slab is expected to be subjected to tension (due to the settling of a dirt fill or heavy load), steel reinforcing rods or welded wire fabric are cast in the concrete. A typical note specifying welded wire fabric in a concrete floor would read as follows:

5″ CONC - 6×6–W10×W10 WWF OVER 4″ ABC

# Waterproofing Foundations

*Waterproofing* of foundation walls is called for in areas where soil and climatic conditions demand protection from underground water. Waterproofing usually consists of mopping the outside of the foundation wall with tar or asphalt and, sometimes, the application of a polyethylene sheet over the tar. Foundations to be waterproofed will have a heavy black line on the exterior wall with a note indicating location. Also, the building specifications may specify the exact material and process to be used.

A layer of crushed rock or gravel is laid below the floor area. This layer is then covered with a heavy plastic vapor barrier to keep the dampness in the ground from transferring to the slab.

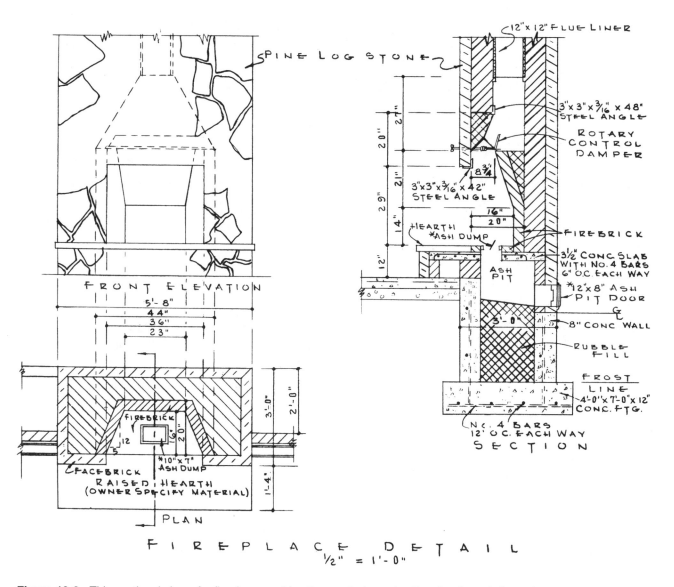

**Figure 12-6.** *This sectional view of a fireplace provides the needed construction details and dimensions.*

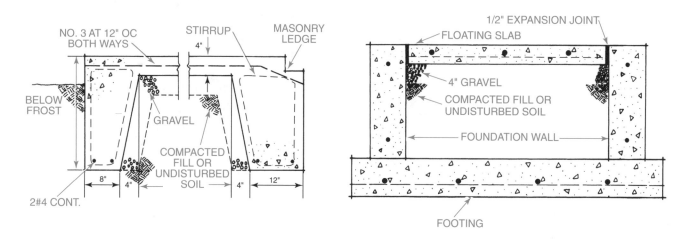

**Figure 12-7.** *A monolithic slab foundation.*

**Figure 12-8.** *A slab floor poured within the foundation walls.*

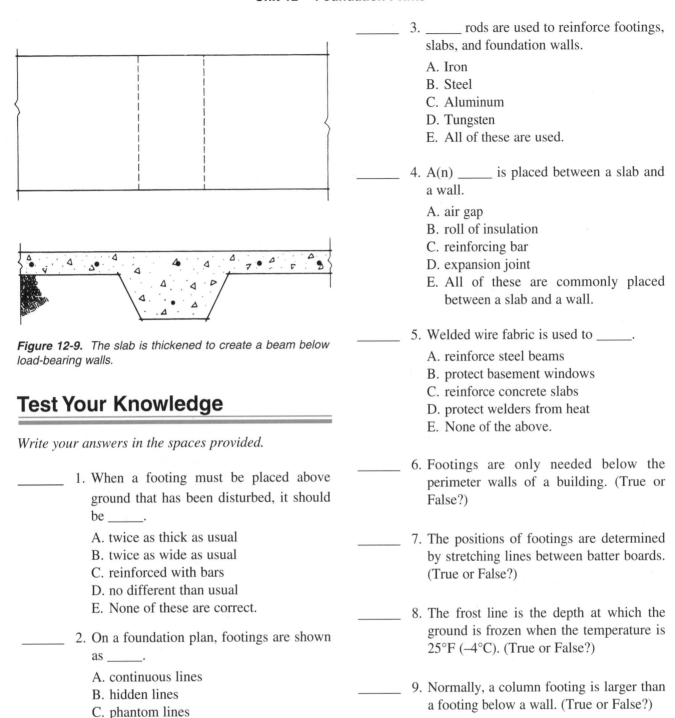

**Figure 12-9.** *The slab is thickened to create a beam below load-bearing walls.*

# Test Your Knowledge

*Write your answers in the spaces provided.*

_____ 1. When a footing must be placed above ground that has been disturbed, it should be _____.

A. twice as thick as usual
B. twice as wide as usual
C. reinforced with bars
D. no different than usual
E. None of these are correct.

_____ 2. On a foundation plan, footings are shown as _____.

A. continuous lines
B. hidden lines
C. phantom lines
D. dotted lines
E. Footings are not shown on foundation plans.

_____ 3. _____ rods are used to reinforce footings, slabs, and foundation walls.

A. Iron
B. Steel
C. Aluminum
D. Tungsten
E. All of these are used.

_____ 4. A(n) _____ is placed between a slab and a wall.

A. air gap
B. roll of insulation
C. reinforcing bar
D. expansion joint
E. All of these are commonly placed between a slab and a wall.

_____ 5. Welded wire fabric is used to _____.

A. reinforce steel beams
B. protect basement windows
C. reinforce concrete slabs
D. protect welders from heat
E. None of the above.

_____ 6. Footings are only needed below the perimeter walls of a building. (True or False?)

_____ 7. The positions of footings are determined by stretching lines between batter boards. (True or False?)

_____ 8. The frost line is the depth at which the ground is frozen when the temperature is 25°F (–4°C). (True or False?)

_____ 9. Normally, a column footing is larger than a footing below a wall. (True or False?)

_____ 10. Foundation walls do not allow water to pass through. (True or False?)

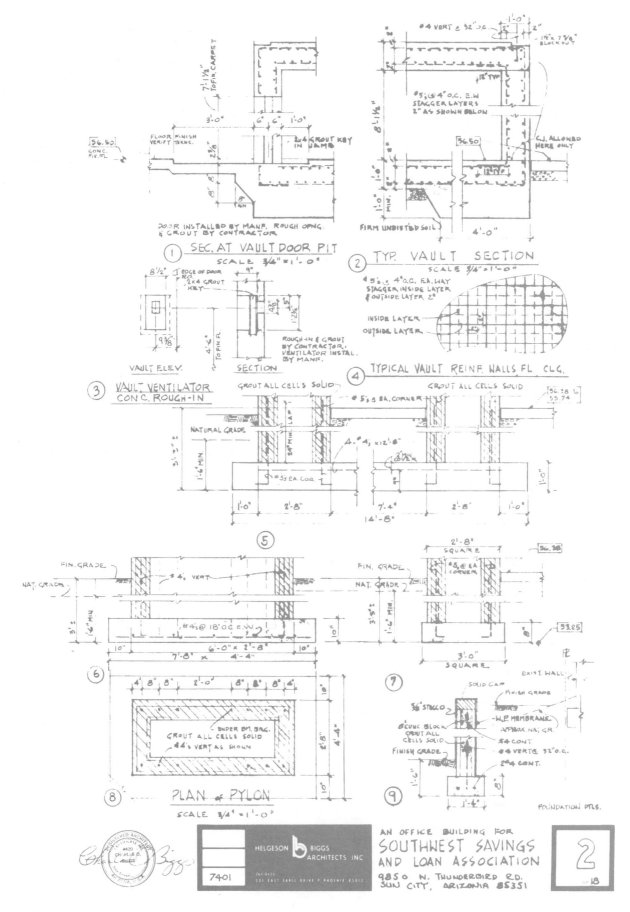

**Figure 12-10.** *Use with Activity 12-1. Sheet 2 of the footing and foundation print.*

**Print Reading Activity 12–1**

# Concrete Foundation for an Office

*Refer to Figure 12-10 from the text and Print 12-1 from the Large Prints supplement to answer the following questions.*

1. What is the scale of the foundation plan?

2. Give the overall size of the building foundation.

3. What is the thickness of the vault floor?

4. What is the wall thickness of the vault?

5. What reinforcing is specified for the vault ceiling?

6. What are the dimensions of the typical footing beneath the exterior wall?

7. How far below natural grade are wall footings located?

8. What reinforcing steel specifications are given for wall footings?

9. What vertical reinforcing rods are to be installed in typical wall footings?

10. What size footings are required for the columns on the south side of the building?

11. How thick are the sidewalks?

12. How many interior bearing wall partitions are there?

13. How far below natural grade are the footings for the pylons on the north side of the building?

14. How far above the pavement does the curbing extend?

1. _____

2. _____

3. _____

4. _____

5. _____

6. _____

7. _____

8. _____

9. _____

10. _____

11. _____

12. _____

13. _____

14. _____

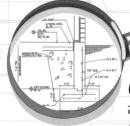

**Print Reading Activity 12–2**

# *Concrete Foundation for a Residence*

*Refer to Print 12-2 from the Large Prints supplement to answer the following questions.*

1. What is used to connect the foundation to the wall forms?

    1. _____

2. In the footings, what is the minimum space required between the reinforcement and the concrete surface?

    2. _____

3. How thick is the floor slab?

    3. _____

4. How wide are the footings that support the slab?

    4. _____

5. What type of reinforcing is used in the slab?

    5. _____

6. What type of reinforcement is used for the square footings in the lower right part of the plan?

    6. _____

7. How thick is the layer of sand or crushed stone beneath the slab?

    7. _____

8. How is the ground next to the foundation sloped?

    8. _____

9. How thick is the vapor barrier beneath the slab?

    9. _____

10. What is the minimum footing depth below the slab surface?

    10. _____

# Commercial Framing Prints

## Technical Terms

| | |
|---|---|
| Beam | Reinforced concrete |
| Bolster | Splicing |
| Chair | Stirrup |
| Column | Structural steel |
| Expansion joint | Ties |
| One-way floor system | Waffle slab |
| Open-web joist | Wide-flange beam |

## Learning Objectives

After completing this unit, you will be able to:

- Recognize various types of concrete floor systems
- Understand concrete reinforcing notation
- Read beam and column schedules
- Identify various structural steel members

Large commercial and industrial buildings are constructed around a framework of reinforced concrete or structural steel, **Figure 13-1.** This type of construction is also used for large residences and light commercial buildings.

Concrete and steel were discussed in Unit 9, *Construction Materials.* Concrete foundations were presented in Unit 12, *Foundation Prints.* The purpose of this unit is to assist you in understanding the applications of reinforced concrete and structural steel.

## Reinforced Concrete

Were it used for only slabs, drives, and walks, concrete would be a valuable building material. However, its applications become even more valuable

**Figure 13-1.** *Steel framing members are used to construct an office building.*

when combined with steel reinforcement in structural applications. The compression strength of concrete and the tension strength of steel make *reinforced concrete* a unique building material.

## Floor Systems

A floor and roof framing system is used to support floors and flat roofs. There are two types of systems:

- **One-Way Floor System:** This system is so named because the floor slab is supported by girders that run parallel to one another (one way) and rest on columns. For heavier construction carrying greater floor loads, this one-way system sometimes uses beams running perpendicular to the one-way girders. See **Figure 13-2.**
- **Two-way floor system:** In this system, the girders and beams (when used) run in two directions. The system is formed by steel "pans" laid over the form support structure. This system is

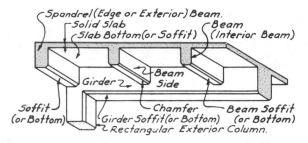

**Figure 13-2.** *This floor slab and girder system is formed by using forms in a monolithic (one continuous) pour and tied directly to the column supports.(Concrete Reinforcing Steel Institute)*

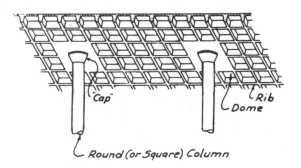

**Figure 13-3.** *Steel "pans" are used to form the support structure for this reinforced, two-way floor system. (Concrete Reinforcing Steel Institute)*

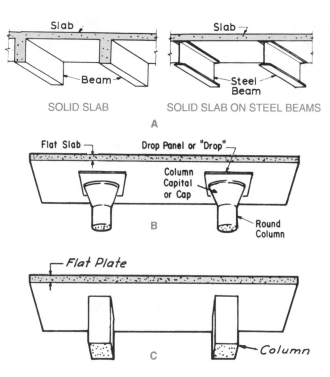

**Figure 13-4.** *Variations on the two-way floor system. A—Slab with beams running between columns. B—Slab with drop panels and capitals above columns. C—Flat plate on columns. (Concrete Reinforcing Steel Institute)*

sometimes referred to as a *waffle slab,* **Figure 13-3.** There are several variations of the two-way system:
- Flat slab with beams running between columns
- Flat slab with flared columns and drop panels
- Flat plate construction with no beams or panels, **Figure 13-4.** This is generally used for light commercial construction (office buildings and apartment houses)

## Steel Reinforcement

Reinforcing steel is used in all of these floor systems. The placement of the steel, which is determined by the designer or engineer, provides maximum resistance to forces of compression, tension, and shear. Reinforcing steel to be placed in concrete is designated with a note on the drawing giving the number of bars, size of bars, and placement:

2 - # 5 × 19'-0" @ 2'-6" O.C.
PLACE ON 1 1/2" BAR CHAIR

The size of the bar is indicated by a number representing eighths of an inch. That is, a No. 5 bar is a bar with a 5/8″ diameter. Identification marks rolled into the bars identify the producer's mill, bar size, type of steel and, for Grade 60, a grade mark indicating yield

strength (Grade 40 and Grade 50 do not show a grade mark). See **Figure 13-5.**

## Expansion Joints

*Expansion joints* are placed between a slab and a wall, and also around columns, **Figure 13-6.** These joints prevent the slab from cracking due to expansion and contraction. They are used with slabs-on-grade that do not settle evenly with the footings and foundations walls. Other expansion joints may be used in long slabs. These usually call for premolded joints and metal coverings.

Some architects indicate on a drawing where it is permissible to make a joint when the pour is terminated at the end of the day. Where no indication is given, the location must be approved by the project engineer or architect.

## Columns and Beams

*Columns* are vertical support members designed to safely carry the anticipated final load of the building and its contents. Concrete columns are reinforced with steel bars or structural shapes, **Figure 13-7.**

Columns are normally specified on the drawing. Otherwise, they are identified by a grid system of numbers and letters on the plan view and specified on a

LINE SYSTEM – GRADE MARKS          NUMBER SYSTEM – GRADE MARKS

Main ribs

Initial of
producing
mill

Bar size

One
line

Type steel
(new billet)

Grade
mark

Main
ribs

Initial of
producing
mill

Bar Size

Type steel
(new billet)

Grade
mark

GRADE 40
GRADE 50

GRADE 60

GRADE 40
GRADE 50

GRADE 60

**N** for new billet (S for supplementary requirements A615—
No. 14 and No. 18 only)

**A** for axle

**I** for rail

**W** for low alloy

**Figure 13-5.** *Identification marks for steel reinforcing bars. (Concrete Reinforcing Steel Institute)*

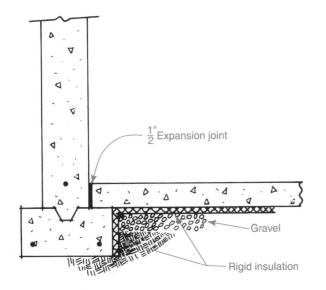

$\frac{1}{2}$" Expansion joint

Gravel

Rigid insulation

**Figure 13-6.** *An expansion joint, made of a flexible material, is placed between the concrete slab and wall.*

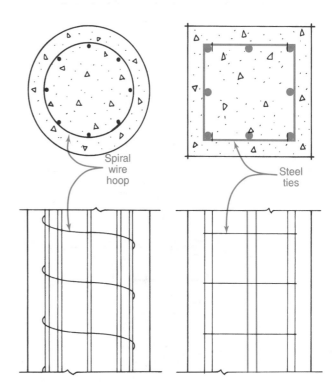

Spiral
wire
hoop

Steel
ties

**Figure 13-7.** *Two types of reinforced concrete columns. Left—Spiral column. Right—Tied column.*

*column schedule,* **Figure 13-8.** Identification should include the size of the column, the number and size of vertical reinforcement, and the size and spacing of *ties* (horizontal reinforcing bars placed around the outside of the vertical bars).

**Beams** are structural members running horizontally beneath a floor system. They are supported at their ends by other beams or columns, **Figure 13-9.** Some beams are rectangular in cross section. Others are thinner at the bottom, where they are reinforced with steel to provide tension strength, and wider at the top to provide compression strength. See **Figure 13-10(A).**

Beams are given added strength by adding *stirrups* (U-shaped steel bars) that hold the horizontal bars in place and increase the resistance to shear stresses, **Figure 13-10(B).** Devices called *bolsters* and *chairs* are used to support reinforcing bars at the desired level, **Figure 13-11.** A chart showing the standard types and

sizes of bar supports and their symbols is included in *Section 7, Reference.*

Beams are normally specified on the drawing. However, if there are many beams, they may be identified on the drawing and specified in a schedule. Identification should include the beam size, the number and size of reinforcing bars at the bottom and top of the beam, and the number, size, and type of stirrups.

## Splicing Reinforcement

*Splicing* of reinforcing bars in columns and beams is necessary when the length of these members exceeds

| COLUMN MARK | SIZE | BASE PLATE | SETTING PLATE | CAP. PLATE |
|---|---|---|---|---|
| A1 | | | | 5″ × 5/8″ × 10″ |
| A2 | | | | 5″ × 5/8″ × 10″ |
| A3 | | | | 5″ × 5/8″ × 10″ |
| B1 | | | | Thru Plate |
| B2 | | | | 5 1/2″ × 5/8″ × 12″ |
| B3 | Typical 4″ ∅ Std. Col. × 10.79 #/Ft. | Typical 9″ × 3/4″ × 9″ Base Plate | Typical 9″ × 1/4″ × 9″ Setting Plate | 5 1/2″ × 5/8″ × 12″ |
| C1 | | | | Thru Plate |
| C2 | | | | 5 1/2″ × 5/8″ × 12″ |
| C3 | | | | 5 1/2″ × 5/8″ × 12″ |
| D1 | | | | Thru Plate |
| D2 | | | | 5 1/2″ × 5/8″ × 12″ |
| D3 | | | | 5 1/2″ × 5/8″ × 12″ |
| E1 | | | | 5″ × 5/8″ × 10″ |
| E2 | | | | 5 1/2″ × 5/8″ × 12″ |
| E3 | | | | 5 1/2″ × 5/8″ × 12″ |

*Figure 13-8.* The schedule contains the specifications for all of the columns in the building.

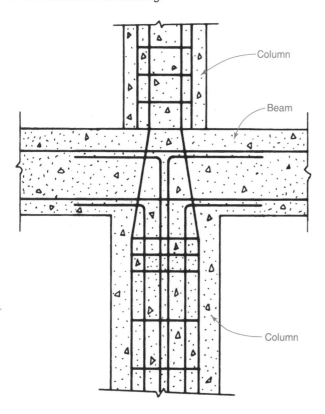

*Figure 13-9.* Beams are tied structurally into columns.

the length of the bars. Splicing is accomplished by overlapping the next bar by a length of a given number of diameters of the bar. A typical splicing note would read:

30 DIA MINIMUM LAP

If No. 4 bars (4/8″ diameter) were specified, the overlap length would be 30 × 4/8″, or 15″.

Reinforcing bars are also added to strengthen wall corners. These corner bars are spliced onto the wall reinforcing bars.

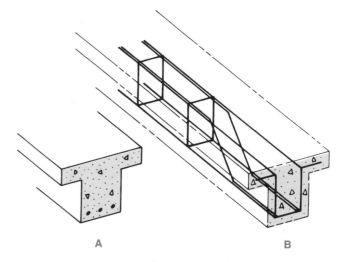

*Figure 13-10.* Cross section of reinforced "T" beams. A—Beam is wider at the top, where compressive strength is needed. Tensile strength is needed in the bottom of the beam, so steel is added. B—Stirrups hold the reinforcing bars in place and make the beam stronger.

Piping and electrical conduit are placed in slabs at the time reinforcing bars are installed, **Figure 13-12.** Electrical conduits are installed with electrical boxes on the ceiling side of the slab, or conduit is stubbed up at a wall location or through a grid system to be located in the floor.

# Structural Steel

*Structural steel* refers to a system of building construction where the framework consists of structural steel shapes. The most widely-used shapes are the *wide-flange beam* (W) and *I-beams* (S). See **Figure 13-13.** Other structural steel shapes include pipes, tubes, angles, and tees.

The framework in heavy construction is designed so floor loads are transferred to columns of steel, so there is no need for load-bearing walls. Often, steel members are encased in concrete or some other fireproofing material to protect them from failing during a fire.

Structural steel members are known as girders, beams, spandrel beams, columns, and trusses. See **Figure 13-14.** Individual members may be dimensioned on the drawing or listed in a schedule if there are a sizable number of members. A typical beam dimension is W12×16, which indicates the following: a wide-flange beam (W), a nominal depth of 12″, and a weight of 16 pounds per linear foot.

## Joists

*Open-web joists* are widely used in light commercial construction for floor and roof structures. Joists support loads more efficiently than wide-flange beams,

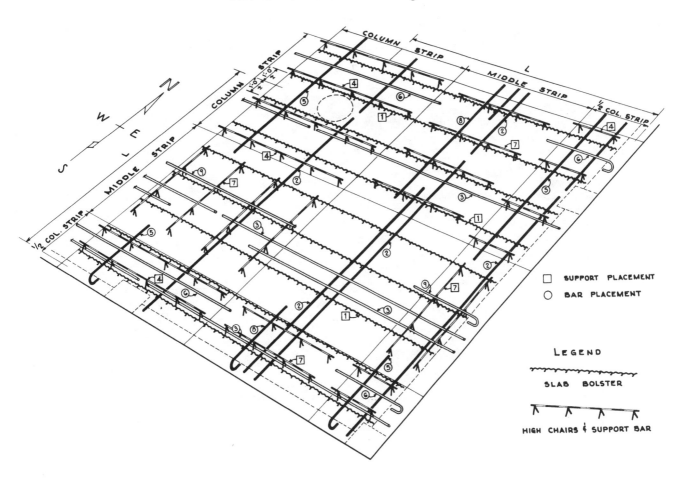

**Figure 13-11.** *Bolsters and chairs hold the reinforcing steel at the correct height in the forms. These are fastened to the forms and wired to the reinforcing bars. (Concrete Reinforcing Steel Institute)*

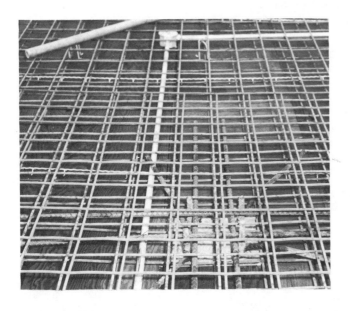

**Figure 13-12.** *Conduit is placed in concrete slabs to serve electrical and telephone circuits. (Wire Reinforcement Institute)*

so they are more affordable. The Steel Joist Institute has standardized the specifications and labeling of these joists.

Steel joists are grouped into three major series: shortspan, longspan, and deep longspan joists. There are two grades of steel used for joists, separated into the J-series and the H-series. The H-series uses a stronger type of steel than the J-series.

Shortspan joists are available in both the J-series and H-series. They are available in depths of 8″ to 30″ and spans up to 60′.

Longspan joists are labeled as LJ and LH series. The L designates longspan. The LJ series has been standardized in depths from 18″ to 48″ and spans to 96′. Deep longspan joists have been standardized in depth from 52″ to 72″ for spans up to 144′.

Open-web joist designations consist of three parts. First, the depth of the joist (in inches) is given. Then the type of joist is given. Finally, a number corresponding to the allowable span is listed. For example, a typical designation for a shortspan joist would be 12J3, which means a shortspan J-series joist 12″ deep. The 3 is a range of allowable span (12′ to 24′ for this size joist).

**Figure 13-13.** *Some structural steel shapes used in construction. (American Iron & Steel Institute)*

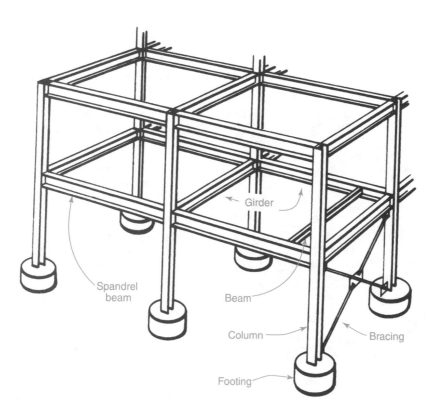

**Figure 13-14.** *Structural steel members.*

The span varies, depending on the load. The heavier the load, the shorter the span. A 60DLH15 is a deep longspan high-strength joist with a depth of 60″. From a load table, the 15 indicates a range of span from 70′ to 120′, depending on the load required.

Steel joists are manufactured as both top-bearing and bottom-bearing. Top-bearing joists are supported at the ends of the top chord. Bottom-bearing joists are supported at the ends of the bottom chords. Longspan and deep longspan joists, **Figure 13-15,** come with parallel chords or pitched chords for roof drainage.

## Connections

Structural steel members are either fastened with bolts or welded. Rivets were once used for connections, but the development of high-strength bolts ended their use. Test procedures are set for these fasteners by the American Society for Testing and Materials (ASTM). The type of bolts or welding electrodes to be used are specified in the drawing notes or in the detail showing the connection. These materials may also be identified in the specifications. For more information, see *Unit 19, Welding Prints.*

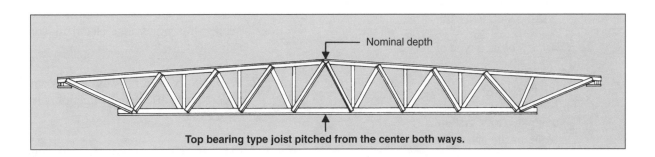
Top bearing type joist pitched from the center both ways.

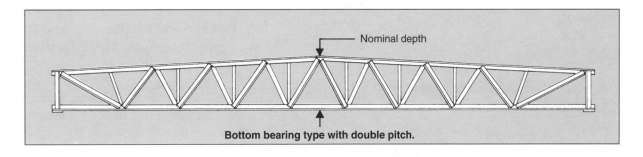
Bottom bearing type with double pitch.

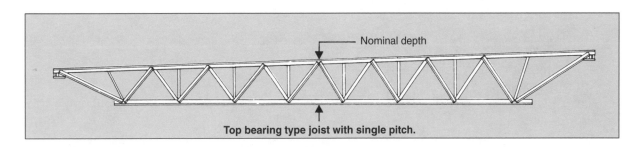
Top bearing type joist with single pitch.

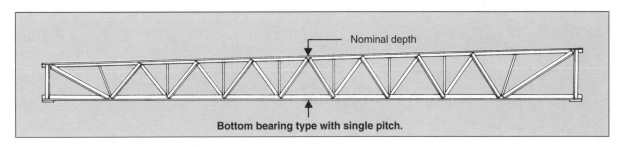
Bottom bearing type with single pitch.

*Figure 13-15.* Open-web joists. (Armco Steel Corporation)

# Test Your Knowledge

*Write your answers in the spaces provided.*

_____ 1. In order to be an effective structural material, concrete must be combined with _____.
 A. plastic rings
 B. a wax coating
 C. steel bars
 D. weathered lumber
 E. All of these products are needed to make concrete useful.

_____ 2. A *waffle slab* is a type of _____.
 A. steel floor system
 B. breakfast food
 C. framing procedure
 D. concrete floor system
 E. None of the above.

_____ 3. The diameter of a No. 5 reinforcing bar is _____.
 A. 5″
 B. 5/8″
 C. 5/16″
 D. 5 mm
 E. None of the above.

_____ 4. If the minimum lap for reinforcing bars is 40 diameters, how long would the splice be for a #4 bar?
 A. 16″
 B. 20″
 C. 40″
 D. 160″
 E. None of the above.

_____ 5. Which of the following is not a horizontal (beam) member?
 A. Spandrel
 B. Girder
 C. Joist
 D. Truss
 E. All of the above.

_____ 6. After slabs are cast, holes are cut where needed for pipes and electrical conduit. (True or False?)

_____ 7. A one-way floor system only allows pedestrian traffic in one direction. (True or False?)

_____ 8. Steel is added to concrete to improve tensile (pulling) strength. (True or False?)

_____ 9. Expansion joists placed around a slab expand and prevent the slab from moving. (True or False?)

_____ 10. Steel beams can be protected from fire by encasing them in concrete. (True or False?)

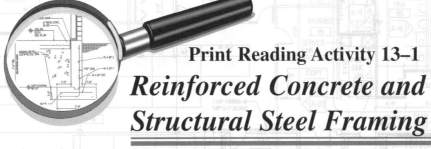

## Print Reading Activity 13–1

# *Reinforced Concrete and Structural Steel Framing*

*Refer to Prints 13-1a and 13-1b from the Large Prints supplement to answer the following questions.*

1. What size steel girders and beams are used to frame the roof of the porte-cochere?

   _____

2. How are the cross beams attached to the girders? _____

   _____

   _____

3. Describe the column at A._____

   _____

   _____

4. How is the beam at A held to column?_____

   _____

   _____

5. Describe how the same beam is anchored to the column at B. _____

   _____

   _____

6. What structural roof material is placed on top of these steel beams? _____

   _____

   _____

7. What elevation level is assigned to the fourth floor?_____

8. How thick is the wall at C (Sheet S-13) and what is the minimum distance permitted between the vertical bar and the opposite wall exterior face?_____

9. What size and at what spacing are the vertical bars between the fourth floor and the roof?

   _____

10. What is the size of the dowel at D anchoring the fourth floor to the wall?

    _____

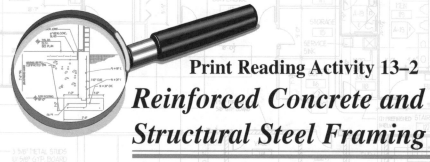

**Print Reading Activity 13–2**

# Reinforced Concrete and Structural Steel Framing

*Refer to Prints 13-2a and 13-2b from the Large Prints supplement to answer the following questions.*

1. Interpret the information given for the column footing at A.

_____

_____

_____

2. Give the top and bottom elevations of the footing at B.

Top _____

Bottom _____

3. Describe the reinforcement around openings in the foundation wall.

_____

_____

_____

4. What reinforcement is required in the foundation wall at Section 3-3?

_____

_____

_____

5. How is each door jamb reinforced?

_____

_____

6. Describe the reinforcement above door openings in Section 6-6.?

_____

_____

7. What specification is given for the concrete?

_____

_____

8. Give the specifications for the reinforcing steel.

   _____

   _____

9. How is the floor joist at C secured to the foundation wall?

   _____

   _____

10. Give the steel beam size at D and explain the sizing.

    _____

    _____

11. Give the size of the beam at E and explain the sizing.

    _____

    _____

12. How is the beam secured to the masonry wall at F?

    _____

    _____

13. Give the size of the roof joist at G and explain the sizing.

    _____

    _____

14. How far on centers are the joists at G?_____

15. What size, type, and spacing of floor joists are required at H? _____

*These open web steel joists will support a metal deck, in which a reinforced concrete slab will be cast.*

*This slab will serve as the floor for a large warehouse.*

# Residential Framing Prints

Bearing partition
Bird's mouth
Blocking
Bridging
Collar beam
Common rafter
Cripple stud
Header
Hip rafter
Jack rafter
Joist
Knee walls
Ledger

Plank-and-beam
Purlin
Ribbon
Ridge
Riser
Rough sill
Sill plate
Sole plate
Span
Stringer
Subfloor
Valley rafter
Winder

## Learning Objectives

After completing this unit, you will be able to:
• List the differences between heavy framing and light framing
• Recognize the construction of floor frames, roof frames, and wall frames
• Read framing drawings
• Explain the difference between platform and balloon framing
• Understand stair details and terms
• Recognize metal framing systems

The framing systems commonly used for residential construction are similar to large steel and concrete frames. Beams and joists are used to support floors. Columns are used in situations where a wall would be inappropriate, such as open areas.

However, there are several differences between heavy commercial frames and light residential frames:
• Wood members are commonly used, rather than structural steel or concrete. Wood is lightweight and easily installed.
• Many more members are used in residential frames, because the wood is relatively weak as compared to concrete or steel.
• Walls are also constructed as a frame, with wood studs spaced every 12″–24″.
• The weight from a floor is supported by the entire length of the wall, rather than being supported by columns.
• The term *joist* is commonly used to refer to a floor-supporting beam. The term *rafter* is used to refer to the angled roof-supporting beams.
• Residential framing plans may include additional information: the roofing material, sheathing, and finish details.

Light gage steel is sometimes used in residential frames instead of wood. However, the framing systems do not change significantly when steel members are used.

## Wood Framing

Wood is the most widely-used residential construction material. Its availability and affordability lead to its popularity. The methods of wood framing are widely-known. Wood has proven to be a durable, dependable material for houses.

There are several frames included in a house. The manner in which each of these frames is shown on prints is described in the following sections.

# Floor Frames

The basic components of a floor frame are shown in **Figure 14-1**:

- **Sill Plate:** This board is attached to the top surface of the foundation wall. Anchor bolts cast in the concrete are used for the connection. A 2×6 member is often used for the sill plate.
- **Header:** The header is nailed to the top of the sill plate, at its exterior edge. The header is positioned with its longer cross-sectional dimension vertical. The header is the same size as the joists that attach to it.
- **Joists:** The end of these floor-support beams rest on the sill plate. The ends are nailed to the header. Joists are normally spaced 12″–16″ apart. Common lumber sizes used as joists are 2×8, 2×10, and 2×12.
- **Subfloor:** The joists and header are covered with subflooring. Normally, a board material, such as plywood, is used. The subfloor is nailed to the joists. The finished floor will cover the subfloor.

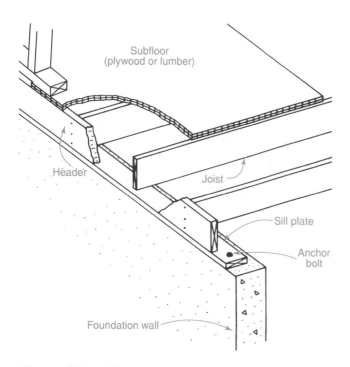

**Figure 14-1.** *Components of a floor frame (platform construction).*

Additional floor framing members are shown in **Figure 14-2**:

- **Double Header:** When an opening that disrupts the framing pattern is needed, a double header is installed perpendicular to the joists. The same size member as the joists is used.
- **Double Trimmer:** Two joists are nailed together next to an opening.
- **Tail Joist:** These joists are interrupted by an opening. They normally run between the double header and the sill plate.
- **Ledger:** A small piece of lumber, such as a 2×2, is nailed to the side of the double header, at its bottom edge. This piece serves as a ledge on which the tail joists rest. Notches must be cut into the joists.
- **Bridging:** These small members are connected between the sides of adjacent joists. Bridging provides lateral stability for the joists and helps to transmit load between the joists. Many types of bridging are used: joist-sized members, crossed 2×4s, or crossed aluminum bars.

The floor framing system is often shown on the floor plan. The size of the members are given. Joists will be specified in manner similar to the following:

2×12 JOISTS 16″ O.C.

A 2×12 member is used for each joist. The joists are spaced 16″ from one another. The *O.C.* is an abbreviation of "on center," meaning the distance between the centers of the joists. Joists shown on a plan represent the joists *above* the level. For example, joists shown on a foundation plan would be located above the basement and below the first floor.

## *Dimensioning Floor Frames*

Normally, dimensions for exterior walls are given to the outside of the stud wall for frame and brick veneer buildings. See **Figure 14-3**. As noted in Unit 8, *Dimensioning,* some architects follow the practice of starting the dimensions for single-story frame buildings at the surface of the wall sheathing (which should align with the foundation wall). A note may be added to the drawing to read:

NOTE: EXTERIOR DIMENSIONS ARE TO
OUTSIDE EDGE OF STUDS; INTERIOR
DIMENSIONS ARE TO CENTER
OF STUDS

The drawings should be checked carefully to verify the dimensioning practice followed.

Usually, interior walls of frame construction are dimensioned to their edges and sometimes to their centerlines. Masonry interior walls are dimensioned to their faces, with the wall thickness also dimensioned.

When studying the floor plans of buildings with two or more stories, note the adjoining stairs, chimneys, and load-bearing partition walls.

In certain style buildings, the floor is cantilevered out over the foundation wall. In these cases, special framing details are shown. See **Figure 14-4.** Houses

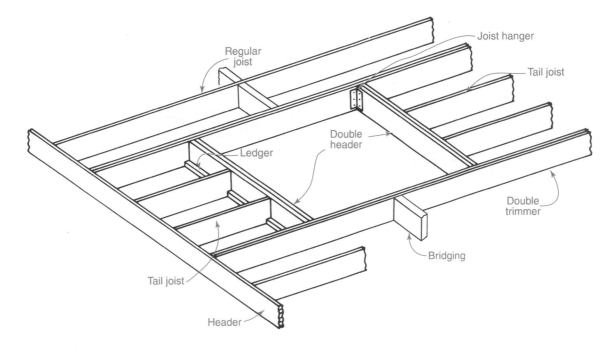

**Figure 14-2.**  *Additional floor framing members.*

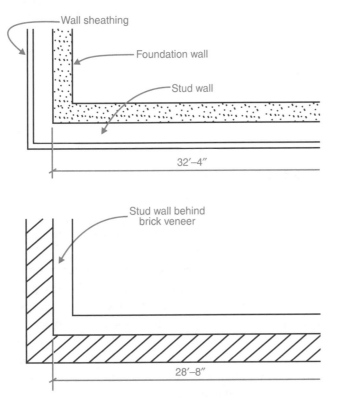

**Figure 14-3.**  *Dimensions shown are to the face of the stud wall.*

having second stories smaller than the first are called one-and-a-half story houses. These houses usually involve *knee walls* (a short wall joined by a sloping ceiling) and dormers.

Split-level houses have floor plans in which the levels are separated by a half-flight of stairs. Many variations are called for in framing of this type of structure, so the plans should be studied carefully.

## Wall Frames

There are three basic types of light frame construction: platform, balloon, and plank-and-beam. The construction worker should be familiar with the three types and be able to distinguish between them on drawings.

*Platform framing,* also know as *Western framing,* is the most widely-used type. It gets its name from its appearance. The first floor is built on top of the foundation, so it resembles a platform when the subflooring is complete.

The first-floor wall sections are raised and a second-floor platform is built on top of these walls. Then, the second-floor wall sections are raised and another platform for the second-story ceiling is constructed. See **Figure 14-5.** Each floor is a separate unit built on the structure below.

*Balloon framing* is not used to any large extent today. In this type of framing, the studs extend from the first floor sill plate to the top floor plate, as in **Figure 14-6.** Second floor joists rest on a member called a *ribbon,* which is set into the studs. Balloon framing has some advantages: it reduces lumber shrinkage problems in masonry veneer and stucco structures. It also simplifies running ducts and electrical conduit from floor to floor.

The main disadvantage of balloon framing is in the tendency of the walls to act as flues in spreading fires

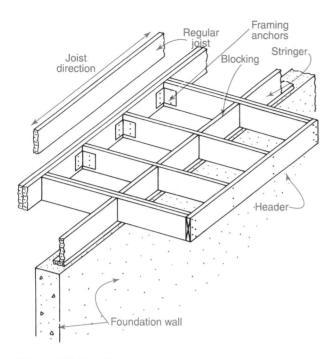

**Figure 14-4.** *Pictorial detail showing the framing of a cantilevered floor.*

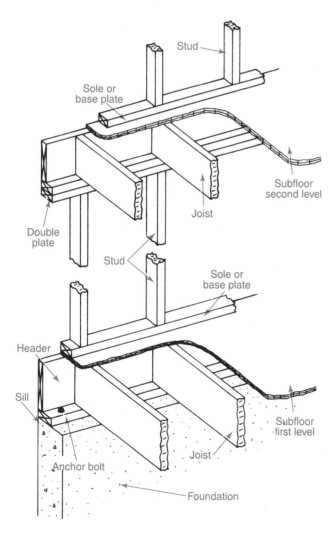

**Figure 14-5.** *An example of platform framing.*

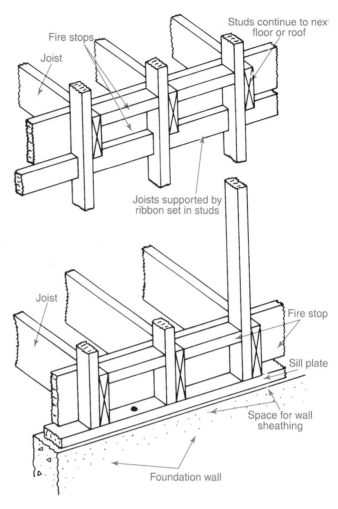

**Figure 14-6.** *Details of balloon framing.*

from floor to floor unless blocking is added. This type of framing also is more difficult to manage in assembling a wall section.

***Plank-and-beam framing*** consists of heavy timber material for posts in wall sections and 2″ thick plank material supporting floor and roof sections. See **Figure 14-7.** The structural members are placed at wider intervals than in other methods of framing. This type of framing lends itself to interesting architectural effects and extensive use of glass and exposed wood sections, as shown in **Figure 14-8.**

Various components of a wall frame are illustrated in **Figure 14-9:**

- **Sole Plate:** This serves as a base for the wall frame. The sole plate is the same size member as the studs (normally 2×4 or 2×6) and is nailed to the subfloor.
- **Studs:** Studs are the vertical members in the wall frame, running from the sole plate to the top plate. Studs are normally 2×4 or 2×6 members.

*Figure 14-7.* Plank-and-beam framing using transverse beams. Longitudinal beams would run parallel to the ridge beam. *(Brown & Kauffman Architects)*

*Figure 14-8.* A residence making use of the plank-and-beam system of framing. (Marvin Windows and Doors.)

- **Header:** When some studs must be left out to make room for a window or door, a header is used to distribute the weight of the building around the opening. Headers can be constructed in many ways: one of the most common is to turn two 2×4 sideways, insert a 3/8″ spacer (making the assembly 2 5/8″ thick, the same width as a 2×4), and nail the header in place.

- **Trimmer Stud:** A stud is always located on either side of a header. Next to these studs and below the header, trimmer studs are placed. A trimmer stud extends from the sole plate to the bottom of the header. It is attached to both the stud at its side and the header.

- **Rough Sill:** A rough sill is positioned to support a window.

- **Cripple Stud:** These short studs extend between the sole or top plate and the header or rough sill. They are similar to trimmer studs but they don't have an adjacent stud and can be above the header.

- **Blocking:** Blocking is used to stall the spread of fire.

- **Top Plate:** The top plate (shown in **Figure 14-9** as a *double plate*) rests above the studs. The next level of joists or rafters are supported by the top plate.

Interior walls that carry the ceiling or floor load from above are called ***bearing partitions***. Usually, they are located over a beam or bearing wall, **Figure 14-10.**

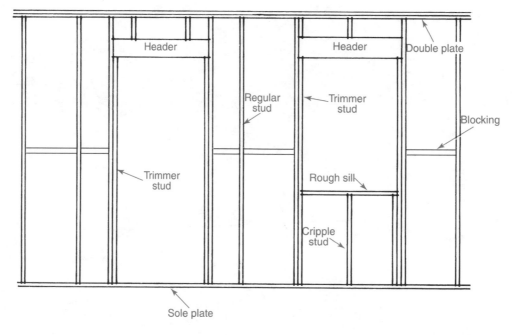

**Figure 14-9.** *Components of a wall frame.*

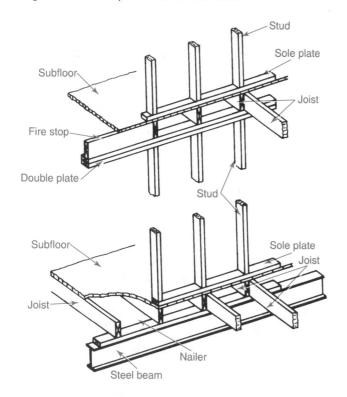

**Figure 14-10.** *Bearing partitions are used to transfer loads from floors above to a bearing structure below.*

## Schedules

Door and window schedules give the number and sizes of the doors and windows in the building. See **Figure 14-11.** Units listed in the schedule are referenced to the plan view with a letter or number. Some architects provide the rough opening size in the schedules to speed construction and ensure a correct fit. If rough opening sizes for doors and windows are not provided, the construction worker must calculate them.

## Sectional Views

Sectional views of walls are drawn to a larger scale and included on the drawings to clarify construction details. The section locations are identified on the plan view with a reference line.

Full sections are cut through the width or length of a building, **Figure 14-12.** They are prepared for buildings with more complex frames, such as split-level houses or those with unusual interiors. These sectional views show features such as floors, walls, and ceilings as sections. Features beyond the cutting plane are shown as they appear in the interior of a building.

### DOOR SCHEDULE

| MARK | TYPE | SIZE | MATERIAL | FRAME | REMARKS |
|------|------|------|----------|-------|---------|
| A | 1 | 3′–0″ × 7′–0″ × 1¾″ | Hollow Metal | Hollow Metal | Closer and Threshold |
| B | 1 | 3′–0″ × 7′–0″ × 1¾″ | Hollow Metal | Hollow Metal | Closer |
| C | 2 | 2′–8″ × 7′–0″ × 1¾″ | Hollow Metal | Hollow Metal | Closer and Kick Pl. |
| D | 2 | 3′–0″ × 7′–0″ × 1¾″ | Hollow Metal | Hollow Metal | Closer |
| E | 2 | 3′–0″ × 7′–0″ × 1¾″ | Hollow Metal | Hollow Metal | Closer |

**Figure 14-11.** *A typical door schedule. (Smith & Neubek & Associates)*

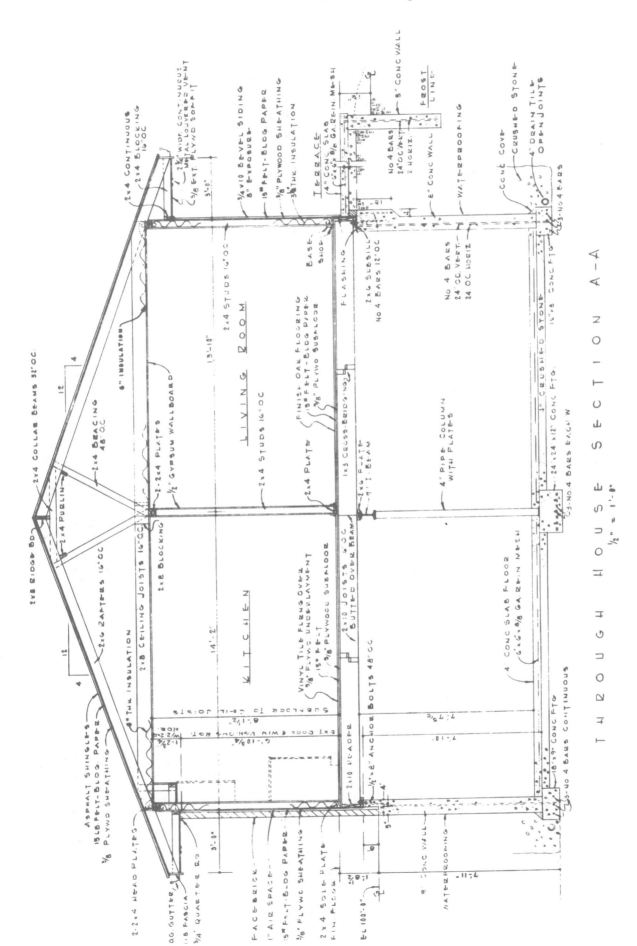

Figure 14-12.   A full section shows the entire building. (Garlinghouse)

# Roof Frames

Construction workers should be familiar with the different types of roofs, and how they are framed. Sketches of various roof styles found in house construction are shown in **Figure 14-13.** The style of the roof is most easily identified in elevation drawings.

Some architects do not supply a roof framing drawing for the more common roofs, such as gables or flat roofs, but rely on the elevation and detail drawings to guide the construction workers. When the roof is more complicated, or when the architect desires to specify the manner of construction, a roof framing plan is prepared, **Figure 14-14.**

**Figure 14-15** illustrates some common terms used in roof framing:

- **Rafter:** The angled members that supports the roof are called rafters. A rafter is normally a 2×6, 2×8, or 2×10 member.
- **Ridge:** A ridge board is the horizontal member at the peak of the roof. The upper end of the rafters are connected to the ridge board.

- **Collar Beam:** This horizontal member ties the rafters together. This makes the roof frame more stable.
- **Rise:** This is the vertical distance between the top plate and the ridge board.
- **Run:** This is the horizontal distance from the wall supporting the bottom of the rafter to the ridge board.
- **Span:** The distance between the walls supporting the rafters is the span. This is equal to twice the run.
- **Bird's Mouth:** In order for the rafter to fit flush on the top plate, this cut must be made. The bird's mouth consists of two cuts: the seat cut and the plumb cut.

**Figure 14-16** shows various types of rafters:

- **Common Rafters:** These rafters run at right angles from the wall plate to the ridge.
- **Hip Rafters:** Rafters that extend from an outside corner of the building to the ridge board, usually at a 45° angle, are hip rafters.

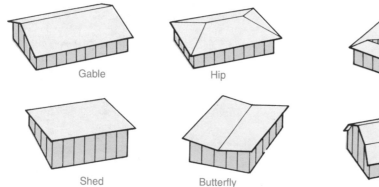

Gable    Hip

Shed    Butterfly

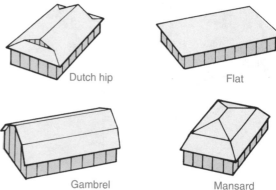

Dutch hip    Flat

Gambrel    Mansard

*Figure 14-13. Common roof styles for residences.*

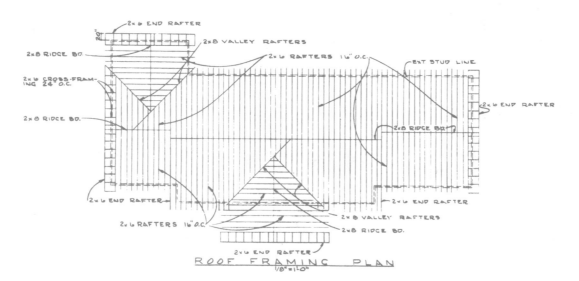

*Figure 14-14. A typical roof framing plan for a residence.*

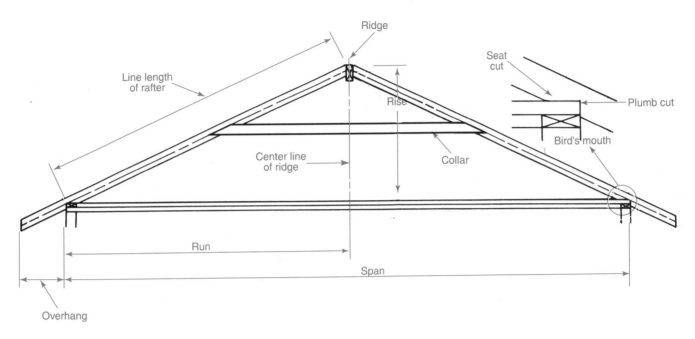

**Figure 14-15.** *Common roof framing terms.*

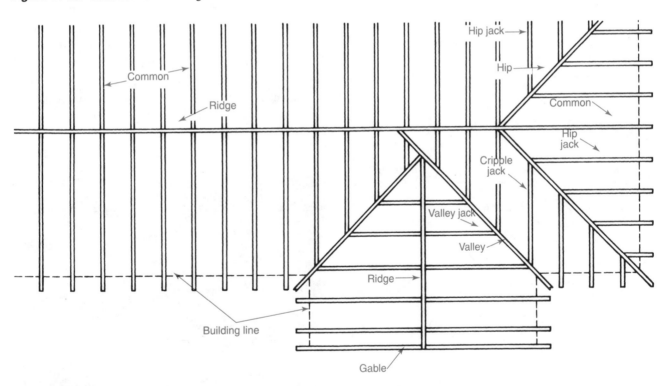

**Figure 14-16.** *Identification of various kinds of rafters.*

- **Valley Rafters:** These rafters extend from the inside corner of a building to the ridge board, usually at a 45° angle.
- **Jack Rafters:** Rafters that do not extend to the ridge board are jack rafters. *Hip jacks* extend from the top plate to a hip rafter. *Valley jacks* extend from the top plate to a valley rafter. *Cripple jacks* run between valley and hip rafters. Another roof framing member is the *purlin,* a hori-

zontal member laid over a truss to support long rafters or the break in gambrel roof rafters.

## Stair Frames

In order to correctly install a staircase, some planning is needed. An elevation view of the stair is normally provided. There are several terms used to describe a stair (refer to **Figure 14-17**):

**Print Reading for Construction**

- **Stringer:** The member running between the lower and upper floors that supports the stairs is the stringer. A 2×8, 2×10, or 2×12 can be used for a stringer, depending on how wide and long the staircase is. The stringers are cut and installed while the wall and floor framing is completed.
- **Tread:** The distance between either the front or the back of adjacent stairs is the tread length. The number of treads in the stairway and the length of each tread is given on the drawing.
- **Riser:** Similar to the tread distance, the riser is the change in elevation between two adjacent

stairs. The number of risers and the height of each is given on the drawing. There is always one more riser than the number of treads.
- **Run:** The total horizontal length of the stairway is the run. The run should be the same as the number of treads multiplied by the tread length.
- **Rise:** If the riser height is multiplied by the number of risers, the vertical distance between floors is found. This distance is the rise.

There are many stair arrangements, three of which are shown in **Figure 14-18.** A modification of the long-L features *winders* (pie-shaped treads) instead of the landing. Using winders conserves space. Also, there are circular winding stairs that gradually change direction as they ascend or descend.

Rough treads are installed for use during construction. These are replaced when finish work is performed.

## Metal Framing

Builders are using metal framing more often in both residential and commercial construction. Components are available for metal framing to meet all construction requirements, **Figure 14-19.** In addition to joists, wall studs, tracks, and blocking, many accessories are manufactured to provide for any need in metal framing, **Figure 14-20.**

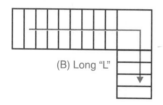

*Figure 14-17.* Terms used to describe a stair.

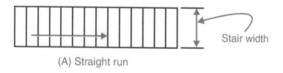
(A) Straight run

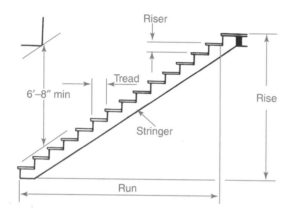
(B) Long "L"

(C) Double "L" and "U"

*Figure 14-18.* Three styles of stairs. A—Straight run stairs are the simplest to design and construct. B—Long-L stairs are used when a change of direction is needed or if the rise is large enough to require a landing. C—Either the double-L or U is used when the stair must turn 180°.

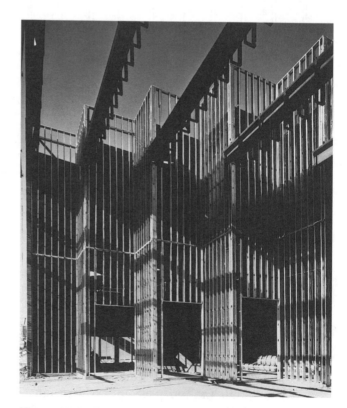

*Figure 14-19.* A variety of metal framing components are used in this commercial building project. (Dale/Incor)

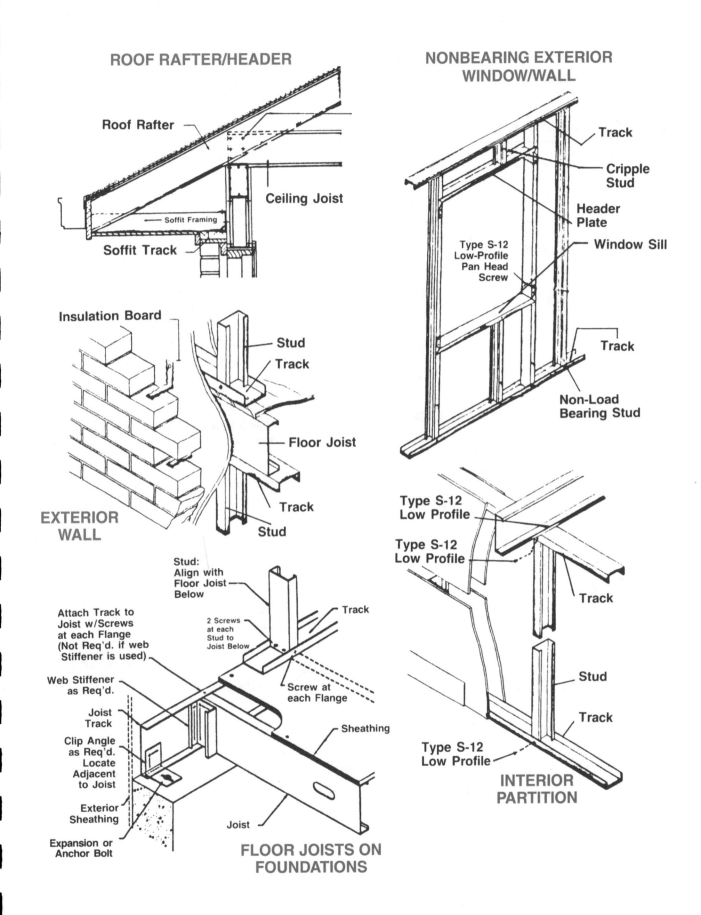

**Figure 14-20.** *Details for residential construction using metal framing.*

Studs and joists are manufactured with punch holes in the web to accommodate plumbing and electrical installations. The punched holes in the web are provided 12″ from each end, with intermediate holes at intervals of 24″.

## Exterior/Interior Finish

The elevation drawings and wall sections show the exterior finish. This includes siding, cornice, roofing, exterior windows, and doors. See **Figure 14-21.** Also, dimensions of ceiling heights, roof pitch, and cornice details are given. Window units are designated with an "O" for a fixed section and an "X" for a sliding section.

Interior finish information may be placed in a finish schedule.

## Test Your Knowledge

*Write your answers in the spaces provided*

_____ 1. Which of the following is *not* a reason for the popular use of wood in residential construction?
  A. It is readily available.
  B. It protects well against fire.
  C. It is relatively affordable.
  D. Dependable construction procedures have been established.
  E. All of these are reasons for the popularity of wood.

_____ 2. Which member rests directly on top of the foundation wall?
  A. Header
  B. Joist
  C. Ledger
  D. Sill plate
  E. None of the above.

_____ 3. Which member is located above a window?
  A. Rough sill
  B. Trimmer stud
  C. Header
  D. Ledger
  E. None of the above.

_____ 4. Which member connects rafters to make the roof frame more stable?
  A. Collar beam
  B. Joist
  C. Hip rafter
  D. Valley rafter
  E. None of the above.

_____ 5. A *winder* is _____.
  A. a member to which joists are attached
  B. a flexible pipe
  C. a stair handrail
  D. a stair tread
  E. None of the above.

_____ 6. A door schedule specifies the order in which doors are to be installed. (True or False?)

_____ 7. A bearing partition is an interior wall that supports load from above. (True or False?)

_____ 8. Sectional views are normally drawn at a larger scale than plan views. (True or False?)

_____ 9. Exterior wall dimensions are normally shown to the outside of a stud wall. (True or False?)

_____ 10. In platform framing, wall studs run continuously from the sill plate to the roof. (True or False?)

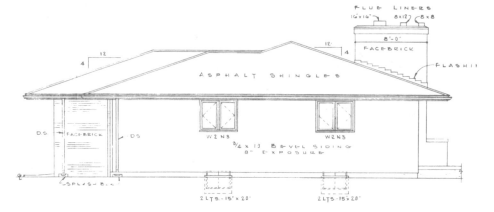

***Figure 14-21.*** *Exterior siding material and finishes are specified on elevation drawings. (Garlinghouse Plan Service)*

**Print Reading Activity 14–1**

# *Wood Framing Prints*

*Refer to Prints 14-1a, 14-1b, 14-1c, and 14-1d from the Large Prints supplement to answer the following questions.*

1. What are the scales of the following drawings:
   Floor plan _____
   Framing plans _____

2. What size are the pipe columns supporting the I-beam? _____

3. How many I-beams are there, and what size are they? _____

4. Give the size of the following members:
   Plate over the I-beam _____
   Subsill on the foundation wall _____

5. Give the following dimensions:
   Overall length to face of studs _____
   Overall width to face of studs_____

6. What is the size of the floor joists, and how are they laid over the beam?
   _____
   _____

7. Describe the floor joist construction under the partitions running parallel to the floor joists.
   _____
   _____

8. What size is the opening in the framing for the fireplace? _____

9. Describe the bridging of the floor joists, including the blocking on the ends of the house.
   _____
   _____

10. What is the width of the foyer to face of studs?_____

11. Give the distance from corner D to the center of rear door. _____

12. Describe the floor framing for the stairway:

Opening size _____

Carriage size _____

Header size _____

Kickplate size _____

Risers (No. and length) _____

Treads (No. and length) _____

13. What type of Section is A-A? _____

14. Give the size of the studs in the regular walls and their spacing.

_____

15. What are the sizes of the headers in the following locations:

Above the garage door _____

Above the front windows _____

Above the front stoop _____

16. How many jamb studs are used to support each end of the garage door header? _____

17. What is the size of the garage doors? _____

18. What size beam is used in the garage to support the ceiling joists? _____

19. What material is used for:

Roof sheathing? _____

Roofing? _____

20. Give the size of the following members:

Common rafters _____

Valley rafters _____

Collar beams _____

Ridge board _____

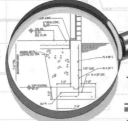

## Print Reading Activity 14–2
# Wood Framing Prints

*Refer to Prints 14-2a, 14-2b, 14-2c, and 14-2d from the Large Prints supplement to answer the following questions.*

1. What size are the valley rafters at the front of the house?

1. _____

2. What is the specification for the steel beams in the basement?

2. _____

3. What is the size and spacing of joists under the kitchen?

3. _____

4. What is the size of the highest ridge board?

4. _____

5. What is the riser height for the stairs?

5. _____

6. What is the size and spacing of studs in exterior walls?

6. _____

7. What size are the rafters above the garage?

7. _____

8. What size are the steel columns in the basement?

8. _____

9. What size are the stair stringers?

9. _____

10. What is the size and spacing of ceiling joists in the screened porch?

10. _____

*Installing a metal partition wall. Metal frames are similar to wood frames, but the metal members are lighter and the different connections are needed.*

*Cutting metal framing members is similiar to cutting wood members.*

# Plumbing Prints

## Technical Terms

Brass pipe
Cleanout
Copper pipe
Control valves
Distribution pipes
Finish plumbing

Galvanized steel pipe
Main
Plastic pipe
Rough-in plumbing
Sweated fittings
Waste stack

## Learning Objectives

After completing this unit, you will be able to:
- Identify various piping systems
- Recognize plumbing fixture symbols on prints
- Explain the three stages of plumbing installation
- Read a piping diagram

In most residences and light commercial buildings, plumbing consists of the water distribution system, sewage disposal system, and piping needed for heating and cooling systems. This unit is designed to familiarize you with the way in which these systems are detailed on construction prints.

Sometimes, piping diagrams are unnecessary. Symbols on the plan drawings locate fixtures such as sinks, water closets, floor drains, and exterior hose bibs. See **Figure 15-1.** The plumber installs the system in accordance with the specifications and local government codes. Larger construction jobs have complete plumbing drawings showing the supply and sewage piping.

## Specifications

The plumbing specifications should be read carefully before the job is started. These specifications

detail the work included in the plumbing contract—piping materials, fixtures, and tests to be performed on the systems.

Plumbers must coordinate their work assignments with other craftspeople because plumbing takes place during three different stages of construction:

- **Stage 1:** Provisions for a water outlet and for the service entrance of the water supply and sewer drain to the building are made prior to the pouring of the foundation.

- **Stage 2:** The next stage is the *rough-in plumbing,* which includes installing water supply pipes and sewage drain pipes. The rough-in work is performed before the slab is poured in slab-in-grade construction and before wall-covering materials are placed on the wall framing. See **Figure 15-2.**

- **Stage 3:** The final stage of the plumber's work is the *finish plumbing,* which includes the setting of fixtures after the walls and floors are finished.

## Water Distribution System

The water distribution system includes the main supply line from the municipal water meter (or other source of supply) to the building. All pipes that take the water from the *main* to the various service outlets (water heaters, sinks, water closets, hose bibs, etc.) are called *distribution pipes.* The distribution system also includes all of the *control valves.*

Symbols for plumbing fixtures are pictorial representations of the fixtures. These symbols are shown on the plan views and on interior elevation views. The most common symbols used for plumbing are shown in

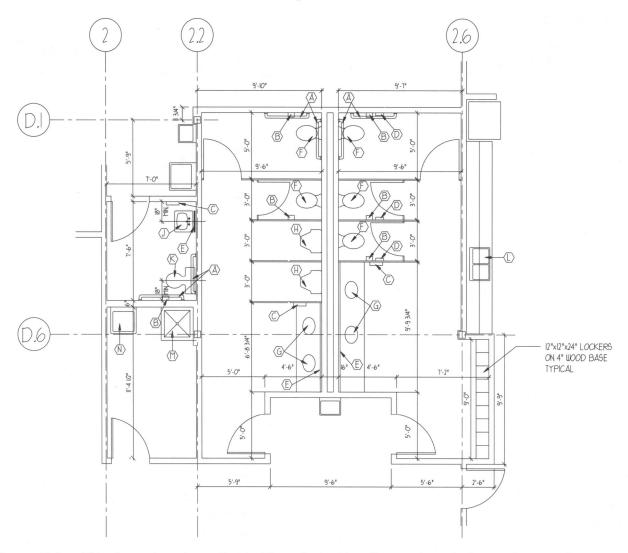

**Figure 15-1.** *This floor plan shows the location of plumbing fixtures in a bathroom for an office building. (Charles E. Smith, Areté 3 Ltd.)*

**Figure 15-2.** *The rough-in plumbing in a large apartment building. (Cooper Development Association, Inc.)*

**Figure 15-3.** Unless the piping layouts are unusual, they generally are not shown on residential drawings. The piping layout is included on commercial projects, however.

## Distribution Piping Materials

Piping materials used for water distribution include copper, which comes in heavy, medium, and light wall thickness. The heavy and medium pipes are suitable for underground and interior plumbing systems. Light pipes are suitable for interior plumbing applications.

*Copper piping* is available in hard and soft tempers. The hard tempers are more suitable for straight runs of exposed pipe, where appearance is a factor. The hard-temper pipe can be bent to a limited radius with proper tools. Soft-temper copper pipe is easily bent by hand or with a tube bender.

Copper piping should not be embedded in concrete slabs, masonry walls, or footings. When it is necessary

LABELS IN FIGURE 15-1: 12"x12"x24" LOCKERS ON 4" WOOD BASE TYPICAL

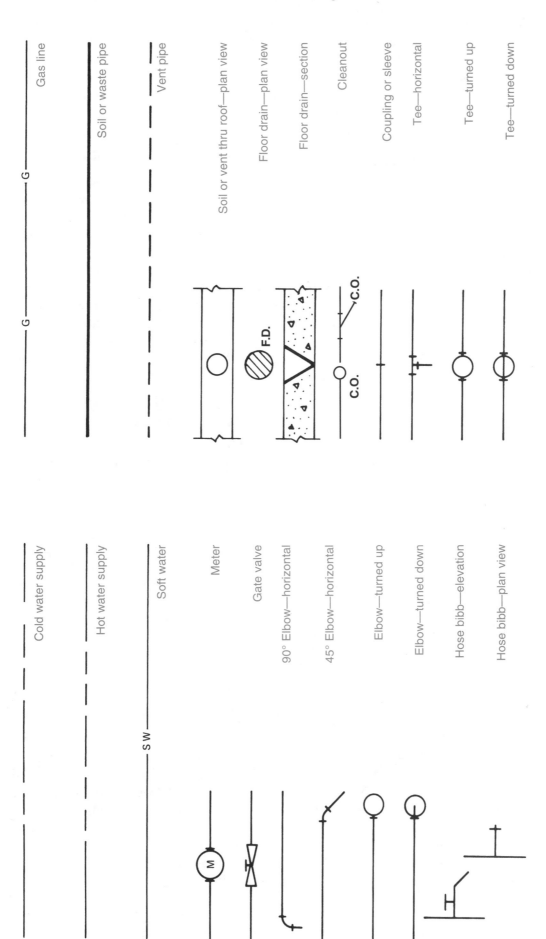

*Figure 15-3. Plumbing symbols used on drawings.*

for the pipe to go through a slab or wall, a sleeve of plastic tape or a larger pipe should be placed between the copper water pipe and concrete. This will permit movement due to expansion of the copper.

Copper has many advantages and is widely used in water distribution systems. Copper pipe should never come into contact with other metals, such as steel pipe or steel reinforcing. Rapid corrosion caused by electrolytic action can be induced. Joints in copper pipe are either sweated or threaded. *Sweated fittings* are soldered using lead-free solder.

*Galvanized steel pipe* has great strength and dimensional stability. The galvanized coating protects the inside and outside of the pipe. There are three grades of wall thickness for galvanized steel pipe: standard weight (S), extra strong (XS), and double extra strong (XXS). The standard weight pipe is used for most residential and light commercial water distribution systems.

*Brass pipe* is used for highly-corrosive water. This type of pipe would be used in situations such as coastal areas where salt water is used for cooling, baths, or other applications.

*Plastic pipe* is used extensively. Three of the most common types are acrylonitrile butadiene styrene (ABS), polyvinyl chloride (PVC), and polybutylene. There are threaded plastic pipes and fittings, but the most common plastic pipes and fittings have solvent-welded joints. Plastic pipe is typically rated according to its wall thickness and its ability to distribute hot water.

## Sewage Disposal System

The sewage disposal system includes a vertical soil (waste) stack, a vent, and a trap for each fixture. The *waste stack* carries the water materials to the building drain, to the building sewer line outside the building, and to the public sewer or septic tank. At the base of each stack, fittings called *cleanouts* (CO) are placed so the drain lines may be cleaned out with a plumber's rod or tape. The installation of sewage disposal systems is carefully controlled by plumbing codes to prevent contamination of the water supply and to keep sewer gases from entering the building.

Piping drawings are provided for most commercial construction projects. Piping can be shown on plan and elevation views, but often an isometric drawing of the system is provided, **Figure 15-4.**

A plan view diagram of a water distribution system and a sewage disposal system is shown in **Figure 15-5.** Note the size of drain pipe specified. Vertical soil pipes or waste stacks serving water closets must have a thicker wall with at least 6″ studs to accommodate a 4″ soil pipe and its joints.

## Sewage Piping Materials

Sewage disposal systems can be made of many different kinds of pipe material. For water distribution systems, piping materials that can pollute the water cannot be used. However, this is not a concern with waste water.

Cast-iron pipe has good qualities of strength and resistance to corrosion. Copper and plastic pipe are used extensively because of ease of installation. Special plastics are used for drainage systems where chemicals are disposed. Clay tile and plastics (ABS and PVC) are used extensively for sewer piping.

## Gas and Fuel Oil Systems

Sometimes, the piping for gas or oil heating systems are included in the plumbing contract. Other than the location of the particular service desired, piping for heating purposes usually is not shown on the drawing. Specifications for the construction job will detail the size and kind of piping to use.

Materials most commonly used for gas piping are black wrought iron, galvanized steel, or yellow brass. Copper tubing is banned by most building codes because it corrodes when exposed to some gases. Black wrought iron pipe is often required by building codes for piping combustible gases, such as natural gas. This pipe is not galvanized, but typically painted black and made of carbon steel.

## Plumbing Codes

Model codes such as the Uniform Plumbing Code and the local government code control all aspects of plumbing work, including the kinds and sizes of pipe, locations of traps and cleanouts, plumbing fixture requirements, venting provisions, and connections to water supply and sewer lines. These codes also specify the leak testing to be conducted on water supply lines and waste lines.

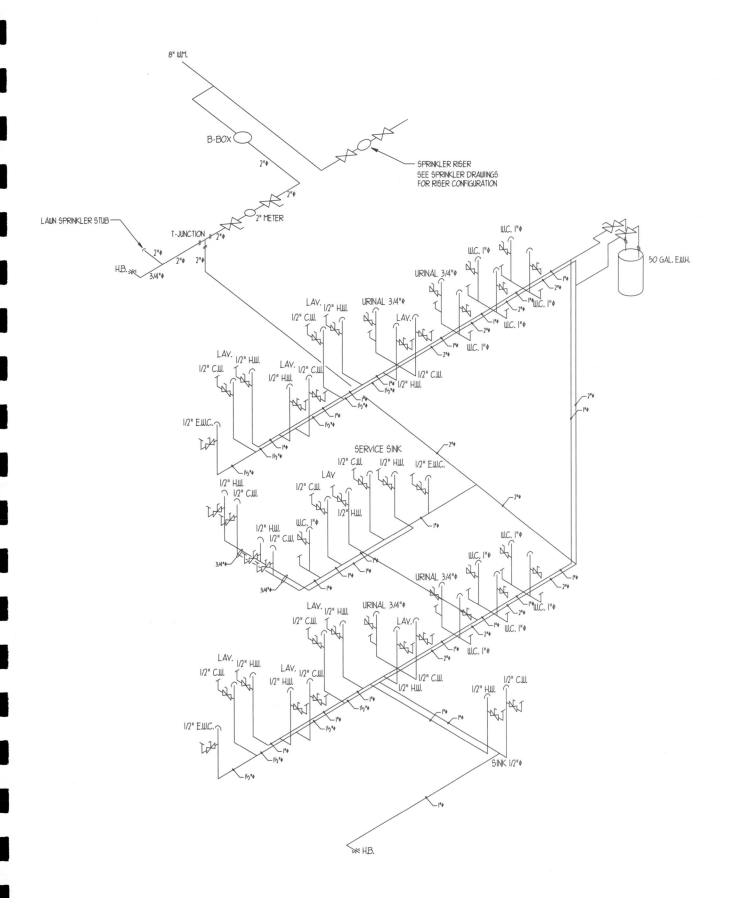

**Figure 15-4.** *An isometric drawing of a water distribution system. The isometric style makes visualization easier. (Charles E. Smith, Areté 3 Ltd.)*

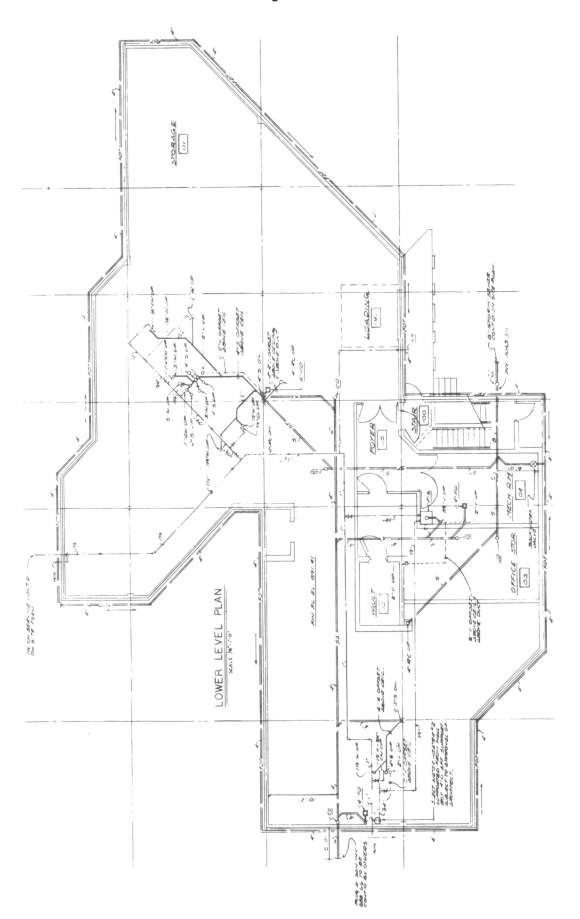

***Figure 15-5.*** *Plumbing diagram of a water distribution system and a sewage disposal system. (Robert E. Hayes & Associates Architects)*

# Test Your Knowledge

*Write your answers in the spaces provided.*

_____ 1. The first stage of plumbing installation is attaching fixture to walls. (True or False?)

_____ 2. Copper pipes should *not* come in contact with concrete. (True or False?)

_____ 3. Cleanouts must be included in the water supply system. (True or False?)

_____ 4. Brass piping is used to transport highly-corrosive products. (True or False?)

_____ 5. Drawings that show the path of pipes through the building are required for all structures. (True or False?)

*The plumber must understand plumbing prints in order to install complex plumbing systems.*

166

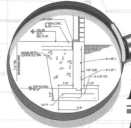

## Print Reading Activity 15–1
# *Residential Plumbing Prints*

*Refer to Print 15-1 from the Large Prints supplement to answer the following questions.*

1. How many roof drains (including overflow drains) are needed?

1. _____

2. Which pieces of equipment are supplied with LP gas?

2. _____
   _____

3. How many hose bibs are provided?

3. _____

4. What size is the deck drain?

4. _____

5. What size are the connections on the water softener?

5. _____

6. What type of drain is specified for the planter in the kitchen?

6. _____

7. How far above grade are the downspout nozzles?

7. _____

8. How many water closets are needed?

8. _____

9. Where is most of the supply piping located?

9. _____

10. What size piping is used to supply the laundry sink?

10. _____

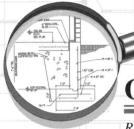

## Print Reading Activity 15–2
# Office Building Plumbing Prints

*Refer to Prints 15-2a and 15-2b from the Large Prints supplement to answer the following questions.*

1. What is the size of the main supply pipe from the meter?_____

2. What is the size of the main pipe as it enters the building?_____

3. List the size of the distribution system pipe:

   A. To electric water heater _____

   B. From electric water heater_____

   C. To service sink_____

   D. Lavatories _____

   E. Water closets _____

   F. Dwyer kitchen unit _____

   G. Electric drinking fountain _____

   H. Hose bib on northwest corner _____

   I. Hose bib on east side _____

4. All supplies are to be valved. Where is this specified?

   _____

5. What must the plumbing contractor do regarding ductwork and electrical services?

   _____

   _____

6. What must the plumbing contractor install between connections of dissimilar metals?

   _____

   _____

7. What is to be done to services to the existing building?

   _____

   _____

8. What type water closet is specified?

   _____

   _____

9. What is the number of the Dwyer Kitchen Unit specified, and what is to be replaced?

   _____

   _____

10. Give the size of the building sewer. _____

11. Where is this waste pipe to be connected?

   _____

12. What size waste pipe is used to drain the electric drinking fountain?_____

13. Give the size of waste pipe serving the:

   A. Water closets _____

   B. Service sink _____

   C. Kitchen Dwyer Unit _____

14. How many floor drains are there? _____

15. Indicate the size of vent through roof for the:

   A. Kitchen Dwyer Unit _____

   B. Drinking fountain _____

# HVAC Prints

## Technical Terms

Duct
Electric radiant
  heating
Evaporative cooling
  systems
Forced-air system
Glass panel heaters

Heating, ventilating,
  and air-conditioning
  (HVAC)
Hydronic heating
Remote cooling
  systems
Series-loop system
Unit cooling systems

## Learning Objectives

After completing this unit, you will be able to:
• Identify the purpose of HVAC systems
• Explain different types of heating and cooling systems
• Identify HVAC symbols on prints

*Heating, Ventilating, and Air-Conditioning (HVAC)* systems produce the movement of air within a building. This air may be heated or cooled and then moved to another location to change the air conditions. The HVAC system makes a space more comfortable for the people occupying it. This treatment involves controlling the temperature, humidity (moisture in the air), and air cleanliness.

During colder periods of the year, the air in a building is heated and moisture is added for comfort. In warmer periods, the air is cooled and moisture is removed.

To accomplish the desired air conditioning in a building, a heating system and a cooling system are needed. Sometimes a system for cleaning and treating the air for desired humidity is also included. In this unit, we shall study heating and cooling systems and how these are shown on drawings.

## HVAC Plans

HVAC plans are prepared by the HVAC subcontractor. Generally, these plans are drawn on the floor plan of the structure for the approval of the architect or homeowner. For larger commercial structures, the heating and cooling plans are prepared by an air-conditioning engineer under the direction of the architect.

Symbols for heating and cooling systems are shown in **Figure 16-1.** A symbol legend is included on the drawing to identify the symbols.

## Heating System

There are three basic types of heating systems used in new construction: forced-air, hydronic (hot water), and electric radiant heating.

In a *forced-air system,* the heated air from the furnace or heat pump chamber is transferred by means of a motor-driven fan through a series of *ducts* (rectangular or round pipes) to registers or diffusers in the various rooms. See **Figure 16-2.** Cool air is gathered through registers near the floor and returned to the heating unit through ducts and a filtering system to be reheated and recirculated.

In residences or light commercial structures, the forced-air heating system is considered to be a closed circuit (no provision for outside air to be added) system. In large commercial structures, provision is made for the addition of fresh air from the outside and no air is returned from kitchens, smoking rooms, and rest rooms.

Sources of heat for forced-air systems are natural gas, liquid petroleum, gas, oil, coal, or electricity. Developments are also taking place in the use of solar energy as a fuel source in forced-air systems.

## AIR CONDITIONING SYMBOLS

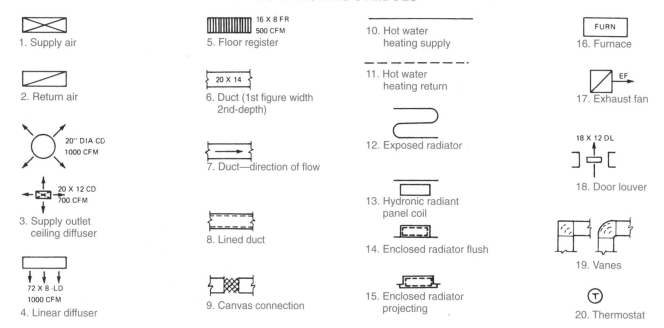

**Figure 16-1.** *Symbols for air-conditioning systems.*

In **Figure 16-2,** note size of ducts specified. Plans often specify the air flow rate at a given point. The flow rate is specified in cubic feet per minute (cfm).

A *hydronic system* begins by heating water to a temperature of 200°F (90°C) in a boiler. Then, the hot water is circulated by a pump and piping system to convectors in the spaces to be heated, **Figure 16-3.** Hydronic systems for residences normally use the *series-loop system* to carry the heated water to the convectors. For larger areas, a one-pipe system or two-pipe system is specified. The latter systems provide more uniform heat for larger area than the series-loop.

When drawings are provided, they usually are superimposed over the floor plan or given in an isometric diagram.

*Electric radiant heating* is usually provided by wires embedded in the ceilings, walls, floors and base-boards of the building. The wires are spaced in a grid pattern, with approximately 1 1/2″ between wires. They are stapled to the gypsum lath of the ceiling or wall and covered with plaster. Floor cables are heavier. These are placed on a grid pattern 1 1/2″ to 3″ below the concrete surface. Radiant heat is given off materials warmed by resistance induced in the wires embedded in the building materials.

*Glass panel heaters* are available for ceiling and wall installation. These panels can be painted, papered, or plastered.

Heating system drawings can be superimposed over the floor plans on a separate diagram provided with appropriate notes. When drawings are not provided, the amount of heat required for each space is noted on the floor plan.

## Cooling Systems

Cooling systems can be grouped as unit systems (window or wall-mounted) and remote systems (refrigeration equipment located away from the area to be conditioned). A third type of system, the evaporator system, is used only in special circumstances.

*Unit cooling systems,* which are installed in a window or space provided in an exterior wall, are used to cool a room. Very little construction is involved in their installation. Units can be purchased to heat as well as cool the air.

*Remote cooling systems* have the condensing unit in a remote space away from the area to be cooled. The evaporator is in the main duct where the fan forces air past the cool coils and circulates the air to the rooms to be cooled or heated. Another variation of this cooling system is with a remote condensing unit and evaporator, and cooled brine or water is circulated to the heat exchangers in each room.

*Evaporative cooling systems* are most effective in dry climates where the relative humidity is low

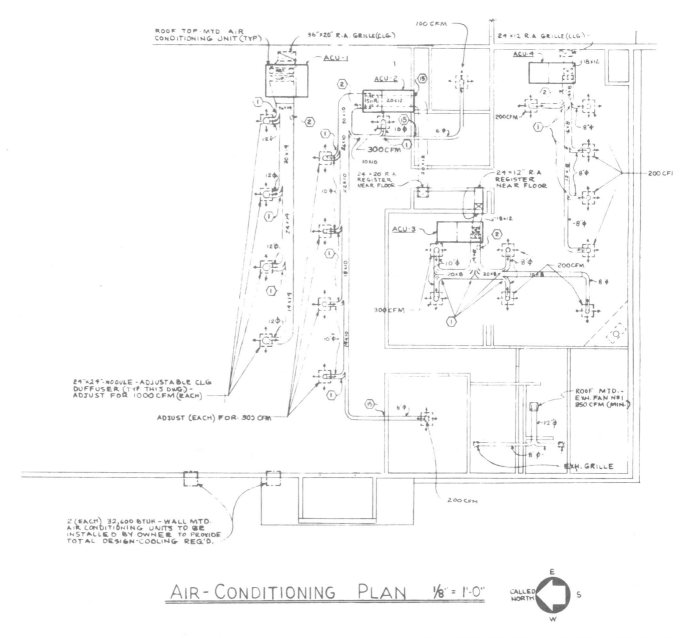

AIR-CONDITIONING PLAN    ⅛" = 1'-0"

**Figure 16-2.** *Forced air HVAC plan with sizes of ducts and diffusers noted. (Henkel, Hovel & Schaefer Architects - Engineer)*

(preferably 20% or less). They will work, but less effectively, at higher levels of humidity. The evaporative system functions by moving air rapidly over a pad of excelsior that is kept moist by a water spray mist. The air is cooled as it passes through the pad, and then carried through a duct system to the rooms. This system of cooling raises the humidity in the space being cooled.

The supply duct layout for an evaporative cooling system is similar to that of a forced-air system. However, the evaporative system has larger ducts, and no return ducts are necessary since outside air is used.

## Air Filters

Most heating and cooling systems provide a means of filtering the air that flows through the system. The filters usually have an adhesive or oil coat that collects lint and dust particles. These filters are either disposable or washable.

Most systems come equipped with a designated space for inserting the adhesive filter. The electrostatic filter usually is a separate unit added to the system. It is noted on the heating and cooling plan, and detailed in the specifications.

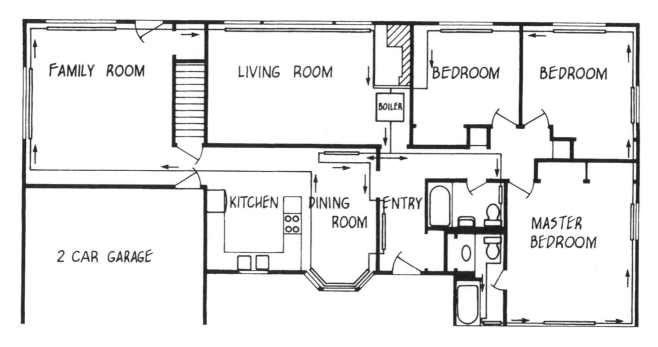

*Figure 16-3.* *A hydronic heating system layout, series-loop type.*

# Test Your Knowledge

*Write your answers in the spaces provided.*

_____ 1. An air-conditioning system changes the temperature of the air, but does nothing to clean the air. (True or False?)

_____ 2. A forced-air heating systems transports air through ducts. (True or False?)

_____ 3. A unit cooling system is the most difficult type of cooling system to install. (True or False?)

_____ 4. To improve comfort during warm weather, moisture should be added to the air. (True or False?)

_____ 5. In a forced-air system, heat is always provided by burning natural gas. (True or False?)

**Print Reading Activity 16–1**

# HVAC Print

*Refer to Print 16-1 from the Large Prints supplement to answer the following questions.*

1. What size and specifications are given for the A/C unit?

2. Where is the A/C condensing unit located?

3. What are the sizes of the refrigeration lines, and how are they brought into the house?

4. Where is the hot air furnace located?

5. What is the size of the supply air duct coming off the furnace? _____

6. Give the size of the supply air duct to the den. _____

7. Indicate how much air is to be supplied:
   A. To sewing room _____
   B. To dining room _____
   C. To kitchen _____
   D. To master bedroom _____

8. Give the number and sizes of the supply air registers:
   A. In living room _____
   B. In foyer _____
   C. In master bedroom _____
   D. In den _____

9. What size return air grille is specified, and where is it located?

10. How many exhaust fans are shown on the plan, and where are they located?

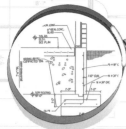

**Print Reading Activity 16–2**
# Commercial HVAC Print

*Refer to Print 16-2 from the Large Prints supplement to answer the following questions.*

1. What is the scale for the A/C floor plan?

1. _____

2. What size is specified for the A/C unit?

2. _____

3. What is the size of the main return air ducts just before they go through the roof?

3. _____

4. What size are the supply air ducts that first enter below the roof?

4. _____

5. Linear diffusers supplying air to the lobby:
   A. How many?
   B. Size?
   C. How much air?

5. A. _____
   B. _____
   C. _____

6. Diffusers supplying workroom:
   A. How many?
   B. Size?
   C. How much air?

6. A. _____
   B. _____
   C. _____

7. Exhaust fans:
   A. How many?
   B. Where located?
   C. Specifications?

7. A. _____
   B. _____
   C. _____

8. What size duct is used to supply the conference room-safe deposit booth area?

8. _____

9. How much air is to be supplied to the conference room?

9. _____

10. Where is the thermostat located?

10. _____

# Electrical Prints

## Technical Terms

Ampere
Branch circuits
Circuit
Circuit breaker
Conductor
Conduit
Distribution Panel
Electrical metallic
 tubing (EMT)
Equipment Schedule
Ground
Ground fault circuit
 interrupter (GFCI)

One-line diagram
Lighting schedule
National Electrical
 Code (NEC)
Panel schedule
Receptacles
Relay
Service Entrance
Voltage
Watt
Wiring diagram

## Learning Objectives

After completing this unit, you will be able to:
• Identify electrical symbols
• Explain various electrical terms
• Recognize different types of electrical drawings

The electrical prints for residential and light commercial buildings usually consist of the outlets and switches shown on the floor plan. Wire routing is left to the electrical contractor and the electrical codes. For large industrial and commercial buildings involving elaborate electrical systems, detailed electrical diagrams are prepared by electrical engineers.

Electricians must be able to read prints in order to plan where circuits will run in the basement, crawl spaces, and attics. They also need to know the direction of floor and ceiling joists. To help you read and understand electrical prints, this unit will explain electrical terms, symbols, diagrams, codes, and circuit calculations.

## Electrical Terms

Following are some common terms used in electrical construction:
- **Ampere:** The unit of measurement of current (electricity flowing through a conductor). Abbreviated as *amps.*
- **Voltage:** The electromotive force that causes current to flow through a conductor (wire).
- **Watt:** The unit of measurement of electrical power. Current (amps) times voltage equals watts. Most appliances are rated in watts.
- **Circuit:** Two or more conductors (wires) carrying electricity from the source (distribution panel) to an electrical device and returning.
- **Circuit Breaker:** A switching device that automatically opens a circuit when it becomes overloaded.
- **Conductor:** A wire or other material used to carry electricity.
- **Conduit:** A channel or pipe in which conductors run. Required by code where conductors need protection.
- **Convenience Receptacle:** An outlet where current is taken from a circuit to serve electrical devices such as lamps, clocks, and toasters. Sometimes called *receptacles.*
- **Service Entrance:** The conductors from the utility pole, service head, and mast that bring the electrical current to the distribution panel.
- **Distribution Panel:** The insulated panel or box, sometimes called a breaker panel, that receives the current from the source and distributes it through branch circuits to various points throughout the building. The panel often contains the main disconnect switch and always

contains fuses or circuit breakers protecting each circuit.

- **Ground:** A wire connecting the circuit or device to the earth to minimize injuries from shock and possible damage from lightning.

# Ground Fault Circuit Interrupters

A *ground fault circuit interrupter (GFCI)* should be installed in areas where moisture may be present or where the use of a tool or appliance, connected to a circuit, can come in contact with a grounded metal surface. The use of GFCIs is defined in the *National Electrical Code (NEC)*. They should be used in the following situations:

- In kitchens where receptacles are within 6'-6" of the sink
- In bathrooms
- In garages where moisture is present or there is direct access to grade, unless the receptacle is not readily accessible or is dedicated to a fixed appliance, such as a freezer
- For exterior receptacles where access to grade is possible

GFCIs open the circuit if a current leakage or fault (to ground) occurs in excess of 0.006 amps. These interruptions occur when the difference in current entering and current leaving the circuit are not identical. The GFCI automatically senses the fault and turns off the power within 25 to 30 milliseconds.

# Electrical Symbols

Some of the more common symbols used on electrical drawings are shown in **Figure 17-1.** Also, a legend of symbols usually is given on the electrical plan.

Any standard symbol can be used to designate some variation of standard equipment by the addition of lower case subscript lettering to the symbol. This would be identified in the legend and, if necessary, further described in the specifications.

# Electrical Prints

There are several different types of drawings used to detail the electrical portion of a project. On small projects, few of the drawings are needed, if any. On larger buildings, many of each type of drawing may be needed.

# Electrical Plans

An electrical plan shows the locations of the distribution panel, receptacles, switches, and lights. See **Figure 17-2.** Broken lines indicate which outlets and switches are connected. However, the path of the wire is not necessarily where the lines are drawn.

The electrical plan may also show the wire and conduit sizes, **Figure 17-3.** The lines on the drawing representing the conduit are used to show the starting and ending points of the conduit run. The line does not show the exact location where the conduit should be located. Conduit is normally located in the field by the electricians.

For larger construction jobs, one electrical plan may be prepared for outlets, another for lighting, and still another for the service entrance. These plans, together with the set of specifications, detail the electrical work to be done and the materials and fixtures to be used.

# Wiring Diagrams

A *wiring diagram,* **Figure 17-4,** is used when wiring details can not be shown clearly on the plan. Wiring diagrams correspond to a specific piece of equipment. The types of wire running between the equipment and its power source, sensors, gauges, and other related equipment are shown.

# Schedules

There are many types of schedules used with electrical drawings:

- **Panel Schedule:** All of the information associated with a circuit breaker box (also called lighting panel or power panel), is included in the panel schedule, **Figure 17-5.** The voltage entering the box, the number and size of the breakers, and a brief description of the devices protected by the breakers are included.
- **Lighting Schedule:** The permanently-mounted light fixtures used in the project can be listed in a lighting schedule. The lamp is marked on the drawing with an identification letter that references the schedule. The brand of fixture, catalog number, and power requirements are listed.
- **Equipment Schedule:** An equipment schedule, **Figure 17-6,** is similar to a lighting schedule. It lists equipment rather than lights. More detailed wiring and power information is included in the equipment schedule, however.

## LIGHTING OUTLETS

| | |
|---|---|
| ○ —⊕— | Ceiling outlet |
| Ⓓ | Drop cord |
| Ⓕ —Ⓕ | Fan outlet |
| Ⓙ —Ⓙ | Junction box |
| Ⓛ PS —Ⓛ PS | Lamp holder with pull switch |
| Ⓧ —Ⓧ | Exit light outlet |
| Ⓛ —Ⓛ | Outlet controlled by low voltage switching when relay is installed in outlet box |
| [○] | Surface or pendant individual fluorescent fixture |
| [OR] | Recessed individual fluorescent fixture |
| Ⓡ —Ⓡ | Recessed incandescent |

## SIGNALING SYSTEM OUTLETS RESIDENTIAL OCCUPANCIES

| | |
|---|---|
| ▣ | Push button |
| ▱ | Buzzer |
| ▭ | Bell |
| ◀ | Outside telephone |
| ◁ | Interconnecting telephone |
| D | Electric door opener |
| CH | Chime |
| TV | Television outlet |
| Ⓣ | Thermostat |

## RECEPTACLE OUTLETS

| | |
|---|---|
| —⊖ | Duplex receptacle outlet |
| —⊖GFCI | Duplex receptacle ground fault circuit interrupter |
| —⊖WP | Weatherproof receptacle outlet |
| ⊞ | Triplex receptacle outlet |
| ⊕ | Quadruplex receptacle outlet |
| ⊖ | Duplex receptacle outlet—split wired |
| ◁ | Single special-purpose receptacle outlet |
| ⊖R | Range outlet |
| ◖DW | Special purpose connection |
| Ⓒ | Clock hanger receptacle |
| ⊙ | Floor single receptacle outlet |
| ⊞ | Underfloor duct and junction box for triple, double, or single duct system as indicated by number of parallel lines |

## PANELS, CIRCUITS, AND MISCELLANEOUS

| | |
|---|---|
| ⏚ | Ground |
| ▬ | Lighting panel |
| ▨ | Power panel |
| —— | Wiring, concealed in ceiling or wall |
| - - - - | Wiring, concealed in floor |
| ◄— | Conduit run to panel board |
| —ⱵⱵⱵ— | *Indicates number of conductors |
| ⬜⌐ | Externally operated disconnect switch |

## SWITCH OUTLETS

| | |
|---|---|
| S | Single pole switch |
| S2 | Double pole switch |
| S3 | Three way switch |
| S4 | Four way switch |
| SK | Key operated switch |
| SP | Switch and pilot lamp |
| SWCB | Weatherproof circuit breaker |
| SWP | Weatherproof switch |
| SL | Switch for low voltage switching system |
| ST | Time switch |
| Ⓢ | Ceiling pull switch |
| ⊖S | Switch and single receptacle |
| ⊖S | Switch and double receptacle |
| SCB | Circuit breaker |
| SRC | Remote control switch |
| SF | Fused switch |
| SLM | Master switch for low voltage switching system |
| SD | Automatic door switch |

*Indicates number of conductors (in this case, 4). Any circuit without cross hatches indicates two-conductor circuit. Some electrical engineers show number of hot conductors with full marks; neutral conductors with half marks (—ⱵⱵⱵ— = 3 hot conductors, 1 neutral).

**Figure 17-1.** *Common symbols used on electrical plan drawings and diagrams.*

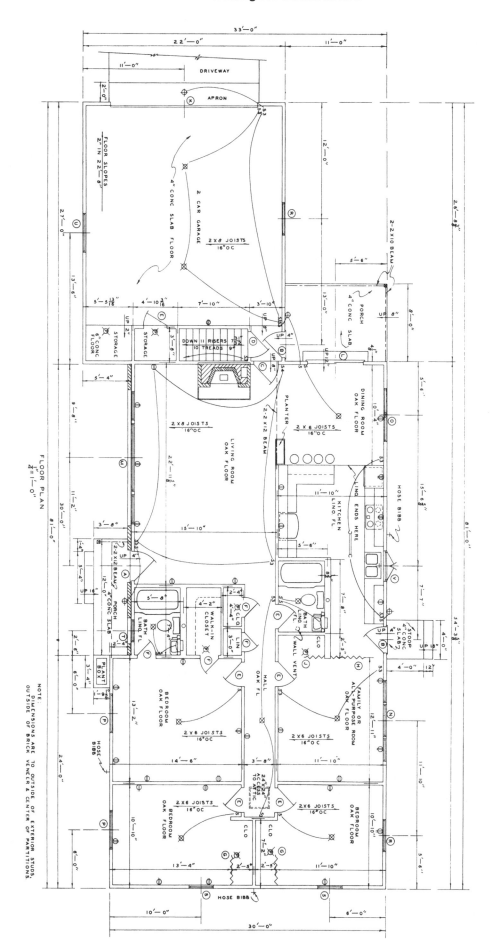

*Figure 17-2. A residential electrical plan.*

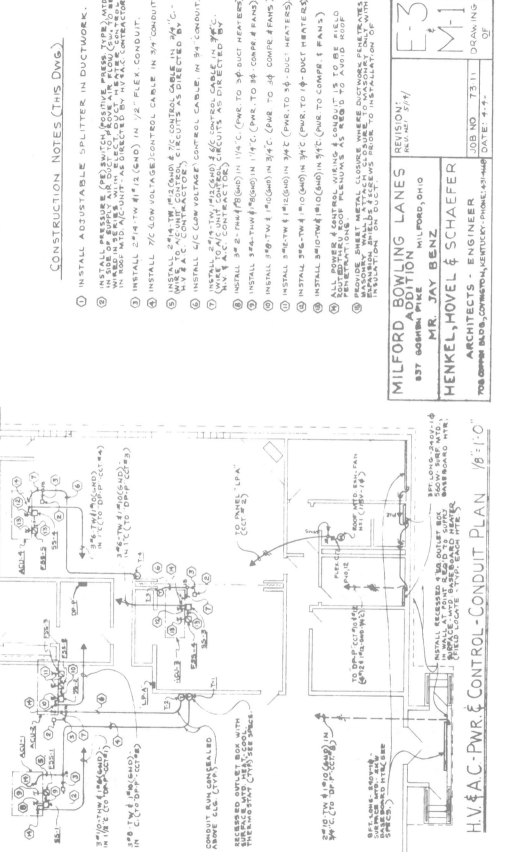

**Figure 17-3.** *An electrical plan with wire and conduit sizes. (Henkel, Hovel & Schaefer, Architects–Engineer)*

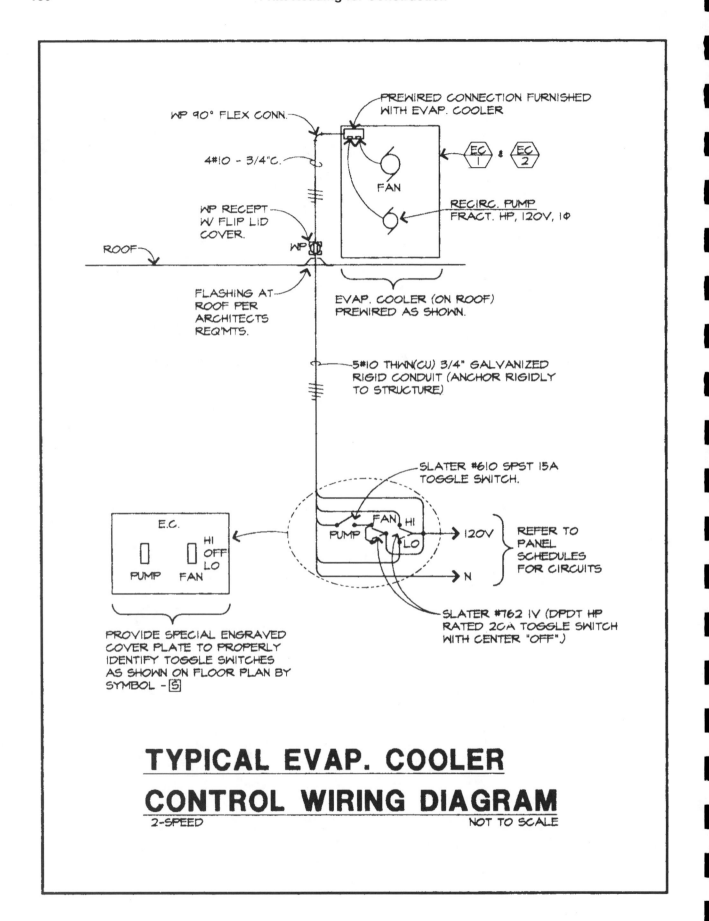

WP 90° FLEX CONN.

PREWIRED CONNECTION FURNISHED WITH EVAP. COOLER

4#10 - 3/4"C.

EC 1  &  EC 2

FAN

WP RECEPT W/ FLIP LID COVER.

RECIRC. PUMP FRACT. HP, 120V, 1∅

ROOF

WP

FLASHING AT ROOF PER ARCHITECTS REQ'MTS.

EVAP. COOLER (ON ROOF) PREWIRED AS SHOWN.

5#10 THWN(CU) 3/4" GALVANIZED RIGID CONDUIT (ANCHOR RIGIDLY TO STRUCTURE)

SLATER #610 SPST 15A TOGGLE SWITCH.

E.C.

HI
OFF
LO

PUMP     FAN

PUMP    FAN    HI
                LO

120V

N

REFER TO PANEL SCHEDULES FOR CIRCUITS

SLATER #762 IV (DPDT HP RATED 20A TOGGLE SWITCH WITH CENTER "OFF".)

PROVIDE SPECIAL ENGRAVED COVER PLATE TO PROPERLY IDENTIFY TOGGLE SWITCHES AS SHOWN ON FLOOR PLAN BY SYMBOL - [S]

# TYPICAL EVAP. COOLER
# CONTROL WIRING DIAGRAM
2-SPEED                    NOT TO SCALE

**Figure 17-4.** *A wiring diagram is used to clearly illustrate the wiring for complicated equipment. (The Fleischer Estancia; Christensen, Cassidy, Billington and Candelaria, Inc., Architects)*

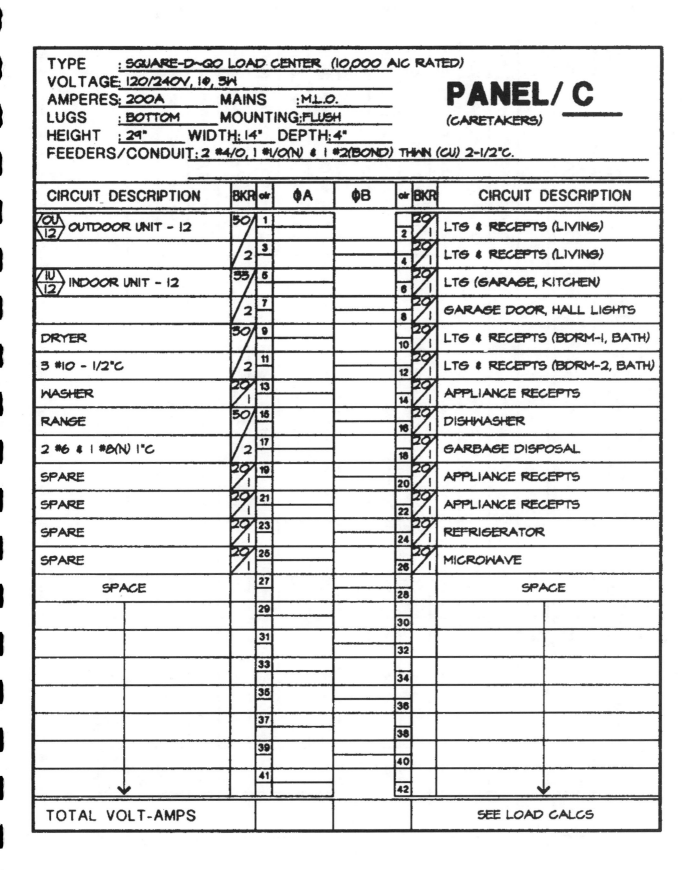

TYPE      : SQUARE-D-QO LOAD CENTER (10,000 AIC RATED)
VOLTAGE: 120/240V, 1Φ, 3W
AMPERES: 200A        MAINS       : M.L.O.         **PANEL/C**
LUGS    : BOTTOM     MOUNTING: FLUSH              (CARETAKERS)
HEIGHT  : 29"    WIDTH: 14"   DEPTH: 4"
FEEDERS/CONDUIT: 2 #4/0, 1 #1/O(N) & 1 #2(BOND) THWN (CU) 2-1/2"C.

| CIRCUIT DESCRIPTION | BKR | clr | ΦA | ΦB | clr | BKR | CIRCUIT DESCRIPTION |
|---|---|---|---|---|---|---|---|
| OU/12 OUTDOOR UNIT - 12 | 50 | 1 | | | | 20 / 2 | LTG & RECEPTS (LIVING) |
| | 2 | 3 | | | | 20 / 4 | LTG & RECEPTS (LIVING) |
| IU/12 INDOOR UNIT - 12 | 35 | 5 | | | | 20 / 6 | LTG (GARAGE, KITCHEN) |
| | 2 | 7 | | | | 20 / 8 | GARAGE DOOR, HALL LIGHTS |
| DRYER | 30 | 9 | | | | 20 / 10 | LTG & RECEPTS (BDRM-1, BATH) |
| 3 #10 - 1/2"C | 2 | 11 | | | | 20 / 12 | LTG & RECEPTS (BDRM-2, BATH) |
| WASHER | 20 / 1 | 13 | | | | 20 / 14 | APPLIANCE RECEPTS |
| RANGE | 50 | 15 | | | | 20 / 16 | DISHWASHER |
| 2 #6 & 1 #8(N) 1"C | 2 | 17 | | | | 20 / 18 | GARBAGE DISPOSAL |
| SPARE | 20 / 1 | 19 | | | | 20 / 20 | APPLIANCE RECEPTS |
| SPARE | 20 / 1 | 21 | | | | 20 / 22 | APPLIANCE RECEPTS |
| SPARE | 20 / 1 | 23 | | | | 20 / 24 | REFRIGERATOR |
| SPARE | 20 / 1 | 25 | | | | 20 / 26 | MICROWAVE |
| SPACE | | 27 | | | 28 | | SPACE |
| | | | 29 | | | 30 | |
| | | | 31 | | | 32 | |
| | | | 33 | | | 34 | |
| | | | 35 | | | 36 | |
| | | | 37 | | | 38 | |
| | | | 39 | | | 40 | |
| | | | 41 | | | 42 | |
| TOTAL VOLT-AMPS | | | | | | | SEE LOAD CALCS |

***Figure 17-5.*** *A panel schedule shows the details of a circuit breaker panel. (The Fleischer Estancia; Christensen, Cassidy, Billington and Candelaria, Inc., Architects)*

# MECHANICAL EQUIPMENT SCHEDULE

| MK | HP | KW | LOAD / EA. | VOLTS-φ | DISC. SW./LPN-RK FUSES | FEEDERS / CONDUIT |
|---|---|---|---|---|---|---|
| **IU — INDOOR UNITS** | | | | | | |
| 1 THRU 4, 6, 8 | 3/4 | 8.0 | 41.7A | 230-1 | 60/2P W (2) 60A | 2 #6&1 #8 (BOND) THHN (CU)-1"C |
| 5, 9 | 1/3 | 5.0 | 25.4A | 230-1 | 60/2P W (2) 35A | 2 #8&1 #8 (BOND) THHN (CU)-3/4"C |
| 7 | 1/5 | 3.0 | 15.2A | 230-1 | 30/2P W (2) 20A | 2 #10&1 #10 (BOND) THHN (CU)-1/2"C |
| 10, 11 | - | 1.0 | 8.3A | 120-1 | MANUAL MOTOR STARTER | 2 #12&1 #12 (BOND) THHN (CU)-1/2"C |
| 12 | 1/2 | 5.0 | 27.0A | 230-1 | 60/2P W (2) 35A | 2 #8&1 #8 (BOND) THHN (CU)-3/4"C |
| **OU — OUTDOOR UNITS** | | | | | | |
| 1, 2, 4, 8 | - | - | 27.9A | 230-1 | HP, 60/2 W(2) 40A | 2 #8&1 #8 (BOND) THHN (CU)-3/4"C |
| 3, 6 | - | - | 36.5A | 230-1 | HP, 60/2 W(2) 50A | 2 #6&1 #8 (BOND) THHN (CU)-1"C |
| 5, 9 | - | - | 15.1A | 230-1 | HP, 30/2 W(2) 20A | 2 #10&1 #10 (BOND) THHN (CU)-1/2"C |
| 7 | - | - | 10.5A | 230-1 | HP, 30/2 W(2) 15A | 2 #12&1 #12 (BOND) THHN (CU)-1/2"C |
| 10, 11 | - | - | 10.0A | 120-1 | HP, 30/2 W(1) 15A | 2 #12&1 #12 (BOND) THHN (CU)-1/2"C |
| 12 | - | - | 25.4A | 230-1 | HP, 30/2 W(2) 35A | 2 #8&1 #8 (BOND) THHN (CU)-3/4"C |
| **EC — EVAP. COOLERS** | | | | | | |
| 1, 2 | 1/2 | - | 9.8A | 120-1 | | SEE CONTROL DIAGRAM THIS SHEET |

*Figure 17-6.* An equipment schedule includes the power requirements for the machinery. *(The Fleischer Estancia; Christensen, Cassidy, Billington and Candelaria, Inc., Architects)*

## One-line Diagrams

*One-line diagrams* are schematic drawings (diagrams). They show which pieces of equipment are electrically-connected and what is used to connect them. See **Figure 17-7.**

# Electrical Circuits

A *circuit* is the path of electricity from a source (distribution panel) through the components (receptacles, lights) and back to the source. Circuits are numbered on the diagram and connected by a heavy line, ending in an arrow that indicates the circuit is connected to the distribution panel.

Electricity is brought into the building by way of the service entrance through the meter and on to the distribution panel. For most residences and light commercial buildings, one distribution panel is sufficient. Large commercial buildings make use of feeder circuits to further distribute the electricity to several distribution panels. Larger conductor sizes should be used in feeder circuits. This helps to avoid excessive voltage drop in branch circuits that otherwise might be in excess of 100′ in length.

*Branch circuits* can be classified as the following:

- General lighting circuits used primarily for lighting and small, portable appliances such as radios, clocks, TV sets, and vacuum cleaners.
- General appliance circuits used for those outlets along the kitchen counter serving toasters, waffle irons, mixers, and other appliances. These circuits are also used for home workshops.
- Individual appliance circuits used for major appliances that require large amounts of electricity, such as range-ovens, washers, dryers, and water heaters.
- Equipment circuits that furnish power to motor-driven equipment.
- Dedicated circuits for computers and other special equipment that cannot tolerate voltage fluctuations or interruptions.

## Circuit Calculations

Calculations for circuits should be made by the electrical contractor if the number of circuits has not been indicated on the drawings or in the specifications. Circuits serving lights and small appliances usually are planned to serve 2400 watts (20 amps × 120 volts = 2400 watts). These circuits normally are wired with #12 gage wire.

Circuits serving individual appliances would be wired with a size of wire and circuit breaker or fuse to safely carry the current required by the appliance. For example, an individual circuit for a 240 volt range-oven using 12,000 watts would require at least a 50 amp circuit (12,000 watts/ 240 volts = 50 amps).

This circuit would be sized at 60 amps, using a #6 gage wire.

# Remote Control and Low-Voltage Systems

The use of a low-voltage (24 volts) wiring system makes it possible to control the switching of any light or outlet in a building from any location in the building. The lights or outlets are wired using standard wire sizes of #12 or #14 wire. The switches are operated through a low-voltage system using bell wire. The switch (located anywhere in the building) in the low-voltage system activates a *relay* (electrically-operated switch) at the outlet, which turns the device ON or OFF. This system is gaining popularity because of its flexibility. Low-voltage (12 or 24 volts) wiring for doorbells or chimes can be wired with bell wire.

# Electrical Codes

It is the architect's responsibility, with the assistance of his consulting engineers, to design a building to meet existing codes. This includes the provisions of the NEC and any state or local codes. In the case of residential or light commercial buildings where no detailed electrical diagram or specifications are provided, the electrical subcontractor or individual is responsible for meeting the provisions of the codes.

# Types and Sizes of Conductors

Conductors (wires) in building projects are specified as copper. Aluminum is also used, but on the exterior of the building only. Copper is a more efficient conductor. Sizes of wire are designated by gage numbers based on the diameter of the wire. Some wire sizes are shown in **Figure 17-8.** Note that as the size number decreases, the wire size increases. Most residential wiring calls for #12 copper wire or #10 aluminum wire. The smallest conductor permitted in branch circuits by the NEC is #14 copper. Circuits of 240 volts use #10 size copper wire. Wire sizes are increased with longer runs.

The National Electrical Code uses letters to designate the type of conductor insulation. This governs the

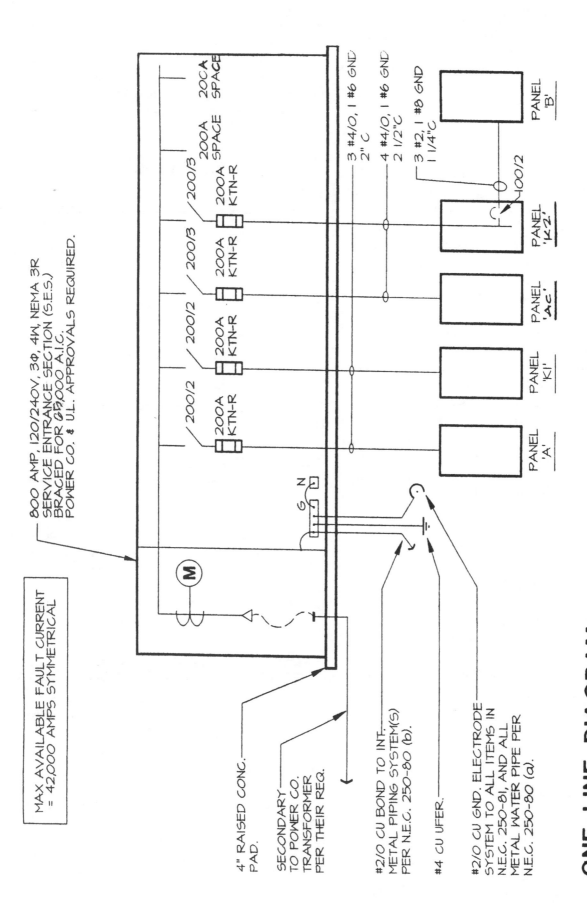

## ONE LINE DIAGRAM

NOTE: CONDUCTOR SIZES BASED ON 'XHHW' COPPER          NO SCALE

*Figure 17-7. Example of a one-line diagram. (The Fleischer Estoncia; Christensen, Cassidy, Billington, and Candeleria, Inc., Architects)*

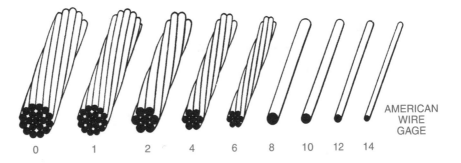

**Figure 17-8.** *Relative sizes of electrical conductors (wires).*

use of electrical conductors. Some of the more common designations are listed in **Figure 17-9.** For more specific applications, check the latest edition of the National Electrical Code.

The abbreviations *AWG* and *MCM* are found on some electrical prints. *AWG* refers to *American Wire Gage,* which is a means of specifying wire diameter. *MCM* refers to *thousand circular mills,* which designates the thickness of the insulation.

| TYPES OF CONDUCTOR INSULATIONS | |
|---|---|
| **LETTER DESIGNATION** | **TYPE OF INSULATION** |
| RH | Heat-Resistant Rubber |
| RHH | Heat-Resistant Rubber |
| RHW | Moisture and Heat-Resistant Rubber |
| RUH | Heat-Resistant Latex Rubber |
| RUW | Moisture-Resistant Latex Rubber |
| T | Flame-Retardant Thermoplastic |
| TW | Flame-Retardant, Moisture Resistant Thermoplastic |
| THHN | Flame-Retardant, Heat-Resistant Thermoplastic |
| THW | Flame-Retardant, Moisture- and Heat-Resistant Thermoplastic |
| THWN | Flame-Retardant Moisture- and Heat-Resistant Thermoplastic |
| XHHW | Moisture-and Heat-Resistant Cross-Linked Synthetic Polymer |
| MTW | Moisture-, Heat- and Oil-Resistant Thermoplastic |
| TFE | Extruded Polytetrafluorethylene |
| TA | Thermoplastic and Asbestos |
| MI | Mineral Insulation (Metal Sheathed) Magnesium Oxide |

**Figure 17-9.** *Types of wire and cable insulations. (National Electrical Code)*

# Conduit

*Conduit* is classified as rigid (pipe) or *electrical metallic tubing (EMT).* EMT also is referred to as *thin-wall.*

Most rigid conduit is galvanized or enameled steel with threaded joints or threadless compression fittings. Conduit comes in 10′ lengths and can be easily bent. Rigid conduit inside dimensions are nominal sizes (1″ is actually 1.049″). Rigid conduit also is available in nonmetallic materials.

Electrical metallic tubing (thin-wall) has thinner walls than rigid conduit and is more easily bent to shape. It usually is made of galvanized steel, although it is available in bronze for use in corrosive atmospheres. It is available in sizes up to 4″. Another type of conduit is called *greenfield.* It is a flexible metallic conduit more easily routed in construction.

Conductors also can be run through metal or plastic surface raceways (channels) with snap-on covers. Raceways are also made to be placed in concrete floors that have surface-covered junction boxes at regular intervals so that electrical connections can be made where needed.

# Test Your Knowledge

*Write your answers in the spaces provided.*

_____ 1. With regards to electrical construction, *NEC* stands for _____.

      A. National Electric Company
      B. Nominal Electrical Conductor
      C. Negative Electric Circuit
      D. National Electrical Code
      E. None of the above.

_____ 2. A _____ is used to connect a distribution panel to a light.

      A. receptacle
      B. conductor
      C. relay
      D. GFCI
      E. None of the above

_____ 3. A ground fault circuit interrupter should be installed in a _____.

      A. bathroom
      B. closet
      C. overhead light
      D. lighting panel
      E. None of the above.

_____ 4. For interior wiring, _____ wire is normally used.

      A. aluminum
      B. steel
      C. copper
      D. brass
      E. None of the above.

_____ 5. For exterior wiring, _____ wiring can be used.

      A. aluminum
      B. steel
      C. tungsten
      D. titanium
      E. None of the above.

_____ 6. A lighting schedule is needed on any drawing that includes a permanently-mounted lamp. (True or False?)

_____ 7. A panel schedule includes a list of all the circuits running from the box. (True or False?)

_____ 8. Electrical plans show the precise locations where conduit is to be run. (True or False?)

_____ 9. An ampere is a measure of electrical power. (True or False?)

_____ 10. A wire carrying 12 volts is considered a low-voltage wire. (True or False?)

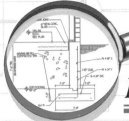

**Print Reading Activity 17–1**

## Residential Electrical Prints

*Refer to Print 17-1 from the Large Prints supplement to answer the following questions.*

1. What type of wiring is to be used on the job?

_____

2. What type of switches and receptacles are to be supplied?

_____

3. What type of switches control the lights at the end of the dining room?

_____

4. How are the ceiling lights in the dining room controlled?

_____

5. How many wall-mounted surface fixtures are there?_____

6. Explain what is required at A in the living room.

_____

7. What type fixture is at B?

_____

8. The light above the stair landing is of what type, and how is it controlled?

_____

_____

9. What type of light is at C, and where is it controlled?

_____

_____

10. Who is to supply the light fixtures? Who is to install?

_____

_____

**Print Reading Activity 17–2**
# Commercial Electrical Prints

*Refer to Prints 17-2a and 17-2b from the Large Prints supplement to answer the following questions.*

1. Which circuits serve the following

   A. Water heater _____

   B. Dwyer kitchen unit _____

   C. Receptacles in safe deposit booths _____

   D. Electric drinking fountain _____

   E. Weatherproof receptacle on column south of the building _____

2. What is "8" in the lounge? _____

3. What circuit serves the accounting machines on the teller line? _____

4. Power is brought to the vault by which circuit? _____

5. What type of light fixtures are called for at D, and on what circuit are they?

   _____

   _____

6. What is to be done about the fixture at E?

   _____

   _____

7. What lights are to be provided for Drive-In-Teller Canopy, and where is the control switch?

   _____

   _____

8. Fill in the following information about the lights on the column on the south walk:

   A. Type _____

   B. Where positioned _____

   C. What circuit _____

   D. How controlled _____

9. Where is the conduit (circuit 33) at H run?

   _____

   _____

10. What is the fixture at J, and where is it positioned?

   _____

   _____

# Masonry Prints

## Technical Terms

| | |
|---|---|
| Ashlar | Face brick |
| Backing wall | Fire brick |
| Bond beam | Flashing |
| Cavity wall | Grout |
| Common brick | Isolation joint |
| Composite wall | Lintel |
| Concrete masonry unit | Mortar |
| (CMU) | Single wythe wall |
| Construction joint | Stretchers |
| Expansion joints | Veneer walls |

## Learning Objectives

After completing this unit, you will be able to:
- Identify several types of masonry walls
- Describe masonry materials
- Recognize symbols used on drawings to represent masonry

Masonry structures are made of a number of smaller units held together with a bonding material known as *mortar.* In this unit, you will study types of masonry construction and learn how each type lends itself to simplified construction procedures and a variety of design textures.

Various masonry walls are shown in **Figure 18-1.**

## Masonry Materials

There are two basic components in masonry construction: masonry units and mortar. Masonry units are manufactured as brick, concrete block, stone, and clay tile. Mortar is a cementitious material that bonds the individual units together.

## Brick

Brick walls can be laid up as *single wythe walls* of 8″ or more in thickness. These can be solid or have two or more cells in them. Sometimes the cells of the brick are filled with granular insulation.

*Composite walls* are used in commercial construction. The *face brick* is placed in front of less expensive concrete block, hollow brick, or structural clay tile. The face brick is normally used to improve the appearance of the wall. The *backing wall* provides the structural support for the building.

*Cavity walls* consist of two wythes separated by a cavity. The cavity reduces the transfer of moisture, heat, and sound. The two wythes are tied together with reinforcing wire. The surface of the rear brick adjacent to the cavity is *parged* (coated with mortar) to provide additional waterproofing. Metal flashing is installed to collect moisture and drain it outdoors through weep holes in the mortar.

*Veneer walls* are similar to composite walls. In both walls, face brick is used to hide the actual support structure. In composite walls, that support structure is another type of masonry block. With veneer walls, the support structure is some type of frame.

### Brick Symbols

Brick is indicated on plan and section drawings with 45° crosshatch lines. For *common brick,* the lines are widely-spaced; for face brick, the spacing is narrower. See **Figure 18-2.** *Fire brick* is shown on plan drawings with the usual 45° lines indicating brick, plus vertical lines that designate it as fire brick.

On elevation drawings, brick normally is shown by horizontal lines. A note identifies the type of brick. Some architects only draw horizontal lines around the outer surface of brick walls.

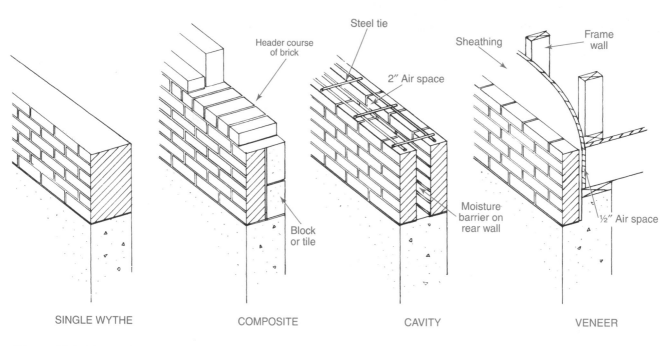

**Figure 18-1.** Types of masonry walls.

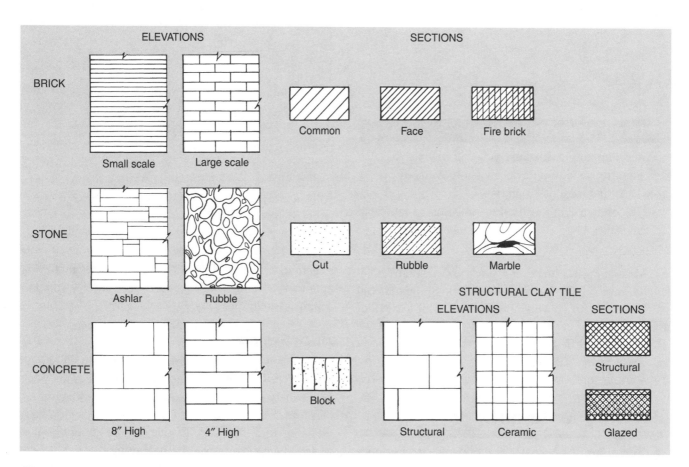

**Figure 18-2.** Masonry material symbols.

## Brick Bonds

There are several types of brick bonds, so construction workers should be familiar with those more widely used. A *bond* is the brick-laying pattern. Bonds are designed to improve appearance, add strength, or tie a wythe wall to a backing wall.

The bonds most widely used are common bond, running bond, English bond, English cross bond, Flemish bond, and stacked bond. See **Figure 18-3.**

When bricks are laid end to end in a course, they are called *stretchers.* A running bond contains only stretchers.

In some bonds, such as the common bond (sometimes called American bond), every sixth or seventh course is turned 90°. This is done to improve appearance or to tie the face brick with the backing wall. Bricks laid in this manner are called a header course.

## Brick Positions

Bricks can be positioned in different ways. These positions are used by the architect to develop a design or style in the building, as well as to add to the structural strength of the brickwork. Each position has a name that identifies it. For example, the most common position is the stretcher, **Figure 18-4,** which is laid in a flat

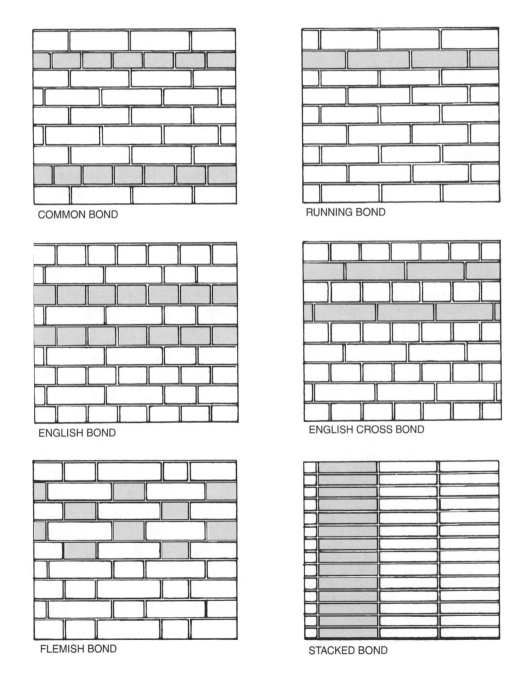

COMMON BOND

RUNNING BOND

ENGLISH BOND

ENGLISH CROSS BOND

FLEMISH BOND

STACKED BOND

*Figure 18-3.* *Different bonds vary the appearance of brick structures.*

position, lengthwise with the wall. Bricks in stretcher positions make up a large portion of most walls.

## Concrete Block

Concrete block comes in many varieties: plain, colored, special designs, and slump block, which simulates adobe brick or stone. See **Figure 18-5.** Concrete block, like brick, can be laid in a variety of bond patterns to produce strength as well as a design effect.

A *concrete masonry unit (CMU)* is the most popular variety of concrete block. Including a mortar joint, a CMU is 8″ high, 8″ deep, and 16″ long.

### Concrete Block Symbols

Symbols for concrete block in plan and section views are the same as concrete with the addition of lines crosswise of the run, **Figure 18-2.** The elevation view symbol for concrete block is the same as poured concrete with lines added to represent the block pattern.

## Stone

Stone masonry can be laid in solid walls of stone or in composite walls backed with concrete block or tile. It is also used as a veneer. Stone walls are classified according to shape and surface finish of the stone, such as rubble, ashlar, and cut stone.

*Rubble* consists of stones as they come from the quarry or are gathered from a field or stream. Such stones can be smooth with rounded edges or rough and angular. **Figure 18-6** illustrates patterns of rubble stone masonry. The random rubble wall consists of stones laid in an irregular pattern with varying sizes and shapes. Other rubble patterns are coursed, mosaic, and strip.

*Ashlar* stones are squared stones that have been laid in a pattern but not cut to dimensions, **Figure 18-6.** There are several ashlar patterns:

- **Regular:** Uniform continuous height.
- **Stacked:** Tends to form columns.
- **Broken Range:** Squared stones of different sizes laid in uniform courses, but broken range within a course.
- **Random Range:** Neither course nor range remain uniform.
- **Random Ashlar:** Course is not uniform and ends are broken, not square.

*Cut stones,* also known as dimensional stones, are cut and finished at the mill to meet the specifications of a particular construction job. Each stone is numbered for location. Unlike ashlar masonry, which is laid largely at the design of the mason, cut stones are laid according to the design of the architect.

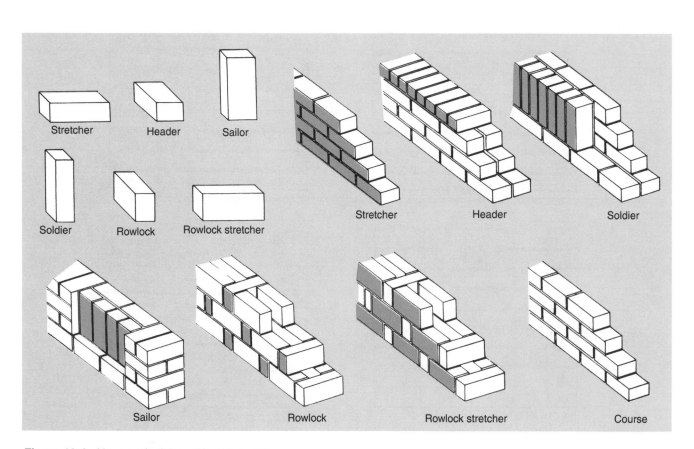

*Figure 18-4. Names of brick positions in a wall.*

**Figure 18-5.** *This type of concrete block is called* slump block. *(National Concrete Masonry Association)*

# Masonry Accessories

Besides the masonry units and mortar, additional details are needed in masonry construction. Bond beams, joints, lintels, and flashing are needed to complete a wall.

## Bond Beams

Concrete masonry walls are usually reinforced horizontally and vertically by constructing a reinforced beam or column within the wall. This is done by pouring *grout* (a watery concrete mixture) around reinforcing steel inserted in the units. Special channel blocks are used to form the horizontal bond beams, using reinforcing steel and mortar or grout. Vertical pilasters or *bond beams* are formed by inserting reinforcing bars in a vertical cell after the wall is laid, then filling the cell with grout.

## Lintels

*Lintels,* made of steel or reinforced concrete, are members placed in masonry walls above door and window openings. Lintels are supported on either side of the opening. They can be made of precast concrete, steel, or other materials. The door and window schedule will often include the size and type of lintel used.

## Joints

Joints are specified to control movement of materials and cracks in surfaces. Isolation, control, and

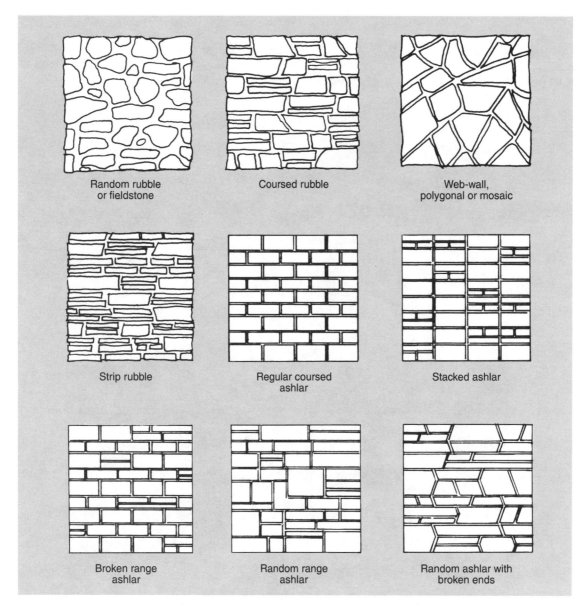

*Figure 18-6.* Stone masonry walls.

construction joints compensate for movement due to moisture or thermal changes, **Figure 18-7.**

There are several types of joints:

- An *isolation joint* is formed of molded material and is suitable for floating slabs against walls or around pilasters.
- A *tooled control joint* is formed using a tool and a straightedge. The joint is suitable for open areas such as walks, drives, floors, and pads.
- A *sawed control joint* is formed by a saw kerf. This joint is used in the same instances as a tooled control joint.
- A *construction joint* is located at the edge of a slab. It is formed by a wood or metal key against a bulkhead. The joint is painted, oiled, or treated with curing compound to prevent the next slab from binding at the joint.

Buildings must be designed for the effects of thermal expansion and contraction, which cause materials to move. All building materials react in their own way to changes in temperature and moisture absorption. *Expansion joints* are designed to absorb this change in movement of materials.

Expansion joints in vertical surfaces are usually butt joints between two bricks. A strip of flexible material, such as bitumen felt, is used as an expansion joint also.

## Flashing

*Flashing* is a wide strip of weather-resistant metal, such as aluminum, copper, or galvanized iron. It is used to prevent the penetration of water in joints. Flashing is installed over joints, so that water cannot penetrate the wall.

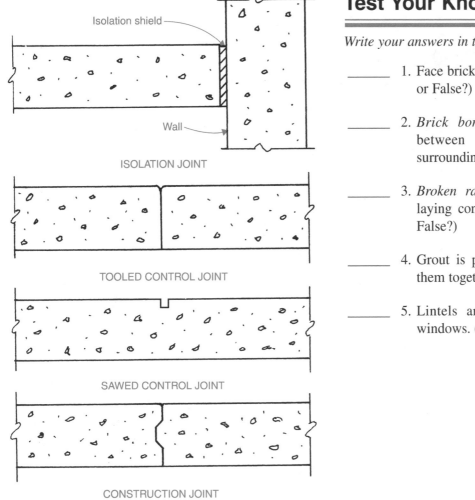

**Figure 18-7.** *Various joints used in concrete construction.*

Labels within figure:
- Isolation shield
- Wall
- ISOLATION JOINT
- TOOLED CONTROL JOINT
- SAWED CONTROL JOINT
- CONSTRUCTION JOINT

# Test Your Knowledge

*Write your answers in the spaces provided.*

_____ 1. Face brick is used in a veneer wall. (True or False?)

_____ 2. *Brick bond* refers to the connection between a brick and the mortar surrounding it. (True or False?)

_____ 3. *Broken range* is a pattern used when laying concrete masonry units. (True or False?)

_____ 4. Grout is placed between bricks to hold them together. (True or False?)

_____ 5. Lintels are located above doors and windows. (True or False?)

## Print Reading Activity 18–1
# *Masonry Residence*

*Refer to Prints 18-1a, 18-1b, and 18-1c from the Large Prints Supplement to answer the following questions*

1. What is the scale of:
   A. The floor plan
   B. The transverse section

   1. A. _____
      B. _____

2. Give the dimensions for the following:
   A. Foundation exterior length
   B. Foundation exterior width
   C. Exterior length from stud face to stud face
   D. Exterior width from stud face to stud face

   2. A. _____
      B. _____
      C. _____
      D. _____

3. Give the distance from the stud face at corner A of the house to:
   A. Center of garage door opening.
   B. Stud face at B
   C. Center of living room window opening
   D. Center of front door opening
   E. Center of opening for garage side door

   3. A. _____
      B. _____
      C. _____
      D. _____
      E. _____

4. Give the distance from the stud face at corner C to:
   A. Center of opening for rear window of bedroom
   B. Family room door center opening

   4. A. _____
      B. _____

5. What material is used for the exterior wall?

   5. _____

6. What type masonry unit construction is the exterior wall?

   6. _____

7. How much air space is to be provided between the masonry and wall sheathing?

   7. _____

8. How far below the top of the foundation wall is the recess for the stone veneer?

   8. _____

9. What is the overall plan size of the fireplace and barbecue (excluding the hearth)?

9. _____

10. What are the dimensions of the hearth?

10. _____

11. What material is used for the fireplace exterior?

11. _____

12. What material is used to line the combustion chamber?

12. _____

13. What material is used as backup for the stone and fire brick?

13. _____

14. Give the size of the lintel used across the opening of:
    A. The fireplace
    B. The barbecue

14. A. _____
    B. _____

15. What are the dimensions of the fireplace opening:
    A. Height
    B. Width
    C. Depth

15. A. _____
    B. _____
    C. _____

**Print Reading Activity 18–2**
# Masonry Office Building

*Refer to Prints 18-2a and 18-2b from the Large Prints supplement to answer the following questions.*

1. How many linear feet of masonry wall are needed for the perimeter of the building (rounded to the nearest 10′)?

1. _____

2. What is the size of the block?

2. _____

3. What reinforcement is provided in the top of the north wall?

3. _____

4. How are the masonry walls connected to the roof and ceiling framing?

4. _____

_____

_____

5. What size are the anchor bolts?

5. _____

6. What is the anchor bolt spacing?

6. _____

7. What covers the exterior surface of the block walls?

7. _____

8. How many brick courses would be needed in an 8′–0″ tall wall?

8. _____

9. What size steel beam is used above the overhead doors?

9. _____

10. How many expansion joints are needed in the wall perimeter?

10. _____

# Welding Prints

## Technical Terms

American Welding
  Society (AWS)
Arrow side
Basic weld symbol
Contour symbol
Field weld symbol
Finish symbol
Groove angle

Melt-through symbol
Other side
Reference line
Spot weld
Tail
Weld all-around
  symbol
Weld dimensions

## Learning Objectives

After completing this unit, you will be able to:
* Identify different portions of a welding symbol
* Explain weld details based on the welding symbol on a print

Welding is one of the principal means of fastening members in structural steel work, **Figure 19-1.** The *American Welding Society (AWS)* has developed standard procedures for using symbols to indicate the location, size, strength, geometry, and details of a weld. The welding symbols studied in this unit will assist you in reading and interpreting drawings involving welding processes.

## Welding Symbols

It is important to distinguish between the *weld symbol* and the *welding symbol*. The weld symbol indicates the specific type of weld. The welding symbol consists of the weld symbol and the following elements:

* The *reference line* is the horizontal line portion of a welding symbol, **Figure 19-2.** It has an

**Figure 19-1.** A welder at work.

arrow at one end and a tail at the other. In some instances, the reference line may be vertical.

* An arrow is used to connect the welding symbol reference line to one side of the joint to be welded. This is considered the *arrow side* of the joint. The side opposite the arrow is termed the *other side* of the joint.

* Notes are placed within the *tail* for designating the welding specification, process, or other reference. See **Figure 19-3.**

* The *basic weld symbols* for various types of welds are shown in **Figure 19-4.** If the symbol is above the reference line, the weld is placed on the arrow side of the joint. If the symbol is below the reference line, the weld is made on the other side of the joint. If both symbols are present, the

weld is made on both sides of the joint. See **Figure 19-5.** A more comprehensive list of weld symbols and their applications are shown in Section 7, *Reference.*

- *Weld dimensions* are drawn on the same side of the reference line as the weld symbol, **Figure 19-6(A).** When the dimensions are covered by a general note, the welding symbol need not be dimensioned, **Figure 19-6(B).** When both welds have the same dimensions, one or both can be dimensioned, **Figure 19-6(C).** The pitch of staggered intermittent welds is shown to the right of the length of the weld, **Figure 19-6(D).**

Other supplementary symbols used with the welding symbol are discussed under the following:

- A *contour symbol* next to the weld symbol indicates fillet welds that are to be flat-faced,

**Figure 19-7(A);** convex, **Figure 19-7(B);** or concave-faced, **Figure 19-7(C).**

- The *groove angle,* **Figure 19-8(A),** is shown on the same side of the reference line as the weld symbol. The size (depth) of groove welds is shown to the left of the weld symbol, **Figure 19-8(B).** The root opening of groove welds, **Figure 19-8(C),** is shown inside the weld symbol.

- *Spot welds* are specified by their diameter, **Figure 19-9(A);** strength in pounds, **Figure 19-9(B);** pitch (center-to-center), **Figure 19-9(C);** and number of welds, **Figure 19-9(D).**

- The *weld all-around symbol,* **Figure 19-10,** indicates that the weld extends completely around a joint.

- The *field weld symbol,* **Figure 19-11,** consists of a small line and triangle originating at the intersection of the reference line and arrow. This symbol identifies welds to be made at the construction site, rather than in the assembly shop.

- A *melt-through symbol* indicates the welds where 100% joint or member penetration is required in welds made from one side. See **Figure 19-12(A).** When melt-through welds are to be finished by machining or some other process, a contour symbol is added, **Figure 19-12(B).**

- A *finish symbol* indicates the finishing method to be used (C = chipping, G = grinding, M = machining, R = rolling, H = hammering). See **Figure 19-12(B).**

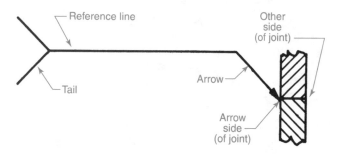

*Figure 19-2. Basic welding symbol.*

*Figure 19-3. Tail section designating arc welding.*

| Groove | | | | | | | |
|---|---|---|---|---|---|---|---|
| Square | ‖ Scarf* | V | Bevel | U | J | Flare-V | Flare-bevel |
|  |  |  |  |  |  |  |  |

| Fillet | Plug or slot | Spot or projection | Seam | Back or backing | Surfacing | Flange | |
|---|---|---|---|---|---|---|---|
|  |  |  |  |  |  | Edge | Corner |
|  |  |  |  |  |  |  |  |

*Used for brazed joints only

*Figure 19-4. Basic weld symbols. (American Welding Society)*

ARROW SIDE          OTHER SIDE          BOTH SIDES

**Figure 19-5.** *Location of welds.*

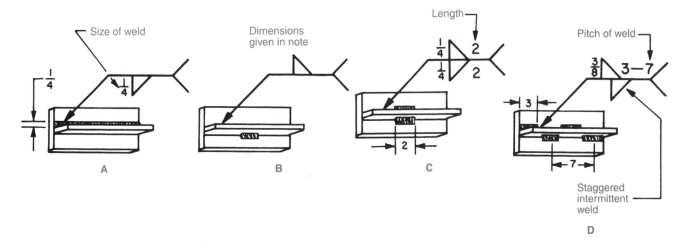

**Figure 19-6.** *Examples of weld dimensions.*

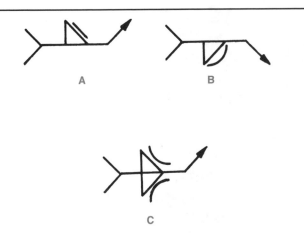

**Figure 19-7.** *Contour symbols.*

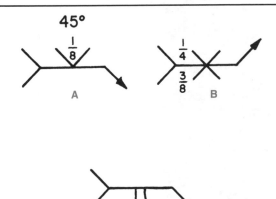

**Figure 19-8.** *Groove symbols.*

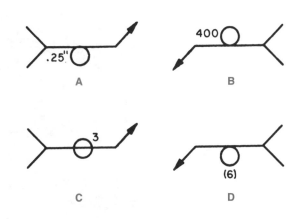

**Figure 19-9.** *Spot weld symbols.*

**Figure 19-10.** *The weld all-around symbol is a small circle around the intersection of the reference line and the arrow.*

**Figure 19-11.** *Field weld symbol*

A                    B

*Figure 19-12.* *Melt-through symbol.*

# Test Your Knowledge

*Write your answers in the spaces provided.*

_____ 1. The American Welding Society develops welding standards. (True or False?)

_____ 2. On the welding symbol, the arrow touches the tail. (True or False?)

_____ 3. A weld symbol above the reference line signifies a weld on the arrow side of the joint. (True or False?)

_____ 4. If a weld is to be made in the field (at the site), a note must be included within the tail. (True or False?)

_____ 5. The size of the weld does not need to be included within the welding symbol. (True or False?)

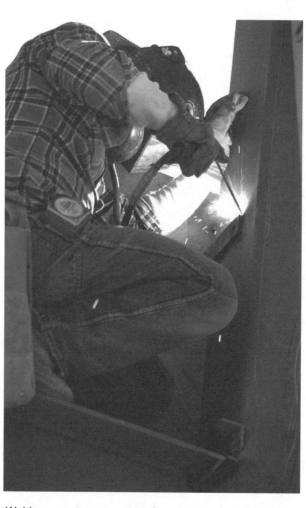

*Welders must wear protective masks and clothing to prevent injuries from heat and sparking.*

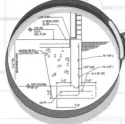

## Print Reading Activity 19–1
# *Industrial Welding Prints*

*Refer to Prints 19-1a, 19-1b, and 19-1c from the Large Prints supplement to answer the following questions.*

1. Give the weld specification for joining the lateral bracing to the rafters.

   _____

   _____

2. How is the clip plate fastened to the rafter?

   _____

   _____

3. Give the weld specification for joining the rafter to the center column.

   _____

   _____

4. Give the dimensions of the bar stock used to form part 5-6. What type weld is required?

   _____

   _____

5. What weld is required for joining parts 5-5 and 5-6?

   _____

6. Give the size of the steel channels used to construct the center column.

   _____

7. What type and size beam is used for rafter 6-14?

   _____

8. What is the number of the gusset used for rafter clip 6-10?

   _____

9. How are the gussets to be welded in the rafter clips?

   _____

   _____

10. What is the weld specification for joining the rafter clips to the girders?

    _____

    _____

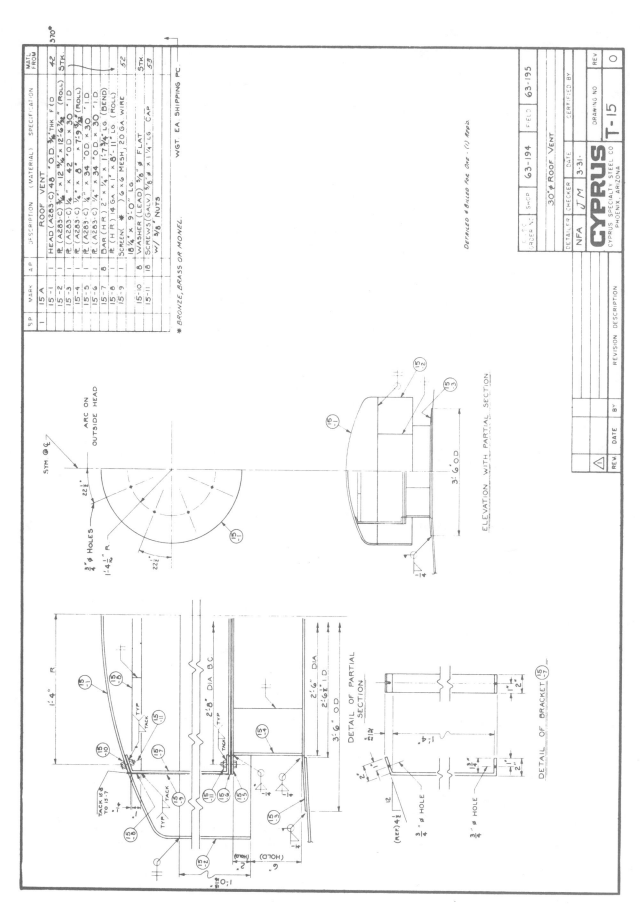

*Figure 19-13. Roof vent welding print studied in Activity 19-2.*

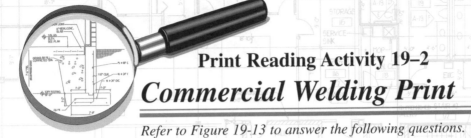

**Print Reading Activity 19–2**

# Commercial Welding Print

*Refer to Figure 19-13 to answer the following questions.*

1. Give the name and drawing number of the assembly.

   _____

   _____

2. What is part number 15-1, and what size is it?

   _____

   _____

3. Give the weld specification for joining pans 15-1 and 15-2.

   _____

   _____

4. Give the weld specification for joining parts 15-3 and 15-4.

   _____

   _____

5. What is the size of part 15-4?

   _____

6. How is part 15-4 to be welded to 15-5?

   _____

   _____

7. What is part 15-9? To what and how is it to be welded?

   _____

   _____

8. Machine screws are used to hold the brackets supporting the head. How many brackets are there, and how are the nuts to be held in place?

   _____

   _____

9. What type weld is used to fasten part 15-8 to the brackets?

   _____

   _____

10. Give the specification for welding the Roof Vent to the Tank.

   _____

   _____

# Section 5

# Estimating

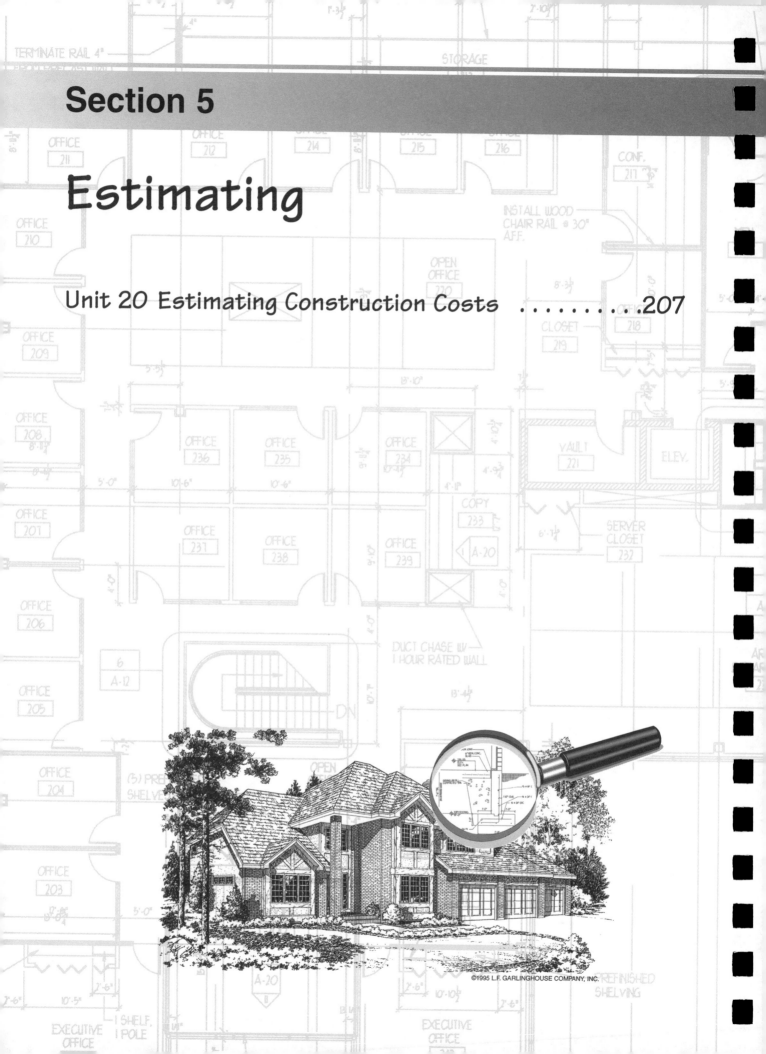

©1995 L.F. GARLINGHOUSE COMPANY, INC.

# Estimating Construction Costs

## Technical Terms

Approximate method     Takeoff
Detailed method

## Learning Objectives

After completing this unit, you will be able to:
- Use the approximate and detailed methods of estimating
- Recognize the proper method for a given situation

Estimating the cost of a construction job is one of the most important operations in a contracting business. If the estimator is careless and misses items that are included in the contract or does not compute accurately, the business could suffer a severe loss. If some items are included more than once (by carelessness or by overlapping subcontractor bids), the contractor may bid too high and lose the job to competition.

Estimating can be a relatively simple procedure. A systematic approach must be used. Reasonable care must be given to the details of preparing the estimate. In this unit, you will have an opportunity to study the general procedure used in estimating building costs.

## Estimating Methods

There are several ways to estimate the costs for a project. Broadly classified, these are called the approximate and detailed methods. Each has a place in construction.

## Approximate Method

The *approximate method* is used by architects or contractors to determine a *rough estimate* of cost. The number of square or cubic feet in a construction project is multiplied by the cost per unit to get an approximate cost.

The accuracy of the estimate is affected by many variables. A more accurate estimate will result if the following are true:
- The cost per unit was arrived at on a sound basis of experience
- Costs have not increased since the unit cost was established (or an appropriate increase is included).
- The construction project to be built is nearly identical to the previous one being compared.

The approximate method of estimating is used in helping an owner decide whether or not to build. This method is usually used early in the project planning stages when drawing and specifications are incomplete.

## Detailed Method

The *detailed method* is the only sound basis of cost estimation when the project is unique in structure, size, site, geographic area, or any other aspect. The detailed method involves:
- A careful study of the completed prints and specifications.
- Creating *takeoffs* (lists) of all material costs, labor costs, equipment costs (depreciation or rental fees), energy costs, overhead, and profit.

### Steps in Preparing a Detailed Estimate

The following steps will assist you in developing a systematic approach to detailed estimates:

1. Study the construction prints.

2. Study the construction specifications.

3. Create labor and material takeoffs (this usually follows the headings of the specifications).

4. Price labor and materials and calculate total costs.

5. Add other costs.
   A. Fees for permits.
   B. Utilities and fuel—equipment fuel, energy for tools, electric, gas, telephone, water and sewer hookups.
   C. Insurance protection for workers and materials.
   D. Overhead for business or office operation.
   E. Profit for job.

## Forms for Preparing a Detailed Estimate

Most contractors develop sets of forms that suit their particular need in preparing an estimate. **Figure 20-1** shows a portion of a typical Estimate Takeoff and Cost Sheet. For clarification, sample entries have been made on the sheet under the various headings. Extra copies of the estimate sheet appear in the Section 7, *Reference*.

## Checking a Detailed Estimate

Having completed a detailed estimate, the estimator should carefully check through the prints and specifications for all items in the contract. Then, if all things have been considered, the estimate should be checked by the approximate method, preferably by another person. The cost can be roughly compared to a similar local project that has already been completed. This manner of checking will help avoid any serious loss due to omission of an item or an error in calculations.

### ESTIMATE TAKEOFF AND COST SHEET

| Item No. | Item Identification | Location on Job | Cost | | | Total Cost |
| --- | --- | --- | --- | --- | --- | --- |
| | | | Labor | Material | Equipment | |
| 02100 | Site preparation | Lot No. 163 | $350 | | $150 | $500 |
| 03300 | Concrete slab (Job Performed) | Driveway (Identify with Project) | $500 | $325 | $75 | $900 |
| | (Number assigned to an item) | | | | | |
| 950 | Amount of bid | | | | | $185,275.00 |

Project:_____

**Figure 20-1.** *Form suitable for estimating the cost of construction of houses and light commercial building projects.*

# Print Reading Activity 20–1

# *Estimating Construction Costs*

*Refer to Prints 20-1a through 20-1f from the Large Prints supplement to answer the following questions. Use the detailed method of estimating. Include all costs except the price of the lot.*

*Compute labor and materials for the entire job or only those jobs you will directly perform or supervise and get cost estimates on those phases you plan to subcontract. Whichever plan your instructor directs you to follow, you are responsible for the estimate of costs for the entire project.*

*The following outline will help you in organizing the estimate.*

## Outline for Preparing a Detailed Estimate

1. Prepare a cost estimate using the form "Estimate Takeoff and Cost Sheet" shown in Figure 20-2. Extra forms appear in the Section 7, *Reference*.

2. Consider each of the following items, and enter your estimates on the cost estimate form.

   A. Plans and specs
   B. Building permits and fees
   C. Utilities
   D. Excavation and fill
   E. Concrete footings, foundations, floors
   F. Unit masonry
   G. Steel beams and columns
   H. Framing lumber
   I. Finish lumber
   J. Hardware
   K. Roofing
   L. Windows and screens
   M. Doors and screens
   N. Electric wiring
   O. Electric fixtures
   P. Sheet metal ducts and gutters
   Q. Air conditioning
   R. Plumbing
   S. Insulation
   T. Gypsum board
   U. Cabinets
   V. Counter tops
   W. Tile
   X. Floor sanding
   Y. Painting and decorating
   Z. Glazing and mirrors
   AA. Floor coverings
   AB. Window cleaning
   AC. Built-ins and accessories
   AD. Range-oven
   AE. Vent hood
   AF. Dishwasher
   AG. Garbage disposal
   AH. Tub-shower enclosures
   AI. Fireplace mantel
   AJ. Clean up
   AK. Insurance protection

   In addition to these items, you may want to consider business overhead, finance charges, and profit on the job.

3. The list of materials that follows was prepared by the Garlinghouse Plan Service. It includes all items except nails, screws, paints, caulking, flashing, hardware, and electrical, plumbing, and air conditioning materials. Use this list as a basis of your estimate, adding the other items omitted here and items other than materials listed under Step 2.

4. When you have completed your detailed estimate of costs, check your estimate by using the approximate method. Your instructor will assist you in arriving at an approximate cost per unit for your area.

## ESTIMATE TAKEOFF AND COST SHEET

Project _____

| Item No. | Item Identification | Location on Job | Cost | | | Total Cost |
|---|---|---|---|---|---|---|
| | | | Labor | Material | Equipment | |
| | | | | | | |

*Figure 20-2.* *Estimating form for Activity 20-1.*

# Materials List
## Plan No. 350
## Garlinghouse Plan Service

| | |
|---|---|
| 54 | 4×8×16 solid concrete blocks for exterior walls |
| 1600 | Norman bricks for terrace wall |
| 7000 | Norman bricks for exterior veneer |
| 21 1/2 yd³ | Concrete for basement floor slab |
| 7 yd³ | Concrete for garage floor slab and apron |
| 6 yd³ | Concrete for terrace, porch, entrance platform and steps |
| 13 yd³ | Concrete for footings |
| 57 yd³ | Concrete for foundation walls |
| 200 lin. ft. | 4″ drain tile |

### STRUCTURAL STEEL

| | |
|---|---|
| 1 | W8×17, 59′-1″ long |
| 1 | W8×17, 26′-4″ long |
| 5 | 4″ steel pipe columns 7′-2″ long with plates |
| 7 | L3×3×1/4×44″ long steel angle lintels over basement windows |
| 1 | 13 1/2″×3/8″×20′-0 3/4″ long steel plate for flitch beam |
| 1 | Complete gas vent |
| 3400 lin. ft. | No. 4 reinforcing rods |
| 3000 ft² | 6×6×W2.0×W2.0 welded wire fabric |
| 7 | 36″Ø, 24″ high galvanized steel areaways |
| 70 | 1/2″Ø, 10″ long anchor bolts |

### LUMBER

| | | |
|---|---|---|
| 5 | 2×8×8′ long | |
| 1 | 2×8×12′ long | *First Floor Joists and Headers* |
| 131 | 2×10×14′ long | |
| | | |
| 1 | 2×6×8′ long | |
| 7 | 2×6×11′ long | *Subsills* |
| 15 | 2×6×14′ long | |
| | | |
| 324 lin. ft. | 1×3 | *Cross Bridging* |
| | | |
| 14 | 2×6×10′ long | |
| 75 | 2×6×14′ long | *House Ceiling Joists* |
| 18 | 2×6×16′ long | |
| | | |
| 17 | 2×4×l0′ long | |
| 1 | 2×8×8′ long | *Porch Ceiling Joists* |
| 16 | 2×8×22′ long | |
| 8 | 2×6×12′ long | |
| | | |
| 10 | 1×6×8′ long | *Collar Beams* |
| | | |
| 14 | 2×4×16′ long | *Roof Bracing* |
| 24 | 2×4×10′ long | |
| | | |
| 4 | 2×12×14′ long | |
| 3 | 2×12×12′ long | *Wood Beams* |
| 1 | 2×12×16′ long | |
| | | |
| 8 | 6×6×7′ long | *Turned Wood Posts* |
| | | |
| 310 lin. ft. | 2×4 | *Cornice Nailing Blocks* |
| | | |
| 66 lin. ft. | 2×4 | |
| 158 lin. ft. | 2×12 | *Window and Door Headers and Sill Framing* |
| 40 lin. ft. | 2×14 | |

| | | |
|---:|---|---|
| 3 | 2×12×14′ long carriage | |
| 12 | 2×10×3′-6″ long treads | |
| 2 | 2″Ø×12′ long hand rail | *Basement Stairs* |
| 2 | 2×4×4′ long railing posts | |
| | | |
| 500 | 2×4×8′ long | |
| 11 | 2×8×8′ long | *First Floor Exterior Wall and Partition Studs* |
| | | |
| 125 | 2×4×12′ long | |
| 3 | 2×8×10′ long | *Head and Sole Plates* |
| | | |
| 8 | 2×6×8′ long | |
| 880 lin. ft. | 2×4 | *Rafter Ties* |
| | | |
| 72 | 2×4×8′ long | *Garage Studs* |
| | | |
| 18 | 2×4×12′ long | *Head and Sole Plates* |
| | | |
| 6 | 2×6×14′ long | |
| 6 | 2×6×16′ long | |
| 81 | 2×6×20′ long | *Common and Jack Rafters* |
| 56 | 2×6×22′ long | |
| | | |
| 4 | 2×8×26′ long | |
| 2 | 2×8×26′ long | *Hip Rafters* |
| | | |
| 2 | 2×8×26′ long | *Valley Rafters* |
| | | |
| 1 | 2×8×12′ long | |
| 2 | 2×8×14′ long | *Ridge Boards* |
| 1 | 2×8×16′ long | |
| 1920 ft² | 5/8″ plyscord plywood | *First Floor Sub Flooring* |
| 1760 ft² | 3/8″ plyscord plywood | *Wall Sheathing* |
| 1460 ft² | 3/8″ plyscord plywood | *Roof Sheathing* |
| 3680 ft² | 15 lb. asphalt felt | *Flooring Paper and Sheathing Paper* |
| 40 sq. | 18″×3/8″ to 3/4″ handsplit-resawn Red Cedar shakes | *Roofing material* |
| 1900 ft² | Polyethylene | *Vapor Barrier* |
| 8000 ft² | 30 lb. roofing felt | |
| 1216 ft² | 1/2″ gypsum wallboard | *Garage Walls and Ceiling Finish* |
| 192 ft² | 3/8″ plywood | *Porch Ceiling* |
| 8 | 1′-6″×3′-10″ shutters | |
| 250 lin. ft. | frieze molding | |
| 512 ft² | 3/8″ plywood | *Soffit* |
| 115 lin. ft. | 1×6 beam casing | |
| 278 lin. ft. | 1×2 fascia trim | |
| 278 lin. ft. | 1×8 fascia | |

## INTERIOR WALL AND CEILING FINISH

| | | |
|---:|---|---|
| 6784 ft² | 1/2″ gypsum wallboard | |

## MILLWORK

| | | |
|---:|---|---|
| 2 | outside door frames, openings 5-0×6-8, jambs 1 5/16″×4 3/8″ | |
| 1 | outside door frame, opening 2-8×6-8, jambs 1 5/16″ × 4 3/8″ | |
| 1 | outside door frame, opening 2-8×6-8, jambs 1 5/16″×4 1/2″ | |
| 1 | inside door frame, opening 6-0×6-8, jambs 3/4″×4 1/2″ | |
| 1 | inside door frame, opening 5-0×6-8, jambs 3/4″×4 1/2″ | |
| 5 | inside door frames, openings 4-0×6-8, jambs 3/4″×4 1/2″ | |
| 2 | inside door frames, openings 3-0×6-8, jambs 3/4″×4 1/2″ | *Doors* |
| 2 | inside door frames, openings 2-8×6-8, jambs 3/4″×4 1/2″ with stops | |
| 3 | inside door frames, openings 2-6×6-8, jambs 3/4″×4 1/2″ with stops | |
| 5 | inside door frames, openings 2-0×6-8, jambs 3/4″×4 1/2″ with stops | |
| 1 | recessed door frame, opening 2-6×6-8 | |

| | |
|---|---|
| 1 | recessed door frame, opening 2-0×6-8 |
| 1 | garage door frame, opening 18-0×7-0, jambs 3/4″×5 3/8″ with stops |
| 4 | outside entrance doors 2-6×6-8×1 3/4 |
| 1 | outside service door 2-8×6-8×1 3/4 |
| 2 | inside doors 3-0×6-8×1 3/8 |
| 3 | inside doors 2-8×6-8×1 3/8 |
| 6 | inside doors 2-6×6-8×1 3/8 |
| 16 | inside doors 2-0×6-8×1 3/8 |
| 1 | garage door 18-0×7-0×1 3/8 |
| 1 | combination door 2-8×6-8×1 1/8 |
| 4 | combination doors 2-6×6-8×1 1/8 |
| 2 | sides of door trim 6-0×6-8, 3/4× 2 1/4 |
| 4 | sides of door trim 5-0×6-8, 3/4×2 1/4 |
| 10 | sides of door trim 4-0×6-8, 3/4×2 1/4 |
| 4 | sides of door trim 3-0×6-8, 3/4×2 1/4 |
| 7 | sides of door trim 2-8×6-8, 3/4×2 1/4 |
| 8 | sides of door trim 2-6×6-8, 3/4×2 1/4 |
| 12 | sides of door trim 2-0×6-8, 3/4×2 1/4 |

## WINDOWS

All Andersen windows are to be complete with frames, sash, interior trim, exterior trim, screens, storm sash and hardware.

| | |
|---|---|
| 3 | No. 24-2432-24 Andersen Narroline D. H. window units |
| 3 | No. 2832-28 Andersen Narroline D. H. window units |
| 1 | No. 2432-24 Andersen Narroline D. H. window unit |
| 2 | No. 2832 Andersen Narroline D. H. windows |
| 3 | No. 2432 Andersen Narroline D. H. windows |
| | *Andersen Corporation, Bayport, Minnesota |
| 7 | Alum. basement units, 2 lites 15″×20″ with screens |

## CABINETS AND MISCELLANEOUS MILLWORK

| | |
|---|---|
| 14′-3″ | Kitchen base unit, 36″ high 24″ deep, complete with hardware |
| 6′-9″ | Kitchen wall unit, 30″ high 12″ deep, complete with hardware |
| 5′-9″ | Kitchen wall unit, 18″ high 12″ deep, complete with hardware |
| 2′-3″ | Kitchen oven unit, 84″ high 24″ deep, complete with hardware |
| 1 | 80″ wide 22″ deep 31″ high, lavatory cabinet complete |
| 1 | 62″ wide 22″ deep 34″ high, lavatory cabinet complete |
| 1 | 30″ wide 16″ deep 84″ high, towel cabinet complete |
| 1 | 36″ wide 24″ deep 29″ high, desk complete |
| 352 ft² | 5/8″ (C-REP.D) plywood                    *Flooring Under Vinyl* |
| 1750 | BM 25/32″×2 1/4″ clear oak T. & G. end matched   *Finished Flooring* |
| 70 lin. ft. | 1×12 closet shelving |
| 320 ft² | vinyl flooring |
| 50 ft² | slate tile |
| 540 lin. ft. | 9/16″×3″ base mold |
| 540 lin. ft. | 1/2″×3/4″ base shoe |
| 1820 ft² | 6″ thick ceiling insulation |
| 1300 ft² | 3 1/2″ thick wall insulation |

## MISCELLANEOUS ITEMS

| | |
|---|---|
| 44 lin. ft. | 1 3/8″ closet poles |

While every attempt has been made in the preparation of this material list to avoid mistakes, the maker cannot guarantee against human errors. The contractor must check all quantities, etc. and be responsible for same. Due to the different practices of contractors, variation in climatic conditions, different covering capacities of paints, wide range of hardware requirements and various local building codes and practices, no attempt has been made to figure items such as nails, screws, paint, caulking, flashing, hardware, or electrical, plumbing, and heating materials.

# Section 6

# Advanced Print Reading Projects

©1995 L.F. GARLINGHOUSE COMPANY, INC.

# Advanced Projects

This section of the text contains four comprehensive projects. Each project comprises several quizzes based on a set of drawings from the *Large Prints* supplement. Each quiz focuses on a different aspect of the building; one quiz is based on the foundation, one quiz is based on the site plan, etc.

Project A and Project B involve residential drawings. These projects will test your familiarity with the symbols and conventions used in house construction. Both projects are based on standard home designs.

Project C and Project D involve commercial drawings. Project C is based on a set of drawings for an office building. Project D is based on a combined office and warehouse. These projects are more extensive than the residential construction projects.

As you work through the projects, refer back to the appropriate units when you are unsure of an answer. Your instructor may assign additional activities using the project drawings.

©1995 L.F. GARLINGHOUSE COMPANY, INC.

*Figure A-1.* Two-story brick residence.

# Two-Story Residence

This project is based on drawings for the two-story residence shown in **Figure A-1**. This large, three bedroom, 2 1/2 bath home includes an attached 2 1/2 car garage, a study, and a three season porch. Refer to Prints A-1 through A-9 from the Large Prints supplement when working on the following activities.

**Print Reading Activity A-1**

## Foundation

1. What is the scale of the foundation plan? _____

2. Give the overall length, outside to outside, through the house in line with:
   A. Living room through the garage _____
   B. Garage through the season porch _____

3. How far does the footing for the optional fireplace extend beyond the family room? _____

4. Give the overall length of the footing (excluding the brick veneer) through the house in line with:
   A. Living room through the garage. _____
   B. Garage through the season porch. _____

5. What is the specification for these slabs:
   A. Basement _____
   _____
   B. Garage _____
   _____

6. What are the specifications for the column footings in the garage?
   _____
   _____

7. What additional requirements are given for the footings and wall below the garage doors?
   _____
   _____

8. What specifications are given for the footings for the season porch?
   _____
   _____

*The following questions refer to the alternate block foundation.*

9. Give the following information:

    A. The height of the block wall above the footing? _____

    B. The block size and type for the wall?_____

    C. The top course of a wall with a masonry ledge? _____

10. Give the size of the anchor bolt in the block wall._____

11. How is the wall to be strengthened with reinforcing bars?

    _____

    _____

12. What is the height of the wall for the crawl space?

    _____

    _____

13. What is the size of the footings for the block piers? _____

14. What size block is required for the piers and how are they reinforced?

    _____

    _____

15. How is the grade to be treated for all walls?

    _____

    _____

*Print Reading Activity A-2*
## Floor Plan

1. What is the scale of the print for the second floor plan? _____

2. Give the plate height of the first floor walls. _____

3. What is the difference in the floor level of the living room and the dining room?

   _____

4. What are the dimensions given for the layout of bedroom #3?

   _____

5. Give the door sizes at:
   A. Powder room_____
   B. Laundry _____
   C. Laundry closet_____
   D. Study _____

6. Give the size of the entry door and the size and type of the side light panels.

   _____

7. What is the rough opening size for the window in the:
   A. Kitchen _____
   B. Garage _____
   C. Master bath _____

8. What is the ceiling height in the foyer? _____

9. What size are the column rafters? _____

10. What size bracing is specified for the over framed roof areas?_____

11. What specification pertains to the hip, valley, and ridge boards?

    _____

    _____

12. What size bracing is specified for the rafters? _____

13. What is the size of the skylight specified for the master bedroom area?_____

14. What exterior materials are specified for the siding of the house? _____

15. What are the dimensions for the vanity in the master bath? _____

*Print Reading Activity A-3*
# Plumbing and Electrical

1. How many lavatories are shown on the plans?

1. _____

2. How many water closets are included in the building?

2. _____

3. What type of sink is shown in the kitchen?

3. _____

4. How many interior ceiling lights are installed on the first and second floors?

4. _____

5. How many interior wall-mounted lights are used?

5. _____

6. How many exterior lights are needed?

6. _____

7. How many exhaust fans are used?

7. _____

8. How many GFI duplex receptacles are located inside the building?

8. _____

9. How many weatherproof GFI duplex receptacles are needed?

9. _____

10. How many 3-way switches are needed in the construction?

10. _____

# Estimating

*Estimate the total construction cost using the approximate "square footage" estimate. Then, select one aspect of the construction, such as foundation, framing, interior finishes, roofing and siding, etc. and make a detailed estimate of the cost for that portion of the project. Calculate material and labor costs separately. Use the estimate sheet below.*

| | | | ESTIMATE TAKEOFF AND COST SHEET | | | | |
|---|---|---|---|---|---|---|---|

**ESTIMATE TAKEOFF AND COST SHEET**

Project _____

| Item No. | Item Identification | Location on Job | Cost | | | Total Cost |
|---|---|---|---|---|---|---|
| | | | Labor | Material | Equipment | |
| | | | | | | |

©1995 L.F. GARLINGHOUSE COMPANY, INC.

*Figure B-1.* A split-level residence.

# Split-Level Residence

This project is based on drawings for the split-level residence shown in **Figure B-1.** This three bedroom, two bath home includes a living room with 12′ ceilings and two skylights. Refer to Prints B-1 through B-7 from the Large Prints supplement to answer the following questions.

### Print Reading Activity B-1
## Foundation

1. What is the scale of the basement and foundation plan? _____

2. What are the dimensions of the foundation? _____

3. How many 3″ steel pipe columns are in the basement? _____

4. What are the size of the footings and reinforcing requirements for these columns?

   _____
   _____

5. What size piers are specified for the optional wood deck?

   _____
   _____

6. How far above the footing does the basement foundation wall extend? _____

7. How thick is the foundation wall and what material is specified? _____

8. What specifications are given regarding the anchor bolts and rebars in the wall?

   _____
   _____
   _____

9. What specifications are given for the exterior for the interior treatment of the foundation wall?

_____

_____

_____

10. Give the thickness of the foundation wall (house side) at the front porch location.

_____

11. What is the height of the garage foundation wall? _____

12. What type of drain tile is used? _____

13. Where does the drain tile empty? _____

_____

14. What is the rough opening size for the windows G in the foundation wall?_____

15. Give the specification for the basement floor. _____

_____

_____

*Print Reading Activity B-2*
## *Floor Plan*

1. Give the scale of the drawings for the:
   A. Upper floor plan _____
   B. Elevations _____
   C. Site plan_____
   D. Roof plan_____

2. What are the overall dimensions of the frame walls through the house in line with the:
   A. Master bedroom – breakfast room _____
   B. Bedroom – dining room _____
   C. Master bedroom, window seat – bedrooms 2 & 3 _____
   D. Breakfast room – dining room _____

3. Dimensions shown regarding the location of partition walls are from what part of the exterior walls to what part of the partition walls? _____

   _____

4. What size beam is called for under the bedroom and dining room joists? _____

5. What size are the floor joists and what is their spacing? _____

6. How far does the fireplace extend beyond the exterior wall? _____

7. What size stud and spacing is used in the exterior house walls?_____

8. What size stud and spacing is used in the interior partitions? _____

9. What is the ceiling height in the following areas?
   A. Dining room _____
   B. Living room (level area) _____
   C. Bedroom #2_____
   D. Entry hall_____

10. What thickness vapor barrier is to be installed at exterior walls and ceiling?_____

11. What window model number is used in the master bath? _____

12. What size doors are specified at:
    A. Front hall coat closet_____
    B. Bedrooms_____
    C. Front door _____
    D. Breakfast – porch _____

13. What framing material is to be used as headers above wall openings?_____

14. Give the height of the vanity in the master bath. _____

15. What is the size and spacing specified for the rafters? _____

16. What size ridge board is used? _____

17. What skylights are specified for the living room? _____

18. Where is the access to the optional attic crawl space located?

_____

_____

19. What type of roof material is used?

_____

_____

20. What siding is specified in these locations?
    A.  Above garage on master bedroom _____
    B.  Rear and side elevations _____

*Print Reading Activity B-3*
## Plumbing and Electrical

1. How many of each of the following fixtures are needed:
   A. Bath tubs
   B. Shower stalls
   C. Water closets
   D. Hose bibs
   E. Hot water heater

1. A. _____
   B. _____
   C. _____
   D. _____
   E. _____

2. How many exterior lights are needed?

2. _____

3. How many fans with lights are used?

3. _____

4. How many exhaust fans are required?

4. _____

5. How many smoke detectors are needed?

5. _____

6. How many single-pole switches are installed?

6. _____

7. How many 3-way switches are used?

7. _____

8. How many GFI duplex receptacles are required?

8. _____

9. How many duplex wall receptacles (non-GFI) are needed?

9. _____

10. How many waterproof duplex receptacles are installed?

10. _____

*Print Reading Activity B-4*
# Estimating

Estimate the total construction cost using the approximate "square footage" estimate. Then, select one aspect of the construction, such as foundation, framing, interior finishes, roofing and siding, etc. and make a detailed estimate of the cost for that portion of the project. Calculate material and labor costs separately. Use the estimate sheet below.

**ESTIMATE TAKEOFF AND COST SHEET**

Project _____

| Item No. | Item Identification | Location on Job | Cost | | | Total Cost |
|---|---|---|---|---|---|---|
| | | | Labor | Material | Equipment | |
| | | | | | | |

## ESTIMATE TAKEOFF AND COST SHEET

Project _____

| Item No. | Item Identification | Location on Job | Cost | | | Total Cost |
|---|---|---|---|---|---|---|
| | | | Labor | Material | Equipment | |
| | | | | | | |
| | | | | | | |
| | | | | | | |
| | | | | | | |
| | | | | | | |
| | | | | | | |
| | | | | | | |
| | | | | | | |
| | | | | | | |
| | | | | | | |
| | | | | | | |
| | | | | | | |
| | | | | | | |

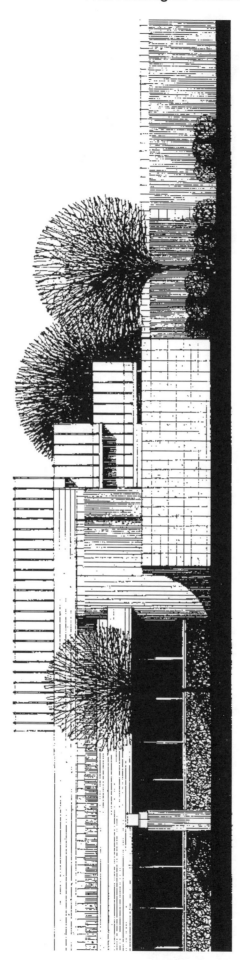

*Figure C-1.* Elevation of an office building.

# Office Building

This project is based on drawings for the office building shown in **Figure C-1.** *This one-story building has 8000 ft²* *of office space. The building houses over 25 offices, two conference rooms, and a reception area. Refer to Prints C-1* *through C-16 from the Large Prints supplement to answer the following questions.*

## Print Reading Activity C-1
## *Site Plan*

1. What is the scale of the:
   A. Site plan_____
   B. Detail site plan_____

2. Give the overall length and width of the building._____

3. What is the legal description of the location of the building?

   _____

   _____

4. What is the elevation of the finished floor? _____

5. Two curb details are provided: one is flush with the pavement and one extends 6″ above the pavement. Where is the flush curb used?

   _____

   _____

6. What type of reinforcement is used in the masonry fence north of the parking lot on the east side of the building?

   _____

   _____

7. How many new gates are required and where are they located?

   _____

   _____

8. Regarding the remodeled fence:

   A.  How far above the grade does the wall extend?_____

   B.  How is this stub wall to be finished? _____

   C.  How is the iron fence supported? _____

       _____

   D.  What type of stringers are used?_____

9.  What are the specifications for the new sidewalk to the east of the building.

     _____

     _____

10.  How many parking spaces are to be provided? How many of these are for handicapped?

     _____

     _____

*Print Reading Activity C-2*
# Foundation

1. What is the scale of the foundation plan? _____

2. Describe the footing below the south wall. _____
   _____

3. How far above the finished floor are the tops of the building walls? _____

4. How many cubic feet of concrete are needed for the footing and pier below column C8? _____

5. How many bond beams (for reinforcing) are in the walls? _____

6. What is the size and spacing of the vertical reinforcing rods in the walls?
   _____
   _____

7. How much lap is required with vertical bars in the wall?
   _____
   _____

8. What are the specifications for the floor slab?
   _____
   _____

9. How many separate areas are to have tile installed? _____

10. How far below the finished floor are piers for columns located? _____

*Print Reading Activity C-3*
# Framing

1. What is the scale of the roof plan? _____

2. What is the specification and spacing of the ceiling joists over the main building?

   _____

   _____

3. What supports the ends of the joists over the center section of the building?

   _____

4. What size are the joists in the prefab deck? What is their spacing?

   _____

5. What is the roof decking and how is it placed? _____

   _____

   _____

6. What is the purlin size for Level 1 of the entrance roof? Level 2? _____

7. Interpret the weld symbols shown in Detail 10 on Sheet 3.

   _____

   _____

8. Where is the framing section detail found for the support for A/C unit located near column C5?

   _____

9. For the 5'-0" extension over the piers on the south side of the building, what type of roofing is used?

   _____

10. What is the slope of the roof?_____

## *Floor Plan*

1. What is the scale of the floor plan? _____

2. What is the width of the waiting room? _____

3. What are the dimensions in the general manager's office? _____

4. What are the overall dimensions for the five lumber sales offices? _____

5. What is the ceiling height above the
   A. Lumber sales offices? _____
   B. General offices? _____

6. What ceiling material is specified for these offices? _____

7. What floor covering and base is indicated for the waiting room?

   _____

   _____

8. What floor covering and base is indicated for the lunch room?

   _____

   _____

9. What size is the exterior window in Conference Room I? _____

10. What sheet details the framing of doors and windows on the front of the building? _____

11. The cabinet, tile walls, and toilets are detailed on which sheet? _____

12. On the sliding window, what is the height from the floor to the stainless steel counter? _____

13. What are the riser and tread sizes on the steps behind the reception desk?

    _____

    _____

14. What material is specified for the counter tops in the lunch room? _____

15. On what sheets are the framing details for the folding doors found?

    _____

    _____

*Print Reading Activity C-5*
# HVAC

1. How many registers are supplied by HP-8?

2. How many registers return air to HP-1?

3. Where is the thermostat for HP-3 located?

4. What size are the supply ducts for HP-1?

5. What part of the building is serviced by the largest heat pump?

6. What size duct is run to locker ventilating sections?

7. What areas are serviced by HP-6?

8. Where are the combustion air louvers installed?

9. Where is the thermostat that controls the temperature in the men's locker room?

10. What is the largest duct size and where is it used?

1. _____

2. _____

3. _____

4. _____

5. _____

6. _____

7. _____

8. _____

9. _____

10. _____
_____
_____

*Print Reading Activity C-6*
## Plumbing

1. Give the manufacturer and model of water heater.

1. _____

    _____

2. What is the size of the pipe for domestic water service to the building?

2. _____

3. The main building shut-off valve is to be located within a space of _____ above ground level.

3. _____

4. What type of flush valves are used in the urinals?

4. _____

    _____

5. How many hose bibs are required?

5. _____

6. How many roof drains are there?

6. _____

7. What is the slope of all waste piping below the building?

7. _____

8. How far beneath the finished floor elevation is the waste piping leaving the building?

8. _____

9. Where does the north roof drains carry the water?

9. _____

10. How much is the condensate drain piping sloped?

10. _____

*Print Reading Activity C-7*
# Electrical

1. How many amps are required for the facility as planned at present?

1. _____

2. How many light poles are in the parking lot?

2. _____

3. Which two circuits supply the exterior lights?

3. _____

4. Four different types of exterior lights are attached to the building structure. Which manufacturers supply these lights?

4. _____

_____

5. How many lights are supplied by Circuit 12?

5. _____

6. For which three lighting circuits are wires delivered to the computer and storage room?

6. _____

7. How many exit signs are used in the building?

7. _____

8. How high above the floor is the outlet for the television in the conference room located?

8. _____

9. Which circuit provides power to the refrigerator in the lunch room?

9. _____

10. Where are the light switches for the general office located?

10. _____

*Print Reading Activity C-8*
## Estimating

*Estimate the total construction cost using the approximate "square footage" estimate. Then, select one aspect of the construction, such as foundation, framing, interior finishes, roofing and siding, etc. and make a detailed estimate of the cost for that portion of the project. Calculate material and labor costs separately. Use the estimate sheet below.*

### ESTIMATE TAKEOFF AND COST SHEET

Project _____

| Item No. | Item Identification | Location on Job | Cost | | | Total Cost |
|---|---|---|---|---|---|---|
| | | | Labor | Material | Equipment | |
| | | | | | | |

***Figure D-1.*** *Rendering of two-story office builing with attached warehouse.*

# Office and Warehouse

This project is based on drawings for the office and warehouse shown in **Figure D-1.** This building has over 15,000 ft² of office space on two floors, plus over 50,000 ft² of warehouse space. The office provides workspace for over 70 employees and contains four conference rooms, a photo studio, and a classroom. Refer to Prints D-1 through D-46 from the Large Prints supplement to answer the following questions.

*Print Reading Activity D-1*

## Site Plan

1. What is the scale of the site plan? _____

2. How wide are the parking spaces? _____

3. How thick are the concrete sidewalks? _____

4. The asphalt in the parking lot consists of two layers of material. Describe these layers.

_____

_____

_____

5. How does the asphalt in the dock areas differ from the asphalt in the parking lot?

_____

_____

_____

6. What type of reinforcement is needed for the curbing at the entrance to the parking lot?

_____

7. Along the north side of the building is a 5'-0" square concrete stoop. Why is the stoop needed?

_____

_____

_____

8. How wide is the sidewalk leading to the main (east) entrance of the office? _____

9. What slope is used for the curb ramp at the end of the sidewalk?_____

10. What is the setback distance for the front (east side) of the building? _____

*Print Reading Activity D-2*
# Architectural Drawings

1. What is the difference between the door to the vault on the first floor and the door to the vault on the mezzanine level?

   _____

   _____

   _____

2. What color are the pipe rails around the loading dock areas painted?_____

3. What type of lights are used in Room 200 (large conference room)?

   _____

4. What is the specification for the ceiling tile in the office?

   _____

   _____

   _____

5. In the stair located behind the reception area, how many risers are needed? _____

6. What is the narrowest space between racks in the warehouse?_____

7. What two sizes of overhead doors are used in the loading dock areas? _____

8. What is the elevation of the top of most of the precast wall panels?_____

9. What size are the lockers in the women's rooms? _____

10. How thick are the bathroom mirrors?_____

11. In the stairs next to the elevator, what are the dimensions of the landing? _____

12. How wide between masonry blocks is the opening for the elevator door? _____

13. How far below the first floor is the top of the slab at the bottom of the elevator pit? _____

14. What is the finish floor elevation in the warehouse?_____

15. How many large (4′×8′) skylights are in the roof?_____

16. What type of finish is used on the door to the VP Sales office? _____

17. What is the maximum distance between handrail supports on the stairs?_____

18. What color glass is used in the doors at the main (east) entrance to the office?_____

19. The walls around the vault in the office are composed of three layers. What are these layers?

_____

_____

20. In the copy area on the mezzanine level, how many wall-mounted cabinets are needed? _____

21. What is the minimum allowable width and depth for the elevator car? _____

22. What types of treads are used in the stairs?

_____

_____

23. What is used for the interior finish of skylight shafts in the office?

_____

_____

24. On the mezzanine level, what is the distance between the finished floor and the finished ceiling?

_____

25. What type of roofing system is used?

_____

_____

_____

*Print Reading Activity D-3*
## *Structural Drawings*

1. What size columns are used around the perimeter of the office? _____

2. How are joists supported by exterior precast walls?

   _____

   _____

   _____

3. What type of member is used for the majority of the framing in the canopy above the employees' entrance?

   _____

4. What is the loading dock slab specification?

   _____

   _____

   _____

5. How thick are the exterior precast wall panels?_____

6. At what elevation is the bottom of the trench foundation? _____

7. How are the roof beams supported at the east and west exterior walls?

   _____

   _____

   _____

8. What is placed above the roof joists in the warehouse?_____

9. What size is the wall footing under the office building? _____

10. What type of joists are used to support the mezzanine floor above the lunch room?_____

11. What is the change in elevation from the west edge of the loading dock slab to the trench drain?

   _____

12. How is the 1 1/2″ metal roof deck attached to the roof joists?

   _____

   _____

   _____

13. What size columns are used in the warehouse? _____

14. What is the size of the footing under the column located at column lines B and 4?_____

15. What reinforcement is included in the slab at the bottom of the elevator pit?

   _____

   _____

*Print Reading Activity D-4*
## Plumbing Drawings

1. How many connections to the storm sewers are needed?

1. _____

2. What size pipe is connected to the drinking fountains?

2. _____

3. How many roof drains (including overflow drains) are needed?

3. _____

4. How many hose bibs are needed?

4. _____

5. How many water closets are needed?

5. _____

6. Where is the water meter located?

6. _____
   _____

7. Where is the water heater located?

7. _____
   _____

8. Where is the sump located?

8. _____
   _____

9. How many cleanouts are provided in the waste piping?

9. _____

10. What size pipe is to be connected to the sanitary sewer?

10. _____

*Print Reading Activity D-5*
## HVAC Drawings

1. How many thermostats are in the warehouse? _____

2. How many exhaust fans are in the warehouse? _____

3. What type of liner is used in supply ducts? _____
_____
_____

4. Which roof-mounted HVAC units supply air to the first floor?_____
_____

5. Where is the thermostat controlling RTU-3 located?_____
_____

6. What size stack is needed for the roof-mounted heating units (UH-1)? _____

7. What is the maximum amount of air that can be supplied to the lunch room? _____

8. What is the minimum allowable distance between outdoor intake openings and exhaust openings?
_____

9. What rooms are serviced by the two EF-2 exhaust fans?
_____

10. Which units are fueled by natural gas? _____
_____

*Print Reading Activity D-6*

# Estimating

*Estimate the total construction cost using the approximate "square footage" estimate. Then, select one aspect of the construction, such as foundation, framing, interior finishes, roofing and siding, etc. and make a detailed estimate of the cost for that portion of the project. Calculate material and labor costs separately. Use the estimate sheet below.*

**ESTIMATE TAKEOFF AND COST SHEET**

Project _____

| Item No. | Item Identification | Location on Job | Cost | | | Total Cost |
|---|---|---|---|---|---|---|
| | | | Labor | Material | Equipment | |
| | | | | | | |

# Section 7

# Reference Section

©1995 L.F. GARLINGHOUSE COMPANY, INC.

# Abbreviations

## A

| | |
|---|---|
| AB | Anchor Bolt |
| ABC | Aggregate Base Course |
| ABS | Acrylonitrile Butadiene Styrene |
| AC | Alternating Current |
| ACI | American Concrete Institute |
| ACOUS | Acoustical |
| ACP | Asbestos Cement Pipe |
| ACT | Actual |
| ADD'L | Additional |
| AFF | Above Finished Floor |
| AGGR | Aggregate |
| AH | Air Handling Unit |
| AIA | American Institute of Architects |
| AIR COND | Air Conditioning |
| AISC | America Institute of Steel Construction |
| AISI | American Iron and Steel Institute |
| ALT | Alternate |
| AL | Aluminum |
| AMP | Ampere |
| AMT | Amount |
| ANSI | American National Standards Institute |
| AP | Access Panel |
| APPD | Approved |
| APPROX | Approximate |
| ARCH | Architectural |
| ASA | American Standards Association |
| ASB | Asbestos |
| ASPH | Asphalt |
| ASTM | American Society for Testing and Materials |
| AUTO | Automatic |
| AUX | Auxiliary |
| AWG | American Wire Gage |
| AV | Air Vent |
| @ | At |

## B

| | |
|---|---|
| B | Bathroom, Bottom |
| B/ | Bottom of |
| BASMT | Basement |
| BBL | Barrel(s) |
| BBR | Base Board Radiation |
| BC | Bolt Circle |
| BD | Board |
| BD FT | Board Feet |
| BEV | Beveled |
| BF | Bottom of Footing |
| BLDG | Building |
| BLK | Block |
| BLKG | Blocking |
| BLR | Boiler |
| BM | Beam, Bench Mark |
| BOT | Bottom |
| BP | Base Plate, Bedroom |
| BR | Brass |
| BRG | Bearing |
| BRK | Brick |
| BRKT | Bracket |
| BRZ | Bronze |
| BTU | British Thermal Unit |
| BUS | Busway |

## C

| | |
|---|---|
| C | Celsius |
| C or COND | Conduit |
| C/C, C to C | Center to Center |
| CAB | Cabinet |
| CB | Catch Basin |
| CD | Ceiling Diffuser |
| CEM | Cement |
| CER | Ceramic |
| CFM | Cubic Feet per Minute |
| CHAM | Chamfer |
| CHR | Chilled Water Return |
| CHS | Chilled Water Supply |
| CI | Cast Iron |
| CIP | Cast-in-Place Concrete |
| CIR | Circuit |
| CIR BKR | Circuit Breaker |
| CIRC | Circumference |
| CJ | Construction Joint, Control Joint |
| CKT | Circuit |
| CL | Center Line, Closet |
| CLG | Ceiling |
| CLK | Caulk |
| CLR | Clear |
| CMU | Concrete Masonry Unit |
| CO | Cleanout |
| COL | Column |
| COM | Common |
| COMP | Composition |
| CONC | Concrete, Concentric |
| CONN | Connection |
| CONT | Continuous |
| CONTR | Contractor |
| CP | Candle Power, Concrete Pipe |

| | |
|---|---|
| CR | Ceiling Register |
| CSK | Countersink |
| CT | Ceramic Tile |
| CU | Copper, Cubic |
| CW | Cold Water |
| CWS | Cold Water Supply |

## D

| | |
|---|---|
| DC | Direct Current |
| DEC | Decorative |
| DEG | Degree |
| DET | Detail |
| DF | Drinking Fountain |
| DH | Double-Hung |
| DIA or ∅ | Diameter |
| DIAG | Diagram, Diagonal |
| DIM | Dimension, Dimmer |
| DISC | Disconnect |
| DIV | Division |
| DMPR | Damper |
| DN | Down |
| DO | Ditto |
| DP | Duplicate |
| DR | Dining Room, Drain, Door |
| DS | Down Spout |
| DW | Dish Washer, Dry Wall |
| DWG | Drawing |
| DWL | Dowel |

## E

| | |
|---|---|
| EA | Each |
| EB | Expansion Bolt |
| EF | Exhaust Fan |
| EL, ELEV | Elevation |
| ELEC | Electric |
| ELVR | Elevator |
| EMER | Emergency |
| EMT | Electrical Metallic Tubing |
| ENAM | Enamel |
| ENC | Enclosure |
| ENGR | Engineer |
| ENT | Entrance |
| EQ | Equal |
| EQUIP | Equipment |
| EQUIV | Equivalent |
| EST | Estimate |
| EW | Each Way |
| EWC | Electric Water Cooler |
| EXC | Excavate |
| EXCL | Exclude |

| | |
|---|---|
| EXH | Exhaust |
| EXIST | Existing |
| EXP | Expansion |
| EXP JT | Expansion Joint |
| EXT | Exterior |
| EXTN | Extension |

## F

| | |
|---|---|
| F | Fahrenheit |
| F BRK | Fire Brick |
| F EXT | Fire Extinguisher |
| FAB | Fabricate |
| FAM RM | Family Room |
| FAO | Finish All Over |
| FBO | Finish by Owner Installed by General Contractor |
| FD | Floor Drain |
| FDN | Foundation |
| FDR | Feeder |
| FH | Fire Hydrant |
| FIG | Figure |
| FIN | Finish |
| FIN FL | Finish Floor |
| FIX | Fixture |
| FL | Flashing, Floor |
| FLEX | Flexible |
| FLG | Flange, Flooring |
| FLR | Floor |
| FLUOR | Fluorescent |
| FP | Fireplace |
| FR | Frame |
| FRG | Furring |
| FS | Floor sink |
| FT | Feet |
| FTG | Fitting, Footing |
| FURN | Furnish |
| FWH | Frostproof Wall Hydrant |
| FX WDW | Fixed Window |

## G

| | |
|---|---|
| GA | Gauge |
| GALV | Galvanized |
| GAR | Garage |
| GC | General Contractor |
| GFCI | Ground Fault Circuit Interrupter |
| GI | Galvanized Iron |
| GL | Glass, Glazed |
| GND | Ground |
| GR | Grade |

| | |
|---|---|
| GRAN | Granular |
| GRTG | Grating |
| GYP | Gypsum |
| GYP BD | Gypsum Board |

## H

| | |
|---|---|
| H | Hall |
| HB | Hose Bib |
| HC | Heating Coil |
| HDW | Hardware |
| HDWD | Hardwood |
| HEX | Hexagonal |
| HGT | Height |
| HM | Hollow Metal |
| HOR | Horizontal |
| HP | Horsepower, High Point |
| HR | Hour |
| HTR | Heater |
| HU | Humidifier |
| HVAC | Heating and Ventilating and Air Conditioning |
| HW | Hot Water |
| HWR | Heating Water Return |
| HYD | Hydraulic |
| HZ | Hertz |

## I

| | |
|---|---|
| ID | Inside Diameter |
| IF | Inside Face |
| INCAND | Incandescent |
| INCL | Include |
| INCR | Increaser |
| INSUL | Insulation |
| INT | Interior |
| INV | Invert |
| ISO | International Standards Organization |

## J

| | |
|---|---|
| J | Junction |
| JAN | Janitor |
| JB | Junction Box |
| JST | Joist |
| JT | Joint |

## K

| | |
|---|---|
| K | Kip (1000 pounds), Kitchen |
| KP | Kick Plate |
| KS | Kitchen Sink |

| | | | | | |
|---|---|---|---|---|---|
| KVA | Kilovolt Amperes | MFR | Manufacturer | PCS | Pieces |
| KW | Kilowatt | MH | Man Hole | PERIM | Perimeter |
| KWY | Keyway | MID | Middle | PERP | Perpendicular |
| | | MIN | Minimum | PH | Phase |
| **L** | | MISC | Miscellaneous | PL | Pilot Light, Plate, Property Line |
| L | Left | MK | Mark | | |
| L & PP | Light and Power Panel | ML | Metal Lath | PL GL | Plate Glass |
| LAB | Laboratory | MLDG | Molding | PLAS | Plaster |
| LAD | Ladder | MN | Main | PLAT | Platform |
| LAM | Laminated | MO | Masonry Opening, Motor-Operated | PLBG | Plumbing |
| LAQ | Lacquer | | | PLWD | Plywood |
| LAT | Lateral | MOD | Modular, Modification | PNEU | Pneumatic |
| LAU | Laundry | | | PNL | Panel |
| LAV | Lavatory | MOR | Mortar | PORC | Porcelain |
| LB | Pound | MS | Manual Starter | PR | Pair |
| LBR | Lumber | MT | Metal Threshold | PREFAB | Prefabricated |
| LDG | Landing | MTD | Mounted | PRESS | Pressure |
| LEV | Level | MTG | Mounting | PRI | Primary |
| LG | Long | MTL | Metal | PROP | Property, Proposed |
| LH | Left-Handed | MULL | Mullion | PRV | Pressure Reducing (Regulating) Valve |
| LIN | Linear | | | | |
| LLH | Long Leg Horizontal | **N** | | PSF | Pounds per Square Foot |
| LLV | Long Leg Vertical | N | North | | |
| LP | Low Point | NA | Not Available | PSI | Pounds per Square Inch |
| LPG | Liquefied Petroleum Gas | NEC | National Electric Code | | |
| | | NEMA | National Electrical Manufacturers Association | PSIG | Pounds per Square Inch Gauge |
| LR | Living Room | | | | |
| LT | Light | | | PTD | Painted |
| LTD | Limited | NF | Near Face | PTN | Partition |
| LTH | Lath | NO | Number | PVC | Polyvinyl Chloride |
| LTR | Letter | NOM | Nominal | PWR | Power |
| LV | Low Voltage | NOR | Normal | | |
| LVR | Louver | NTS | Not to Scale | **Q** | |
| | | | | QUAL | Quality |
| **M** | | **O** | | QT | Quarry Tile |
| | | OC | On Center | QTY | Quantity |
| MAGN | Magnesium | OD | Outside Diameter | | |
| MAINT | Maintenance | OF | Outside Face | **R** | |
| MAN | Manual | OFF | Office | R | Radius, Risers |
| MAS | Masonry | OPNG | Opening | RA | Return Air |
| MATL | Material | OPP | Opposite | RAD | Radiator |
| MAV | Manual Air Vent | OUT | Outlet | RCP | Reinforced Concrete Pipe |
| MAX | Maximum | OVHD | Overhead | | |
| MB | Mixing Boxes (or Units) | | | RD | Roof Drain, Round |
| | | **P** | | REC | Recessed |
| MCM | Thousand Circular Mills | | | RECP | Receptacle |
| | | P | Pump | REF | Reference, Refrigerator |
| MDP | Main Distribution Panel | PAN | Pantry | | |
| | | PAR | Parallel | REG | Register |
| MECH | Mechanical | PART | Partition | REINF | Reinforcing |
| MED | Medium | PASS | Passage | REQ'D | Required |
| MET | Metal | PAV | Paving | RES | Resilient Edge Strip |
| MEZZ | Mezzanine | PC | Pull Chain | RET | Return |

| | |
|---|---|
| RETG | Retaining |
| REV | Revision |
| RFG | Roofing |
| RGH | Rough |
| RGH OPNG | Rough Opening |
| RIV | Rivet |
| RH | Right-Handed |
| RIO | Rough-In Opening |
| RM | Room |
| RV | Relief Valve |
| RWD | Redwood |

## S

| | |
|---|---|
| S | Stretcher |
| S or SW | Switch |
| SA | Supply Air |
| SAD | Supply Air Diffuser |
| SAN | Sanitary |
| SCH | Schedule |
| SCR | Screen, Screw |
| SCUP | Scupper |
| SDG | Siding |
| SDL | Saddle |
| SEC | Secondary |
| SECT | Section |
| SEL | Select |
| SER | Service |
| SEW | Sewer |
| SG | Supply Air Grille |
| SH | Sheet, Shower |
| SHLP | Shiplap |
| SHT | Sheet |
| SHTHG | Sheathing |
| SI | Storm Water Inlet |
| SIM | Similar |
| SJ | Steel Joist |
| SK | Sink |
| SL | Slate, Sleeve |
| SM | Sheet Metal |
| SOV | Shutoff Valve |
| SP | Soil Pipe, Sump Pump |
| SPAN | Spandrel |
| SPEC | Specification |
| SPKR | Speaker |
| SPR | Sprinkler |
| SQ | Square |
| SR | Supply Air Register |
| SST | Stainless Steel |
| ST | Storm |
| STD | Standard |
| STIFF | Stiffener |

| | |
|---|---|
| STIR | Stirrup |
| STL | Steel |
| STM | Steam |
| STN | Stone |
| STOR | Storage |
| STR | Straight, Strainer |
| STRUCT | Structural |
| SUR | Surface |
| SUSP | Suspended |
| SV | Safety Valve |
| SWG | Standard Wire Gauge |
| SYM | Symbol, Symmetric |

## T

| | |
|---|---|
| T | Thermostat, Tread |
| T/ | Top of |
| T & B | Top and Bottom |
| T & G | Tongue and Groove |
| TAN | Tangent |
| TB | Top of Beam |
| TC | Terra Cotta, Top of Concrete, Top of Curb |
| TEL | Telephone |
| TEMP | Temperature, Temporary |
| TEMPL | Template |
| TERM | Terminal |
| TERR | Terrazzo |
| TF | Top of Footing |
| THK | Thick or Thickness |
| THR | Threaded |
| THRU | Through |
| TJ | Top of Joist |
| TM | Top of Masonry |
| TMB | Telephone Mounting Board |
| TOIL | Toilet |
| TP | Top of Pier, Top of Pavement |
| TRANS | Transformer |
| TS | Time Switch, Top of Slab |
| TV | Television |
| TW | Top of Wall |
| TYP | Typical |

## U

| | |
|---|---|
| UG | Underground |
| UH | Unit Heater |
| UL | Underwriters Laboratory |

| | |
|---|---|
| UNFIN | Unfinished |
| UNO | Unless Noted Otherwise |
| UR | Urinal |

## V

| | |
|---|---|
| V | Vent, Volts |
| VAC | Vacuum |
| VAN | Vanity |
| VAR | Varies |
| VC | Vitrified Clay |
| VCJ | Vertical Control Joint |
| VERT | Vertical |
| VEST | Vestibule |
| VF | Vinyl Wall Fabric |
| VOL | Volume |
| VP | Vitreous Pipe |
| VTR | Vent Through Roof |

## W

| | |
|---|---|
| W | Washer (laundry), Waste, Water, Watts |
| W or WTH | Width |
| W/ | With |
| W/O | Without |
| WC | Water Closet |
| WD | Wood |
| WDW | Window |
| WF | Water Fountain, Wide Flange |
| W GL | Wire Glass |
| WH | Water Heater, Weep Hole |
| WHR | Watt Hour |
| WI | Wrought Iron |
| WM | Water Meter |
| WP | Waterproofing, Work Point |
| WR | Washroom |
| WR BD | Weather Resistant Board |
| WS | Weather Strip |
| WT | Weight |
| WV | Water Valve |
| WWF | Welded Wire Fabric |

## Y

| | |
|---|---|
| Y | Wye |

## Z

| | |
|---|---|
| Z | Zinc |

## BUILDING MATERIAL SYMBOLS

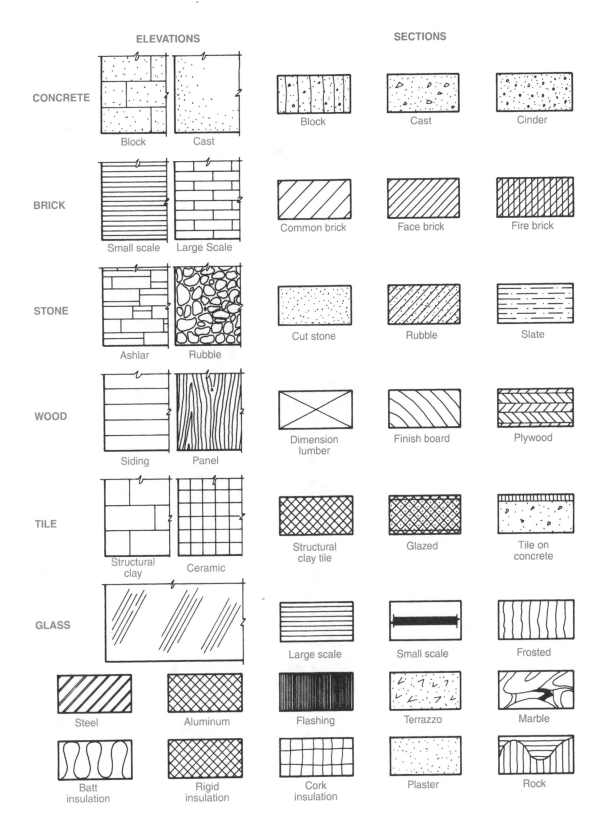

ELEVATIONS

SECTIONS

CONCRETE — Block, Cast | Block, Cast, Cinder

BRICK — Small scale, Large Scale | Common brick, Face brick, Fire brick

STONE — Ashlar, Rubble | Cut stone, Rubble, Slate

WOOD — Siding, Panel | Dimension lumber, Finish board, Plywood

TILE — Structural clay, Ceramic | Structural clay tile, Glazed, Tile on concrete

GLASS — Large scale, Small scale, Frosted

Steel, Aluminum, Flashing, Terrazzo, Marble

Batt insulation, Rigid insulation, Cork insulation, Plaster, Rock

## PLAN SYMBOLS

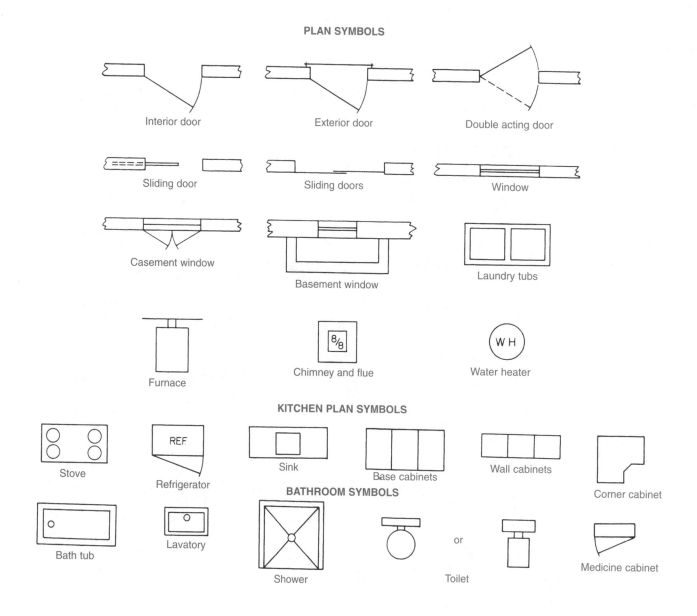

Interior door

Exterior door

Double acting door

Sliding door

Sliding doors

Window

Casement window

Basement window

Laundry tubs

Furnace

Chimney and flue

Water heater

### KITCHEN PLAN SYMBOLS

Stove

Refrigerator

Sink

Base cabinets

Wall cabinets

Corner cabinet

### BATHROOM SYMBOLS

Bath tub

Lavatory

Shower

or

Toilet

Medicine cabinet

# CLIMATE CONTROL SYMBOLS

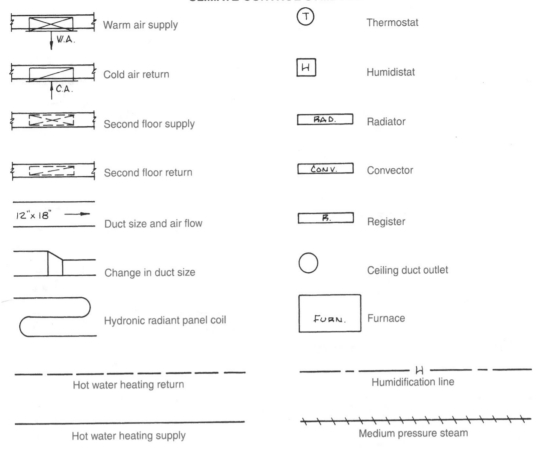

| | | | |
|---|---|---|---|
| Warm air supply | | Thermostat | |
| Cold air return | | Humidistat | |
| Second floor supply | | Radiator | |
| Second floor return | | Convector | |
| Duct size and air flow | | Register | |
| Change in duct size | | Ceiling duct outlet | |
| Hydronic radiant panel coil | | Furnace | |
| Hot water heating return | | Humidification line | |
| Hot water heating supply | | Medium pressure steam | |

# ELECTRICAL SYMBOLS

| | | |
|---|---|---|
| Ceiling outlet fixture | Single receptacle outlet | Single-pole switch |
| Recessed outlet fixture | Duplex receptacle outlet | Double-pole switch |
| Drop cord fixture | Triplex receptacle outlet | Three-way switch |
| Fan hanger outlet | Quadruplex receptacle outlet | Four-way switch |
| Junction box | Split-wired duplex receptacle outlet | Weatherproof switch |
| Fluorescent fixture | Special purpose single receptacle outlet | Low voltage switch |
| Telephone | 230 Volt outlet | Push button |
| Intercom | Weatherproof duplex outlet | Chimes |
| Ceiling fixture with pull switch | Duplex receptacle with switch | Television antenna outlet |
| Thermostat | Flush mounted panel box | Dimmer switch |
| Special fixture outlet A,B,C Etc. | Special duplex outlet A,B,C Etc. | Special switch A,B,C Etc. |

## TOPOGRAPHICAL SYMBOLS

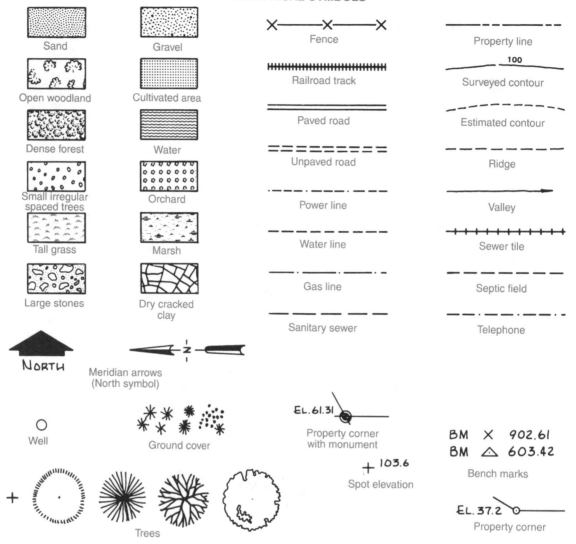

## PLUMBING SYMBOLS

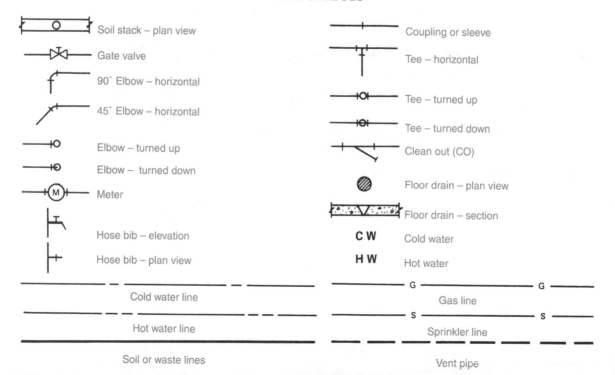

## ASTM STANDARD REINFORCING BARS

| BAR SIZE DESIGNATION | AREA Sq. Inches | WEIGHT Pounds per Ft. | DIAMETER Inches |
|---|---|---|---|
| 3 | .11 | .376 | .375 |
| 4 | .20 | .668 | .500 |
| 5 | .31 | 1.043 | .625 |
| 6 | .44 | 1.502 | .750 |
| 7 | .60 | 2.044 | .875 |
| 8 | .79 | 2.670 | 1.000 |
| 9 | 1.00 | 3.400 | 1.128 |
| 10 | 1.27 | 4.303 | 1.270 |
| 11 | 1.56 | 5.313 | 1.410 |
| 14 | 2.25 | 7.650 | 1.693 |
| 18 | 4.00 | 13.600 | 2.257 |

## STANDARD TYPES AND SIZES OF WIRE BAR SUPPORTS

| SYMBOL | BAR SUPPORT ILLUSTRATION | TYPE OF SUPPORT | STANDARD SIZES |
|---|---|---|---|
| SB | 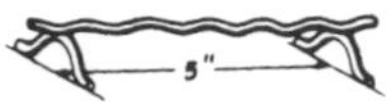 | Slab Bolster | ¾, 1, 1½, and 2 inch heights in 5 ft. and 10 ft. lengths |
| SBU* | 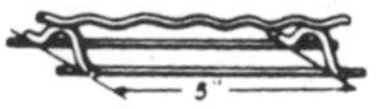 | Slab Bolster Upper | Same as SB |
| BB |  | Beam Bolster | 1, 1½, 2; over 2″ and 5″ heights in increments of ¼″ in lengths of 5 ft. |
| BBU* | 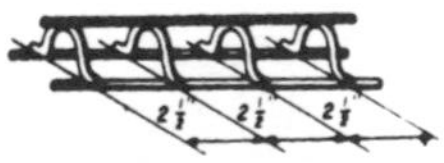 | Beam Bolster Upper | Same as BB |
| BC |  | Individual Bar Chair | ¾, 1, 1½, and 1¾″ heights |
| JC |  | Joist Chair | 4, 5, and 6 inch widths and ¾, 1, and 1½ inch heights |
| HC |  | Individual High Chair | 2 to 15 inch heights in increments of ¼ in. |
| HCM* | 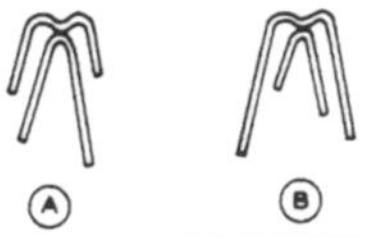 | High Chair for Metal Deck | 2 to 15 inch heights in increments of ¼ in. |
| CHC |  | Continuous High Chair | Same as HC in 5 foot and 10 foot lengths |
| CHCU* | 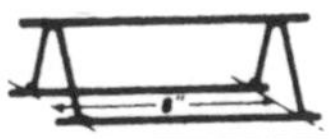 | Continuous High Chair Upper | Same as CHC |
| CHCM* | 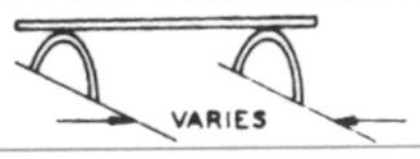 | Continuous High Chair for Metal Deck | Up to 5 inch heights in increments of ¼ in. |
| JCU** | 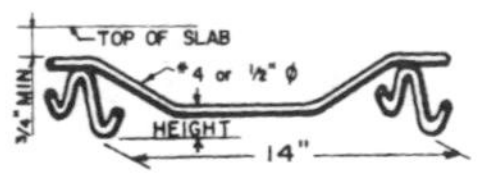 | Joist Chair Upper | 14" Span. Heights -1″ through +3½ vary in ¼″ increments |

\* Available in Class A only, except on special order.
\** Available in Class A only, with upturned or end bearing legs.

(Concrete Reinforcing Steel Institute)

## METRIC MODULES FOR CONSTRUCTION

The Internation Standards Organization (ISO) and the National Forest Products Association recommend 100 millimeters as the basic module for the construction industry. This is about the same as the 4 inch module used in the customary system of measurement. The illustration below shows the metric modules and the customary measurement equivalent.

| METRIC – FEET CONVERSION* | | | | | | | | | | |
|---|---|---|---|---|---|---|---|---|---|---|
| Feet | 1 | 2 | 3 | 4 | 5 | 6 | 7 | 8 | 9 | 10 |
| Metric Module | 300 mm<br>30 cm | 600 mm<br>60 cm<br>0.6 m | 900 mm<br>90 cm<br>0.9 m | 1200 mm<br>120 cm<br>1.2 m | 1500 mm<br>150 cm<br>1.5 m | 1800 mm<br>180 cm<br>1.8 m | 2100 mm<br>210 cm<br>2.1 m | 2400 mm<br>240 cm<br>2.4 m | 2700 mm<br>270 cm<br>2.7 m | 3000 mm<br>300 cm<br>3.0 m |
| Feet | 20 | 30 | 40 | 50 | 60 | 70 | 80 | 90 | 100 | 200 |
| Metric Module | 6000 mm<br>600 cm<br>6 m | 9000 mm<br>900 cm<br>9 m | 12 000 mm<br>1200 cm<br>12 m | 15 000 mm<br>1500 cm<br>15 m | 18 000 mm<br>1800 cm<br>18 m | 21 000 mm<br>2100 cm<br>21 m | 24 000 mm<br>2400 cm<br>24 m | 27 000 mm<br>2700 cm<br>27 m | 30 000 mm<br>3000 cm<br>30 m | 60 000 mm<br>6000 cm<br>60 m |

* Recommended modular conversions

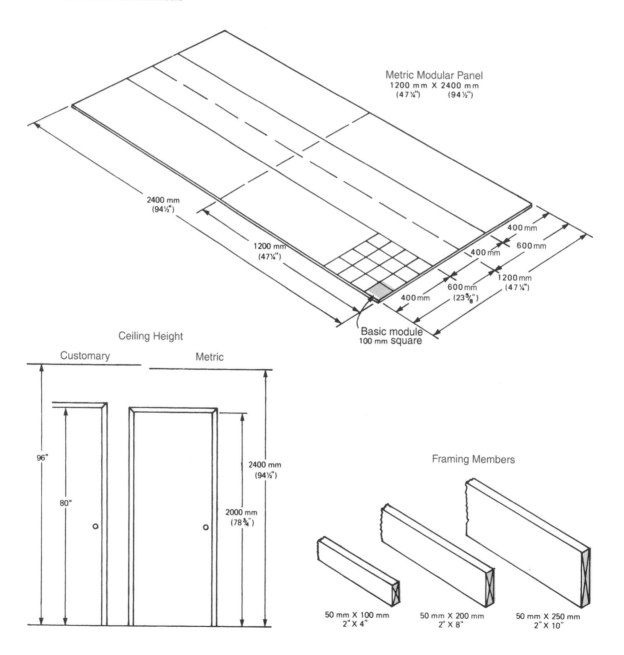

Metric Modular Panel
1200 mm X 2400 mm
(47¼")     (94½")

2400 mm
(94½")

1200 mm
(47¼")

400 mm

400 mm     600 mm

600 mm     1200 mm
(23⅝")     (47¼")

400 mm

Basic module
100 mm square

Ceiling Height

Customary          Metric

96"

80"

2400 mm
(94½")

2000 mm
(78¾")

Framing Members

50 mm X 100 mm
2" X 4"

50 mm X 200 mm
2" X 8"

50 mm X 250 mm
2" X 10"

## METRIC — INCH EQUIVALENTS

| INCHES Fractions | Decimals | Milli-meters | INCHES Fractions | Decimals | Milli-meters |
|---|---|---|---|---|---|
| | .00394 | .1 | 15/32 | .46875 | 11.9063 |
| | .00787 | .2 | | .47244 | 12.00 |
| | .01181 | .3 | 31/64 | .484375 | 12.3031 |
| 1/64 | .015625 | .3969 | 1/2 | .5000 | 12.70 |
| | .01575 | .4 | | .51181 | 13.00 |
| | .01969 | .5 | 33/64 | .515625 | 13.0969 |
| | .02362 | .6 | 17/32 | .53125 | 13.4938 |
| | .02756 | .7 | 35/64 | .546875 | 13.8907 |
| 1/32 | .03125 | .7938 | | .55118 | 14.00 |
| | .0315 | .8 | 9/16 | .5625 | 14.2875 |
| | .03543 | .9 | 37/64 | .578125 | 14.6844 |
| | .03937 | 1.00 | | .59055 | 15.00 |
| 3/64 | .046875 | 1.1906 | 19/32 | .59375 | 15.0813 |
| 1/16 | .0625 | 1.5875 | 39/64 | .609375 | 15.4782 |
| 5/64 | .078125 | 1.9844 | 5/8 | .625 | 15.875 |
| | .07874 | 2.00 | | .62992 | 16.00 |
| 3/32 | .09375 | 2.3813 | 41/64 | .640625 | 16.2719 |
| 7/64 | .109375 | 2.7781 | 21/32 | .65625 | 16.6688 |
| | .11811 | 3.00 | | .66929 | 17.00 |
| 1/8 | .125 | 3.175 | 43/64 | .671875 | 17.0657 |
| 9/64 | .140625 | 3.5719 | 11/16 | .6875 | 17.4625 |
| 5/32 | .15625 | 3.9688 | 45/64 | .703125 | 17.8594 |
| | .15748 | 4.00 | | .70866 | 18.00 |
| 11/64 | .171875 | 4.3656 | 23/32 | .71875 | 18.2563 |
| 3/16 | .1875 | 4.7625 | 47/64 | .734375 | 18.6532 |
| | .19685 | 5.00 | | .74803 | 19.00 |
| 13/64 | .203125 | 5.1594 | 3/4 | .7500 | 19.05 |
| 7/32 | .21875 | 5.5563 | 49/64 | .765625 | 19.4469 |
| 15/64 | .234375 | 5.9531 | 25/32 | .78125 | 19.8438 |
| | .23622 | 6.00 | | .7874 | 20.00 |
| 1/4 | .2500 | 6.35 | 51/64 | .796875 | 20.2407 |
| 17/64 | .265625 | 6.7469 | 13/16 | .8125 | 20.6375 |
| | .27559 | 7.00 | | .82677 | 21.00 |
| 9/32 | .28125 | 7.1438 | 53/64 | .828125 | 21.0344 |
| 19/64 | .296875 | 7.5406 | 27/32 | .84375 | 21.4313 |
| 5/16 | .3125 | 7.9375 | 55/64 | .859375 | 21.8282 |
| | .31496 | 8.00 | | .86614 | 22.00 |
| 21/64 | .328125 | 8.3344 | 7/8 | .875 | 22.225 |
| 11/32 | .34375 | 8.7313 | 57/64 | .890625 | 22.6219 |
| | .35433 | 9.00 | | .90551 | 23.00 |
| 23/64 | .359375 | 9.1281 | 29/32 | .90625 | 23.0188 |
| 3/8 | .375 | 9.525 | 59/64 | .921875 | 23.4157 |
| 25/64 | .390625 | 9.9219 | 15/16 | .9375 | 23.8125 |
| | .3937 | 10.00 | | .94488 | 24.00 |
| 13/32 | .40625 | 10.3188 | 61/64 | .953125 | 24.2094 |
| 27/64 | .421875 | 10.7156 | 31/32 | .96875 | 24.6063 |
| | .43307 | 11.00 | | .98425 | 25.00 |
| 7/16 | .4375 | 11.1125 | 63/64 | .984375 | 25.0032 |
| 29/64 | .453125 | 11.5094 | 1 | 1.0000 | 25.4001 |

## BASIC WELDING SYMBOLS AND THEIR LOCATION SIGNIFICANCE

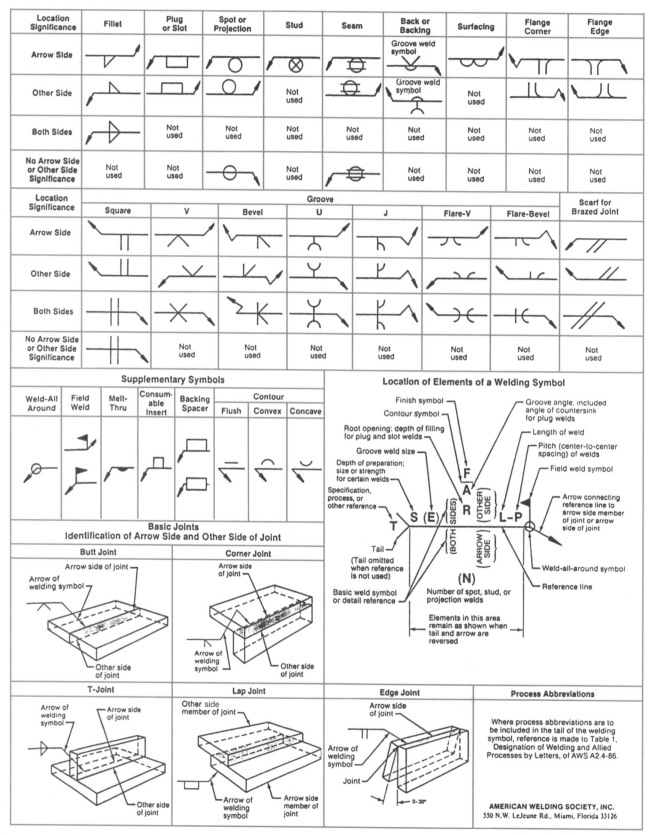

(American Welding Society)

## TYPICAL WELDING SYMBOLS

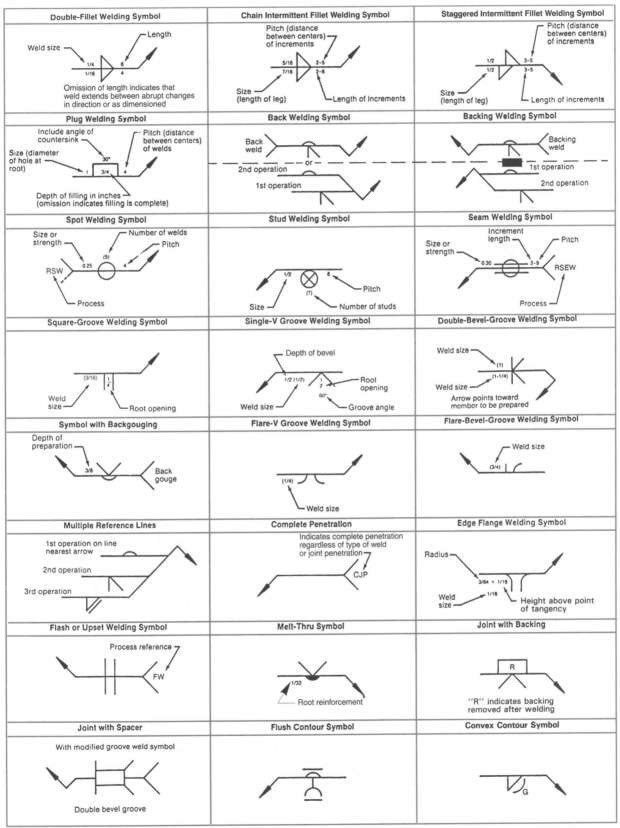

(American Welding Society)

# CSI Specification

## Introductory Information

| | |
|---|---|
| 00001 | Project Title Page |
| 00005 | Certifications Page |
| 00007 | Seals Page |
| 00010 | Table of Contents |
| 00015 | List of Drawings |
| 00020 | List of Schedules |

## Bidding Requirements

| | |
|---|---|
| 00100 | Bid Solicitation |
| 00200 | Instructions to Bidders |
| 00300 | Information Available to Bidders |
| 00400 | Bid Forms and Supplements |
| 00490 | Bidding Addenda |

## Contracting Requirement

| | |
|---|---|
| 00500 | Agreement |
| 00600 | Bonds and Certificates |
| 00700 | General Conditions |
| 00800 | Supplementary Conditions |
| 00900 | Addenda and Modifications |

## Division 1—General Requirements

| | |
|---|---|
| 01100 | Summary |
| 01200 | Price and Payment Procedures |
| 01300 | Administrative Requirements |
| 01400 | Quality Requirements |
| 01500 | Temporary Facilities and Controls |
| 01600 | Product Requirements |
| 01700 | Execution Requirements |
| 01800 | Facility Operation |
| 01900 | Facility Decommissioning |

## Division 2—Site Construction

| | |
|---|---|
| 02050 | Basic Site Materials and Methods |
| 02100 | Site Remediation |
| 02200 | Site Preparation |
| 02300 | Earthwork |
| 02400 | Tunneling, Boring, and Jacking |
| 02450 | Foundation and Load-Bearing Elements |
| 02500 | Utility Services |
| 02600 | Drainage and Containment |
| 02700 | Bases, Ballasts, Pavements, and Appurtenances |
| 02800 | Site Improvements and Amenities |
| 02900 | Planting |
| 02950 | Site Restoration and Rehabilitation |

## Division 3—Concrete

| | |
|---|---|
| 03050 | Basic Concrete Materials and Methods |
| 03010 | Concrete Forms and Accessories |
| 03200 | Concrete Reinforcement |
| 03300 | Cast-in-Place Concrete |
| 03400 | Precast Concrete |
| 03500 | Cementitious Decks and Underlayment |
| 03600 | Grouts |
| 03700 | Mass Concrete |
| 03900 | Concrete Restoration and Cleaning |

## Division 4—Masonry

| | |
|---|---|
| 04050 | Basic Masonry Materials and Methods |
| 04200 | Masonry Units |
| 04400 | Stone |
| 04500 | Refractories |
| 04600 | Corrosion-Resistant Masonry |
| 04700 | Simulated Masonry |
| 04800 | Masonry Assemblies |
| 04900 | Masonry Restoration and Cleaning |

## Division 5—Metals

| | |
|---|---|
| 05050 | Basic Metal Materials and Methods |
| 05100 | Structural Metal Framing |
| 05200 | Metal Joists |
| 05300 | Metal Deck |
| 05400 | Cold-Formed Metal Framing |
| 05500 | Metal Fabrications |

| | |
|---|---|
| 05600 | Hydraulic Fabrications |
| 05650 | Railroad Track and Accessories |
| 05700 | Ornamental Metal |
| 05800 | Expansion Control |
| 05900 | Metal Restoration and Cleaning |

## Division 6—Wood and Plastics

| | |
|---|---|
| 06050 | Basic Wood and Plastic Materials and Methods |
| 06100 | Rough Carpentry |
| 06200 | Finish Carpentry |
| 06400 | Architectural Woodwork |
| 06500 | Structural Plastics |
| 06600 | Plastic Fabrications |
| 06900 | Wood and Plastic Restoration and Cleaning |

## Division 7— Thermal and Moisture Protection

| | |
|---|---|
| 07050 | Basic Thermal and Moisture Protection Materials and Methods |
| 07100 | Dampproofing and Waterproofing |
| 07200 | Thermal Protection |
| 07300 | Shingles, Roof Tiles, and Roof Coverings |
| 07400 | Roofing and Siding Panels |
| 07500 | Membrane Roofing |
| 07600 | Flashing and Sheet Metal |
| 07700 | Roof Specialties and Accessories |
| 07800 | Fire and Smoke Protection |
| 07900 | Joint Sealers |

## Division 8—Doors and Windows

| | |
|---|---|
| 08050 | Basic Door and Window Materials and Methods |
| 08100 | Metal Doors and Frames |
| 08200 | Wood and Plastic Doors |
| 08300 | Specialty Doors |
| 08400 | Entrances and Storefronts |
| 08500 | Windows |
| 08600 | Skylights |
| 08700 | Hardware |
| 08800 | Glazing |
| 08900 | Glazed Curtain Wall |

## Division 9—Finishes

| | |
|---|---|
| 09050 | Basic Finish Materials and Methods |
| 09100 | Metal Support Assemblies |
| 09200 | Plaster and Gypsum Board |
| 09300 | Tile |
| 09400 | Terrazzo |
| 09500 | Ceilings |
| 09600 | Flooring |
| 09700 | Wall Finishes |
| 09800 | Acoustical Treatment |
| 09900 | Paints and Coatings |

## Division 10—Specialties

| | |
|---|---|
| 10100 | Visual Display Boards |
| 10150 | Compartments and Cubicles |
| 10200 | Louvers and Vents |
| 10240 | Grilles and Screens |
| 10250 | Service Walls |
| 10260 | Wall and Corner Guards |
| 10270 | Access Flooring |
| 10290 | Pest Control |
| 10300 | Fireplaces and Stoves |
| 10340 | Manufactured Exterior Specialties |
| 10350 | Flagpoles |
| 10400 | Identification Devices |
| 10450 | Pedestrian Control Devices |
| 10500 | Lockers |
| 10520 | Fire Protection Specialties |
| 10530 | Protective Covers |
| 10550 | Postal Specialties |
| 10600 | Partitions |
| 10670 | Storage Shelving |
| 10700 | Exterior Protection |
| 10750 | Telephone Specialties |
| 10800 | Toilet, Bath, and Laundry Accessories |
| 10880 | Scales |
| 10900 | Wardrobe and Closet Specialties |

## Divisions 11 Equipment

| | |
|---|---|
| 11010 | Maintenance Equipment |
| 11020 | Security and Vault Equipment |
| 11030 | Teller and Service Equipment |
| 11040 | Ecclesiastical Equipment |
| 11050 | Library Equipment |
| 11060 | Theater and Stage Equipment |
| 11070 | Instrumental Equipment |
| 11080 | Registration Equipment |
| 11090 | Checkroom Equipment |
| 11100 | Mercantile Equipment |
| 11110 | Commercial Laundry and Dry Cleaning Equipment |
| 11120 | Vending Equipment |
| 11130 | Audio-Visual Equipment |
| 11140 | Vehicle Service Equipment |
| 11150 | Parking Control Equipment |
| 11160 | Loading Dock Equipment |
| 11170 | Solid Waste Handling Equipment |
| 11190 | Detention Equipment |
| 11200 | Water Supply and Treatment Equipment |
| 11280 | Hydraulic Gates and Valves |
| 11300 | Fluid Waste Treatment and Disposal Equipment |
| 11400 | Food Service Equipment |
| 11450 | Residential Equipment |
| 11460 | Unit Kitchens |
| 11470 | Darkroom Equipment |
| 11480 | Athletic, Recreational, and Therapeutic Equipment |

| 11500 | Industrial and Process Equipment |
| 11600 | Laboratory Equipment |
| 11650 | Planetarium Equipment |
| 11660 | Observatory Equipment |
| 11680 | Office Equipment |
| 11700 | Medical Equipment |
| 11780 | Mortuary Equipment |
| 11850 | Navigation Equipment |
| 11870 | Agricultural Equipment |
| 11900 | Exhibit Equipment |

## Division 12 Furnishings

| 12050 | Fabrics |
| 12100 | Art |
| 12300 | Manufactured Casework |
| 12400 | Furnishings and Accessories |
| 12500 | Furniture |
| 12600 | Multiple Seating |
| 12700 | Systems Furniture |
| 12800 | Interior Plants and Planters |
| 12900 | Furnishings Restoration and Repair |

## Division 13 Special Construction

| 13010 | Air-Supported Structures |
| 13020 | Building Modules |
| 13030 | Special Purpose Rooms |
| 13080 | Sound, Vibration, and Seismic Control |
| 13090 | Radiation Protection |
| 13100 | Lightning Protection |
| 13110 | Cathodic Protection |
| 13120 | Pre Engineered Structures |
| 13150 | Swimming Pools |
| 13160 | Aquariums |
| 13165 | Aquatic Park Facilities |
| 13170 | Tubs and Pools |
| 13175 | Ice Rinks |
| 13185 | Kennels and Animal Shelters |
| 13190 | Site-Constructed Incinerators |
| 13200 | Storage Tanks |
| 13220 | Filter Underdrains and Media |
| 13230 | Digester Covers and Appurtences |
| 13240 | Oxygenation Systems |
| 13260 | Sludge Conditioning Systems |
| 13280 | Hazardous Material Remediation |
| 13400 | Measurement and Control Instrumentation |

| 13500 | Recording Instrumentation |
| 13550 | Transportation Control Instrumentation |
| 13600 | Solar and Wind Energy Equipment |
| 13700 | Security Access and Surveillance |
| 13800 | Building Automation and Control |
| 13850 | Detection and Alarm |
| 13900 | Fire Suppression |

## Division 14 Conveying Systems

| 14100 | Dumbwaiters |
| 14200 | Elevators |
| 14300 | Escalators and Moving Walks |
| 14400 | Lifts |
| 14500 | Material Handling |
| 14600 | Hoists and Cranes |
| 14700 | Turntables |
| 14800 | Scaffolding |
| 14900 | Transportation |

## Division 15 Mechanical

| 15050 | Basic Mechanical Materials and Methods |
| 15100 | Building Services Piping |
| 15200 | Process Piping |
| 15300 | Fire Protection Piping |
| 15400 | Plumbing Fixtures and Equipment |
| 15500 | Heat-Generation Equipment |
| 15600 | Refrigeration Equipment |
| 15700 | Heating, Ventilating, and Air Conditioning Equipment |
| 15800 | Air Distribution |
| 15900 | HVAC Instrumentation and Controls |
| 15950 | Testing, Adjusting, and Balancing |

## Divisions 16 Electrical

| 16050 | Basic Electrical Materials and Methods |
| 16100 | Wiring Methods |
| 16200 | Electrical Power |
| 16300 | Transmission and Distribution |
| 16400 | Low-Voltage Distribution |
| 16500 | Lighting |
| 16700 | Communications |
| 16800 | Sound and Video |

# Glossary

## A

**Adhesive:** A cement, glue, or other material used to hold two or more items together.

**Admixtures:** Materials added to concrete or mortar to alter it in some way.

**Aggregate:** Sand, gravel, rock, or other material used along with cement and water to make concrete.

**Air Infiltration Barrier:** A material such as a sheet of plastic placed in floors and walls to prevent the passage of air.

**Alphabet of Lines:** The accepted drafting practice of using specific line thickness and style to represent various drawing details.

**American Bond:** See Common Bond.

**American Society for Testing and Materials (ASTM):** Organization responsible for setting criteria for the quality of structural materials.

**American Welding Society (AWS):** Organization responsible for welding standards.

**Ampere:** Units used to measure electrical current.

**Anchor:** A device, generally made of metal, used to fasten plates, joists, trusses, and other building parts to concrete or masonry.

**Anchor Bolt:** A metal bolt with one threaded end and one L-shaped end. It is embedded in concrete and is used to hold structural members in place.

**Angle:** With regards to structural steel, an L-shaped member with two perpendicular legs. Common leg lengths are 2–7″, with common thicknesses of 1/8–5/8″.

**Angular Perspective:** See Two-Point Perspective.

**Anodize:** An electrolytic means of coating aluminum or magnesium by oxidizing.

**Approximate Method:** An estimating procedure in which the size of the building is multiplied by a unit cost. Used to determine a rough estimate.

**Apron:** A piece of trim below the window stool and wall support used to conceal the edge of the wall material. Also: a concrete ramp in front of the garage door.

**Areaway:** The open space around foundation walls, doorways or windows to permit light and air to reach the below-ground-level floors.

**Arrow Side:** On a welded joint, the side nearest the welding symbol on the drawing.

**Asbestos:** A mineral material with long thread-like fibers.

**Ashlar:** A stone cut by sawing to a rectangular shape.

**Asphalt:** A mineral pitch used for waterproofing roofs and foundation walls. It also is used with crushed rock to pave drives and parking areas.

**Assumed Benchmark:** An arbitrarily chosen benchmark.

**ASTM:** See American Society for Testing and Materials.

**AWS:** See American Welding Society.

## B

**Backfill:** To replace ground that has been excavated during construction. Also, the material used to replace excavated material.

**Backing Wall:** In masonry, a wall hidden behind a veneer wall.

**Balloon Framing:** Wall framing in which wall studs run the entire height of the building, from foundation to roof plate. Also called **Western Framing.**

**Balusters:** Vertical stair members used to support a hand rail.

**Balustrade:** A row of balusters supporting a common rail.

**Basement Plan:** A drawing showing the top view of the basement, often with foundation details.

**Batten:** A narrow strip of wood placed across the joint between two boards, such as siding.

*Batter Board:* A temporary framework of stakes and horizontal members used in laying out a foundation.

*Beam:* A horizontal structural member used between posts, columns, or walls.

*Bearing:* A measure of direction expressed as degrees east or west of north or south.

*Bearing Partition:* An interior wall that transmits a load from above to a wall, columns, or footings below.

*Benchmark:* A point of known elevation, such as a mark cut on a permanent stone or plate set in concrete, from which measurements are taken.

*Bevel:* A cut on the edge of a board at an angle other than 90°.

*Bevel Siding:* A siding material that is tapered from a thick edge to a thin edge.

*Bird's Mouth:* Two cuts placed in a rafter that allow it to sit on the top plate.

*Blocking:* Wood members placed between wall studs to prevent fire from spreading.

*Blueprint:* A print consisting of white lines against a blue background. The term is used interchangeable with *print*.

*Bolster:* A bent wire device used in holding reinforcing bar in place during the pounding of concrete.

*Bond:* The holding or gripping force between reinforcing steel and concrete. Also, the pattern in which masonry units are laid.

*Bond Beam:* A reinforced concrete beam running around a masonry wall to provide added strength. Vertical bond beams are formed by inserting reinforcing bar in a cell after the wall is laid and filling with grout.

*Branch Circuit:* The various circuits coming out of the breaker panel and running through the building.

*Brass Pipe:* Pipe made primarily of copper and zinc used for corrosive materials.

*Brick Veneer:* A brick wall of single brick, usually covering a frame structure.

*Bridging:* The bracing of joists by crossing diagonal pairs of braces.

*Building Code:* Laws or regulations set up by building departments for uniformity in construction, design, and building practices.

## C

*Cabinet Oblique:* An oblique drawing in which the receding distance is drawn at half scale.

*CADD:* See *Computer-Aided Design and Drafting.*

*Camber:* A slight vertical curve (arch) formed in a beam or girder to counteract deflection due to loading.

*Cant Strip:* A wooden strip used to raise the first course of shingles in plane; an angular board placed at the junction of the roof deck and wall to relieve the sharp angle when the roofing material is installed.

*Cantilever:* A projecting structural member or slab supported at one end only.

*Cast-in-Place Concrete:* Concrete that is cast at the construction site in its permanent location.

*Caulk:* A substance used to seal cracks and joints.

*Caviler Oblique:* An oblique drawing in which the receding faces are drawn at full scale.

*Cement:* The material used in concrete to bind the aggregate together.

*Centimeter:* Unit of length measurement used in the Metric System. One inch is the same length as 2.54 centimeters.

*Chair:* A bent wire or plastic device used to hold reinforcing bars in place during concrete pouring.

*Chamfer:* A beveled outside corner or edge on a beam or column.

*Chord:* The top and bottom member of open-web joist, and the principal members of trusses, as opposed to the diagonals.

*Circuit:* The electric path from the source through the components and back to the source.

*Circuit Breaker:* A protective device for opening and closing an electric circuit. It opens automatically in case of an overload on the circuit.

*Circumference:* The perimeter around a circle.

*Cleanout:* An opening in the waste pipe of the plumbing system for rodding out the drain. Also: an opening at lower part of the fireplace for removing ashes.

*Clerestory:* A windowed area between roof planes or rising above the lower story, that admits light and ventilation.

*CMU:* See *Concrete Masonry Unit.*

*Cold Joint:* Construction joint in concrete occurring at a place where continuous pouring has been interrupted.

*Collar Beam:* A tie between two opposite rafters, well above the wall plate.

*Column:* A vertical structural member.

*Column Schedule:* A list of the details and specifications for all of the columns in a structure.

*Common Bond:* Masonry pattern in which every sixth or seventh course of stretchers is interrupted by a header course. Also called *American Bond.*

*Common Rafter:* A rafter running between the ridge plate and the wall plate.

*Composite Wall:* A masonry wall with a veneer wall in front of a backing wall of less expensive brick.

*Computer-Aided Design and Drafting (CADD):* Preparation of drawings using a personal computer.

*Concrete:* Structural material comprising water, gravel, sand, and cement.

*Concrete Masonry Unit (CMU):* A masonry unit made of concrete measuring 8″×8″×16″ long (including mortar joint).

*Conductor:* A material, usually wires, carrying electrical current.

*Conduit:* Metal or fiber pipe used to carry electrical conductors.

*Construction Joint:* Separation between two placements of concrete; a means for keying two sections together.

*Control Valve:* Valves in a water distribution system used to stop the flow.

*Coping:* The top course or cap on a masonry wall protecting the masonry below from water penetration.

*Corbel:* A stone, masonry, or wood bracket projecting out from a wall.

*Cornice:* That part of the roof extending horizontally out from the wall.

*Course:* A horizontal layer of masonry unit.

*Cripple Jack Rafter:* A rafter running between a valley rafter and a hip rafter.

*Cripple Stud:* A stud that does not run the full height of the wall due to the presence of a header or a rough sill.

*Curtain Wall:* A nonbearing wall between columns.

*Cut Stones:* Stones that are cut to size and finished at a mill prior to being used for construction.

**D**

*Dead Load:* The load on a structure resulting from the weight of its own materials and any other fixed loads, such as a roof-mounted air conditioner.

*Denominator:* The bottom number in fraction.

*Detail Drawing:* A type of drawing showing a specific detail of the construction. Details are normally drawn at a larger scale than other drawings.

*Detailed Method:* Estimating method in which every aspect of construction (including materials, equipment, and labor) are listed and assigned a cost.

*Diameter:* The length of line running between two points on a circle, through the center of the circle.

*Diffuser:* A grille or register over an air duct opening into a room that controls and directs the flow of air.

*Distribution Pipes:* Pipes that deliver supply water to plumbing fixtures.

*Diverter:* A piece, usually metal, used to direct moisture to a desired path or location.

*Divisions:* Different construction categories standardized by the Construction Specification Institute.

*Dormer:* A projection built out from a sloping roof, including one or more vertical windows.

*Double Header:* A header consisting of two headers, used when extra strength is desired.

*Double Trimmer:* A framing detail in which the side of an opening is supported by two members connected together.

*Dowel:* Straight metal bars used to connect or position two sections of concrete or masonry.

*Drywall:* A type of wall covering (gypsum board) used in place of plaster.

*Duct:* A round or rectangular pipe, usually metal, used for transferring conditioned air in a heating and cooling system.

**E**

*Eaves:* The portion of the roof that overhangs the wall.

*Electric Radiant Heating:* A heating system in which electrical resistance is used to generate heat.

*Electrical Metallic Tubing (EMT):* A type of electrical conduit, as called thin-wall.

*Electrical Plan:* A plan view drawing showing the layout of the electrical wiring and fixtures.

*Electrostatic Filter:* A type of filter used in heating systems in which particles are electrically charged and then collected.

*Elevation:* In surveying, the height of a survey marker above sea level; a measurement on a plot or foundation referenced to a known point. In architectural drafting, the drawing of the front, sides, or rear view of a structure.

*EMT:* See *Electrical Metallic Tubing.*

*Evaporative Cooling System:* A cooling system used in areas of low humidity in which air is blown through a damp medium.

*Excavation:* The recess or pit formed by removing the ground in preparation for footings or other foundations.

*Expansion Joint:* Formed in concrete or masonry units by a bituminous fiber strip or foam rod and caulk to allow for expansion and contraction in materials caused by temperature changes and shrinkage.

*Exploded Pictorial Drawings:* A pictorial drawing in which the parts of an assembly are separated to better illustrate the assembling sequence.

**F**

*Face Brick:* A select brick made of clays and chemicals to produce a desired color and effect for use in the face of a wall.

*Fascia:* A finish board nailed to the ends of rafters or lookouts.

*Finish Plumbing:* The final stage of plumbing, in which fixtures are attached to the rough plumbing.

*Fire Brick:* A refractory ceramic brick made to resist high temperatures.

*Fire Stop:* A block placed between studs of a wall to prevent a draft and the spread of fire.

*Flanges:* The parallel faces of a structural beam, connected by the web.

*Flashing:* Sheet metal or other thin material used to prevent moisture from entering a structure, such as around a chimney.

*Float Glass:* The most common method of producing glass. A ribbon of glass floats on a bath of molten tin.

*Floating Slab:* A slab-on-grade foundation in which the footings, foundation walls, and slab are cast at the same time.

*Floor Plan:* A plan view showing room sizes and locations and many construction details. For simple construction, the floor plan may contain all of the needed information.

*Flue:* The passageway in a chimney that provides for the escape of smoke, gases, and fumes.

*Flush Door:* A smooth surface door, without panels or molding.

*Footing:* The base of a foundation wall or column, which is wider to provide a larger bearing surface.

*Forced-Air System:* A heating system that uses a motor-driven fan to distribute the warm air through ducts.

*Foundation Plan:* A plan view shows the dimensions and details of a building's foundation system, including footings, walls, and piers.

*Framing:* The wood or metal structure of a building, which gives it shape and strength.

*Frost Line:* The depth below the ground surface subject to freezing.

*Furring:* Narrow wood strips fastened to a wall or ceiling for use in nailing finished material.

## G

*Gable:* The portion of a wall above the eave line and between the slopes of a double-opened roof.

*Galvanized:* A coating of zinc that protects metal from atmospheric corrosion.

*Gauge:* A scale of measurement for wire sizes and sheet metal thickness.

*Girder:* A principal beam supporting other beams.

*GFCI:* See *Ground Fault Circuit Interrupter.*

*Glass:* Translucent ceramic material.

*Glazing:* Installation of glass in window sashes and doors.

*Grade:* The level of the ground around a building.

*Grade Beam:* A low foundation wall or a beam, usually at ground level, which provides support for the walls of a building.

*Gravel Stop:* The metal strip at the edge of a built-up roof.

*Ground Fault Circuit Interrupter (GFCI):* An electrical receptacle that breaks the circuit if an overload occurs. Used when the receptacle is located near a water source, such as in a kitchen or bathroom.

*Grout:* A cementitious mixture of high water content, prepared to pour easily into spaces in a masonry wall. Made from Portland cement, lime, and aggregate, it is used to secure anchor bolts and vertical reinforcing rods in masonry walls.

*Gusset:* The piece of metal or plywood used to reinforce a joint of a truss.

## H

*Haunch:* Portion of a beam that increases in depth towards the support.

*Header:* The horizontal structural members over a door or window opening. Also: the joists at the end of an opening in the floor supporting tail joists.

*Header Course:* A course of brick laid flat so their long dimension is across the thickness of the wall, and the heads of the course of bricks show on the face of the wall.

*Hip Jack Rafter:* A rafter running between the plate and a hip rafter.

*Hip Rafter:* A rafter running from an outside corner of the building to the ridge board.

*Honeycomb:* Voids or open spaces left in concrete due to a loss or a shortage of mortar or cement paste.

*Horizon Line:* In perspective drawing, an imaginary line on which vanishing points are located.

*Hose Bib:* A threaded water faucet suitable for fastening a garden hose.

*Hydronic Heating:* A heating system that uses hot water to warm the air.

## I

*Improper Fraction:* A fraction in which the numerator is larger than the denominator.

*Insulating Glass:* A window or door glass consisting of two sheets of glass separated by a sealed air space to reduce heat transfer.

*Integrally-Cast:* Element (such as concrete joist and top slab) cast in one piece. See *Monolithic.*

*Invert:* The lowest part of the inside of a horizontal pipe.

*Isometric Projection:* A pictorial drawing positioned so that its principal axes make equal 30° angles with the plane of projection. Used for some detail and schematic layouts on construction drawings.

**J**

**Jack Rafter:** A rafter that is not attached to the ridge board.

**Jamb:** The top and sides of a door or window frame.

**Joist:** One of a series of wood or metal framing members used to support a floor or ceiling.

**K**

**Keyway:** Slotted joint in concrete used to connect portions cast at different times, such as a groove in footing where foundation wall is to be poured.

**Kiln-Dried:** The process of drying wood to a desired moisture content by controlling heat and humidity.

**Kilo:** The metric system prefix meaning one thousand. A kilometer, for example, is 1000 meters; a kilogram .

**Knee Walls:** A short wall.

**L**

**Lally Column:** A vertical steel pipe, usually filled with concrete, used to support beams and girders.

**Laminated Plastic:** Layers of cloth or other fiber impregnated with plastic, formed into sheets of the desired thickness and shape with heat and pressure. Commonly used for cabinetwork.

**Lamination:** A method of constructing by bonding layers of material with an adhesive, such as plastic laminate or a glue-laminated wood beam.

**Landing:** A platform in a flight of stairs to change direction or break a long run.

**Lath:** Gypsum board or metal mesh attached to studs or joists as a base for plaster.

**Ledger:** A horizontal strip of wood attached to the side of a beam to support joists.

**Legend:** A list of symbols used on a drawing and their meanings.

**Lift Slab:** Concrete floor construction in which slabs are cast directly on one another. Each slab is lifted into final position by jacks on top of columns. Floors are secured at each floor level by column brackets or collars.

**Lighting Schedule:** A listing of the brand, quantity, and electrical details of the lamp fixtures to be used in a building.

**Lintel:** Support for a masonry opening, usually steel angles or special form, such as precast stone or concrete.

**Live Load:** All movable objects, including persons and equipment, in a building.

**Longitudinal:** With the long dimension of an object or structure.

**Lookout:** The structural member running from the outside wall to a rafter end, which carries the plancier or soffit.

**Louver:** A ventilated opening in the attic, usually at the gable end, made of inclined horizontal slats to permit air to pass but to exclude moisture. Also used in doors to ventilate.

**Lumber:** Wood that has been cut to specific dimensions for structural use.

**M**

**Mastic:** Similar to an adhesive, a thick cement, glue, or other material used to seal the joint between two building materials.

**Mechanical Plan:** Plan drawing showing location of mechanical equipment, often showing HVAC system and piping.

**Meter:** Metric unit of measurement, equal to 39.37″.

**Mil:** Unit of thickness measurement, equal to 1/1000 of an inch (.001″).

**Minute:** A unit of angular measure equal to 1/60th of a degree.

**Modular Measurement:** The design of a structure to use standard size building materials. In the customary system of measurement the module is 4". In the metric system, the recommended module is 100 millimeters.

**Monolithic:** Concrete cast in one continuous pour.

**Mortar:** Cementitious substances used as a binding agent for masonry units.

**N**

**National Electric Code (NEC):** Handbook of standards and guidelines for electrical installation.

**NEC:** See **National Electric Code.**

**Nominal Size:** A general classification term used to designate size of commercial products but not identical to the actual size of the item. For example, a 2×4 (nominal) board is actually 1 1/2″×3 1/2″.

**Nonferrous Metals:** Metals containing little or no iron.

**North Arrow:** An arrow shown on a plan view drawing indicating the orientation of the structure.

**Numerator:** The top number in a fraction.

**O**

**Oblique Drawing:** A drawing in which one plane of the object is parallel to the paper. The receding faces can be drawn at any angle: 30 and 45 are the most common.

**One-Line Diagram:** An electrical schematic drawing.

**One-Point Perspective:** A perspective drawing that only uses one vanishing point.

**One-Way Floor System:** A floor system in which the slab is supported by beams that run in only one direction.

**Open Web Steel Joist:** A truss type joist with top and bottom chords and a web formed of diagonal members. Some manufacturers make a joist with chords of wood and a steel web and refer to it as a truss joist.

**Orthographic Projection:** The projection of an object as viewed from six different perpendicular directions. The basis of architectural plan and elevation drawings.

## P

**Panel Door:** A door of solid frame strips with inset panels.

**Panel Schedule:** A list of the electrical details and all of the circuits controlled by a breaker panel.

**Parapet Wall:** A wall extending above the roof line.

**Parallel Perspective:** See **One-Point Perspective.**

**Parge:** To coat with mortar.

**Partition:** An interior wall that divides an area.

**Perpendicular Projectors:** In orthographic projection, lines between views that connect common points.

**Perspective Drawing:** A drawing in which the lines moving away from the viewer converge, producing a drawing similar to the way objects actually appear.

**Pictorial Drawing:** A drawing in which an object is shown as it actually appears.

**Pier:** A heavy column of masonry between two openings used to support other structural members.

**Pilaster:** A column projecting on the outside or inside of a masonry wall to add strength or decorative effect.

**Pitch:** Roof slope expressed as the ratio of rise divided by span.

**Plancier:** The board or panel forming the underside of the eave or cornice.

**Plan North:** An assumed north direction (differing from True North) that is aligned with the building orientation.

**Plan View:** A drawing shows one floor of a building from directly above.

**Plaster:** A material consisting of gypsum and water (or Portland cement, sand, and water) used for interior wall surfaces.

**Plat:** A drawing of a parcel of land indicating lot number, location, boundaries, and dimensions. Contains information about easements and restrictions.

**Platform Framing:** A wall framing method in which wall studs run the length of a single story.

**Plenum:** A chamber in an air conditioning system that receives air under pressure before distribution to ducts.

**Plot Plan:** See **Site Plan.**

**Plumb:** Perpendicular or vertical. Also: to make something vertical.

**Plumbing Plan:** A plan drawing showing the layout of the water distribution and drainage systems.

**Plywood:** A composite lumber material consisting of layers of wood glued together with their grains orientated perpendicular.

**Pocket Door:** A door that slides into a partition or wall.

**Portland Cement:** Cement normally combined with water and aggregate to make concrete.

**Posttensioned Concrete:** Prestressed concrete in which the pretensioning steel is stressed after the concrete is cast.

**Precast Concrete:** Concrete that is cast into members in a factory and then transported to the construction site.

**Prestressed Concrete:** Concrete in which steel is tensioned (stretched) and anchored to compress the concrete.

**Pretensioned Concrete:** Prestressed concrete in which the pretensioning steel is stressed before the concrete is cast.

**Print:** A copy of a drawing.

**Proper Fraction:** A fraction that has a numerator smaller than its denominator.

**Property Line:** A line shown on a site plan representing the limits of a plot of land.

**Proportion:** The size of a portion of an object relative to the entire object or another portion.

**Purlin:** A horizontal roof member between the plate and ridge board used to support rafters or trusses.

## R

**Raceway:** Work channels set in floor to receive electrical wiring.

**Radius:** The distance from the center of a circle to the edge of the circle.

**Rafter:** One of a series of structural members of a roof. The rafters of a flat roof are sometimes called roof joists.

**Receptacle:** An electrical outlet into which appliances and other electrical devices can be connected by means of a plug.

**Register:** A grille used to cover an air duct opening into a room.

**Reinforced Concrete:** Concrete cast with steel bars, which provide additional strength.

**Reinforcing Bars:** Steel bars placed within forms and surrounded by concrete. The surface of reinforcing bars is normally deformed to improve the bond between the bar and the concrete.

*Rendering:* A pictorial drawing showing what a structure will look like when the project is finished.

*Ribbon:* In balloon framing, the member attached to the studs and used to support joists.

*Ridge:* The board at the peak of a roof.

*Rise:* The vertical distance from the plate to the ridge of a roof.

*Riser:* The vertical portion of a stair.

*Roof Jack:* The sheet metal device placed around a pipe projecting through the roof to prevent moisture from entering.

*Rough Sill:* A horizontal member running between studs below a window opening.

*Rough-In Plumbing:* The second stage of plumbing, in which pipes are installed.

*Rubble:* A type of stone masonry unit taken directly from the quarry, without smoothing or finishing.

*Run:* Horizontal distance from the plate to the ridge of a roof.

*Running Bond:* The most common brick pattern, consisting of offset courses of stretchers.

**S**

*Saddle:* A small, gable roof constructed between a vertical surface (such as the back of a chimney) and a sloped roof to prevent water from standing.

*Scale:* A measuring device with graduations for laying off distances. Also: the ratio of size that a structure is drawn, such as: 1/4″ = 1′-0″.

*Schedule:* A list of details or sizes for building components such as doors, windows, or beams.

*Screed:* A template to guide finishers in leveling off the top of fresh concrete.

*Second:* In angular measurement, a unit equal to 1/60th of a minute and 1/3600 of a degree.

*Sectional View:* Drawing view of a structure as if part of the structure were removed. A sectional drawing is defined by a cutting-plane on another view.

*Septic Tank:* A concrete or metal tank used to reduce raw sewage by bacterial action. Used where no municipal sewage system exists.

*Setback:* The distance from the property boundaries to the building location, required by zoning.

*Sheathing:* The boards or panels that cover the studs and rafters of a building to which finishing materials are applied.

*Shelf Angles:* Structure angles that are bolted to a concrete wall to support brick work, stone, or terra cotta.

*Sill Cock:* See *Hose Bib.*

*Sill Plate:* Wood board attached to the top of a foundation wall on to which the wall frame is attached.

*Single Wythe Wall:* A masonry wall composed of one row of bricks.

*Site Plan:* A drawing showing the location of a building on its plot of land and various details of the land. Also called *Plot Plan.*

*Skewed:* At an angle other than 90°.

*Slab:* A flat area of concrete such as a floor or drive.

*Slab-on-Grade:* A concrete slab supported by ground.

*Sleeper:* Wood strips laid over or embedded in a concrete floor for attaching a finished floor.

*Soffit:* In framing, the underside of a staircase or roof cornice. In masonry, the underside of a beam, lintel, or arch.

*Sole Plate:* This horizontal wood member serves as a base for the studs in a wall frame. It is normally the same size as the studs.

*Span:* The distance between supports for joists beams, girders, and trusses.

*Spandrel Beam:* The beam in an exterior wall of a structure.

*Spandrel Wall:* The portion of a wall above the head of a window and below the sill of the window above.

*Specifications:* The written directions issued by architects or engineers to establish general conditions, standards, and detailed instructions to be used on a project.

*Splicing:* Method of connecting two reinforcing bars at their ends to produce a single, long bar.

*Square:* A unit of measure referring to 100 square feet. Roofing materials and some siding materials are sold on this basis.

*Stirrup:* In reinforced concrete beams, a thin reinforcing bar wrapped around the main reinforcing bars to hold them in position. Stirrups also provide additional reinforcement against shear.

*Story:* The space between two floors of a building or between a floor and the ceiling above.

*Stringer:* Angled members that support stairs.

*Structural Steel:* General name for several types of mild steel normally used in construction.

*Stucco:* A plaster material consisting of Portland cement, sand, and water. Used for exterior wall surfaces.

*Stud:* A vertical wall framing member.

*Subfloor:* Plywood or other board material placed over joists and located below the finished floor material.

*Superstructure:* Frame of the building, usually above grade.

# T

***T-Beam:*** Beam that has a T-shaped cross section.

***Takeoff:*** Computation of a quantity for a cost estimate.

***Termite Shield:*** Sheet metal placed in or on a foundation wall to prevent termites from entering the structure.

***Terra Cotta:*** A type of stone used for its attractiveness. Literally—burnt earth.

***Thermostat:*** An automatic device controlling the operation of air conditioning system.

***Thin-Wall:*** See ***Electrical Metal Tubing.***

***Ties:*** In reinforced concrete columns, thin reinforcing bars wrapped horizontally around the primary, vertical bars. The ties keep the larger bars from moving as the concrete is cast.

***Top Plate:*** The horizontal framing member running above wall studs.

***Topography:*** The locations and details of land features.

***Tracing:*** A drawing or copy of a drawing from which prints are created.

***Transverse:*** Across the short dimension of an object or structure.

***Tread:*** The horizontal length of a stair.

***True North:*** Actual North, as opposed to the arbitrary Plan North.

***Truss:*** A structural unit having such members as beams, bars, and ties, usually arranged as triangles. Used for spanning wide spaces.

***Two-Point Perspective:*** A perspective drawing using two vanishing points. Also called ***Angular Perspective.***

***Typical (TYP):*** This term, when associated with any dimension or feature, means the dimension or feature applies to the locations that appear to be identical in size and shape.

# V

***Valley:*** The internal angle formed by two roof slopes.

***Valley Jack Rafter:*** A rafter running between the plate and a valley rafter.

***Valley Rafter:*** A rafter connecting the inside corner of the building with the ridge board.

***Vanishing Point:*** In perspective drawing, a point on the horizon line where receding lines converge.

***Veneer:*** A thin layer of cabinet wood bonded to a plywood or particle board backing.

***Veneer Wall:*** A single thickness (one wythe) masonry unit wall tied to a backing wall.

***Vent:*** A pipe, usually extending through the roof, providing a flow of air to and from the drainage system.

***Vitrified Clay Tile:*** A ceramic tile fired at a high temperature to make it very hard and waterproof.

***Voltage:*** The measure of an electromotive force.

# W

***Waffle Slab:*** A slab supported by beams running in two directions.

***Watt:*** A measure of electric power.

***Weep Holes:*** Small holes in a wall to permit water to exit from behind.

***Welded Wire Fabric (WWF):*** Wire mesh fabricated by means of welding the crossing joints of steel wires. Normally used to reinforce concrete slabs.

***Western Framing:*** See ***Balloon Framing.***

***Working Drawings:*** A set of drawings which provide the necessary details and dimensions to construct the object. May also include the specifications.

***Wythe:*** A continuous vertical section of masonry, one unit in thickness; sometimes called *withe* or *tier.* Also: a partition between flues of a chimney.

# Index